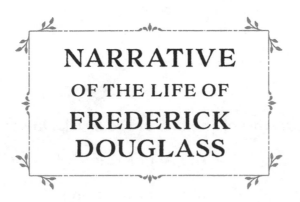

NARRATIVE

OF THE LIFE OF

FREDERICK
DOUGLASS

NARRATIVE

OF THE LIFE OF

FREDERICK DOUGLASS

An American Slave

Written by Himself

BOSTON
PUBLISHED AT THE ANTI-SLAVERY OFFICE,
NO. 25 CORNHILL 1845

Published 2019 by Gildan Media LLC
aka G&D Media
www.GandDmedia.com

Front Cover design by David Rheinhardt of Pyrographx

Interior design by Meghan Day Healey of Story Horse, LLC

Library of Congress Cataloging-in-Publication Data is available upon request

ISBN: 978-1-7225-0226-3

10 9 8 7 6 5 4 3 2 1

CONTENTS

CONTENTS

PREFACE

In the month of August, 1841, I attended an anti-slavery convention in Nantucket, at which it was my happiness to become acquainted with Frederick Douglass, the writer of the following Narrative. He was a stranger to nearly every member of that body; but, having recently made his escape from the southern prison-house of bondage, and feeling his curiosity excited to ascertain the principles and measures of the abolitionists,—of whom he had heard a somewhat vague description while he was a slave,—he was induced to give his attendance, on the occasion alluded to, though at that time a resident in New Bedford.

Fortunate, most fortunate occurrence!—fortunate for the millions of his manacled brethren, yet panting for deliverance from their awful thraldom!—fortunate for the cause of negro emancipation, and of universal liberty!—fortunate for the land of his birth, which he has already done so much to save and bless!—fortunate for a large circle of friends and acquaintances, whose sympathy and affection he has strongly secured by the many sufferings he has endured, by his virtuous traits of character, by his ever-abiding remembrance of those who are in bonds, as being bound with them!—fortunate for the multitudes, in various parts of our republic, whose minds he has enlightened on the subject of slavery, and who have been melted to tears by his pathos, or roused to virtuous indignation by his stirring eloquence against the enslavers of men!—fortunate for himself, as it at once brought him into the field of public usefulness, "gave the world assurance of a MAN," quickened the slumbering energies of his soul, and consecrated him to the great work of breaking the rod of the oppressor, and letting the oppressed go free!

I shall never forget his first speech at the convention—the extraordinary emotion it excited in my own mind—the powerful impression it created upon a crowded auditory, completely taken by surprise—the applause which followed from the beginning to the end of his felicitous remarks. I think I never hated slavery so intensely as at that moment; certainly, my perception of the enormous outrage which is inflicted by it, on the godlike nature of its victims, was rendered far more clear than ever. There stood one, in physical proportion and stature commanding and exact—in intellect richly endowed—in natural eloquence a prodigy—in soul manifestly "created but a little lower than the angels"—yet a slave, ay, a fugitive slave,—trembling for his safety, hardly daring to believe that on the American soil, a single white person could be found who would befriend him at all hazards, for the love of God and humanity! Capable of high attainments as an intellectual and moral being—needing nothing but a comparatively small amount of cultivation to make him an ornament to society and a blessing to his race—by the law of the land, by the voice of the people, by the terms of the slave code, he was only a piece of property, a beast of burden, a chattel personal, nevertheless!

A beloved friend from New Bedford prevailed on Mr. Douglass to address the convention: He came forward to the platform with a hesitancy and embarrassment, necessarily the attendants of a sensitive mind in such a novel position. After apologizing for his ignorance, and reminding the audience that slavery was a poor school for the human intellect and heart, he proceeded to narrate some of the facts in his own history as a slave, and in the course of his speech gave utterance to many noble thoughts and thrilling reflections. As soon as he had taken his seat, filled with hope and admiration, I rose, and declared that Patrick Henry, of revolutionary fame, never made a speech more eloquent in the cause of liberty, than the one we had just listened to from the lips of that hunted fugitive. So I believed at that time—such is my belief now. I reminded the audience of the peril which surrounded this self-emancipated young man at the North,—even in Massachusetts, on the soil of the Pilgrim Fathers, among the descendants of revolutionary sires; and I appealed to them, whether they would ever allow him to be carried back into slavery,—law or no law, constitution or no constitution. The response was unanimous and in thunder-tones—"NO!" "Will you succor and protect him as a brother-man—a resident of the old Bay State?" "YES!" shouted the whole mass, with an energy so startling, that the ruthless tyrants south of

Mason and Dixon's line might almost have heard the mighty burst of feeling, and recognized it as the pledge of an invincible determination, on the part of those who gave it, never to betray him that wanders, but to hide the outcast, and firmly to abide the consequences.

It was at once deeply impressed upon my mind, that, if Mr. Douglass could be persuaded to consecrate his time and talents to the promotion of the anti-slavery enterprise, a powerful impetus would be given to it, and a stunning blow at the same time inflicted on northern prejudice against a colored complexion. I therefore endeavored to instil hope and courage into his mind, in order that he might dare to engage in a vocation so anomalous and responsible for a person in his situation; and I was seconded in this effort by warm-hearted friends, especially by the late General Agent of the Massachusetts Anti-Slavery Society, Mr. John A. Collins, whose judgment in this instance entirely coincided with my own. At first, he could give no encouragement; with unfeigned diffidence, he expressed his conviction that he was not adequate to the performance of so great a task; the path marked out was wholly an untrodden one; he was sincerely apprehensive that he should do more harm than good. After much deliberation, however, he consented to make a trial; and ever since that period, he has acted as a lecturing agent, under the auspices either of the American or the Massachusetts Anti-Slavery Society. In labors he has been most abundant; and his success in combating prejudice, in gaining proselytes, in agitating the public mind, has far surpassed the most sanguine expectations that were raised at the commencement of his brilliant career. He has borne himself with gentleness and meekness, yet with true manliness of character. As a public speaker, he excels in pathos, wit, comparison, imitation, strength of reasoning, and fluency of language. There is in him that union of head and heart, which is indispensable to an enlightenment of the heads and a winning of the hearts of others. May his strength continue to be equal to his day! May he continue to "grow in grace, and in the knowledge of God," that he may be increasingly serviceable in the cause of bleeding humanity, whether at home or abroad!

It is certainly a very remarkable fact, that one of the most efficient advocates of the slave population, now before the public, is a fugitive slave, in the person of Frederick Douglass; and that the free colored population of the United States are as ably represented by one of their own number, in the person of Charles Lenox Remond, whose eloquent appeals have extorted the highest applause of multitudes on both sides of the Atlantic. Let the calumniators of the colored race despise themselves for their baseness and illiberality of spirit, and henceforth cease to talk of the natural inferiority of those who require nothing but time and opportunity to attain to the highest point of human excellence.

It may, perhaps, be fairly questioned, whether any other portion of the population of the earth could have endured the privations, sufferings and horrors of slavery, without having become more degraded in the scale of humanity than the slaves of African descent. Nothing has been left undone to cripple their intellects, darken their minds, debase their moral nature, obliterate all traces of their relationship to mankind; and yet how wonderfully they have sustained the mighty load of a most frightful bondage, under which they have been groaning for centuries! To illustrate the effect of slavery on the white man,—to show that he has no powers of endurance, in such a condition, superior to those of his black brother,—Daniel O'connell, the distinguished advocate of universal emancipation, and the mightiest champion of prostrate but not conquered Ireland, relates the following anecdote in a speech delivered by him in the Conciliation Hall, Dublin, before the Loyal National Repeal Association, March 31, 1845. "No matter," said Mr. O'connell, "under what specious term it may disguise itself, slavery is still hideous. *It has a natural, an inevitable tendency to brutalize every noble faculty of man.* An American sailor, who was cast away on the shore of Africa, where he was kept in slavery for three years, was, at the expiration of that period, found to be imbruted and stultified—he had lost all reasoning power; and having forgotten his native language, could only utter some savage gibberish between Arabic and English, which nobody could understand, and which even he himself found difficulty in pronouncing. So much for the humanizing influence of The Domestic Institution!" Admitting this to have been an extraordinary case of mental deterioration, it proves at least that the white slave can sink as low in the scale of humanity as the black one.

Mr. Douglass has very properly chosen to write his own Narrative, in his own style, and according to the best of his ability, rather than to employ some one else. It is, therefore, entirely his own production; and, considering how long and dark was the career he had to run as a slave,—how few have been his opportunities to improve his mind since he broke his iron fetters,—it is, in my judgment, highly creditable to his head and heart. He who can peruse it without a tearful eye, a heaving breast, an afflicted spirit,—without being filled with an unutterable abhorrence of slavery and all its abettors, and animated with a determination to seek the immediate overthrow of that execrable system,—without trembling for the fate of this country in the hands of a righteous God, who is ever on the side of the oppressed, and whose arm is not shortened that it cannot save,—must have a flinty heart, and be qualified to act the part of a trafficker "in slaves and the souls of men." I am confident that it is essentially true in all its statements; that nothing has been set down in malice, nothing exaggerated, nothing drawn from the imagination; that it comes short of the reality, rather than overstates a single fact in regard to *slavery as it is*. The experience of Frederick Douglass, as a slave, was not a peculiar one; his lot was not especially a hard one; his case may be regarded as a very fair specimen of the treatment of slaves in Maryland, in which State it is conceded that they are better fed and less cruelly treated than in Georgia, Alabama, or Louisiana. Many have suffered incomparably more, while very few on the plantations have suffered less, than himself. Yet how deplorable was his situation! what terrible chastisements were inflicted upon his person! what still more shocking outrages were perpetrated upon his mind! with all his noble powers and sublime aspirations, how like a brute was he treated, even by those professing to have the same mind in them that was in Christ Jesus! to what dreadful liabilities was he continually subjected! how destitute of friendly counsel and aid, even in his greatest extremities! how heavy was the midnight of woe which shrouded in blackness the last ray of hope, and filled the future with terror and gloom! what longings after freedom took possession of his breast, and how his misery augmented, in proportion as he grew reflective and intelligent,—thus demonstrating that a happy slave is an extinct man! how he thought, reasoned, felt, under the lash of the driver, with the chains upon his limbs! what perils he encountered in his endeavors to escape from his horrible doom! and how signal have been his deliverance and preservation in the midst of a nation of pitiless enemies!

This Narrative contains many affecting incidents, many passages of great eloquence and power; but I think the most thrilling one of them all is the description Douglass gives of his feelings, as he stood soliloquizing respecting his fate, and the chances of his one day being a freeman, on the banks of the Chesapeake Bay—viewing the receding vessels as they flew with their white wings before the breeze, and apostrophizing them as animated by the living spirit of freedom. Who can read that passage, and be insensible to its pathos and sublimity? Compressed into it is a whole Alexandrian library of thought, feeling, and sentiment—all that can, all that need be urged, in the form of expostulation, entreaty, rebuke, against that crime of crimes,—making man the property of his fellow-man! O, how accursed is that system, which entombs the godlike mind of man, defaces the divine image, reduces those who by creation were crowned with glory and honor to a level with four-footed beasts, and exalts the dealer in human flesh above all that is called God! Why should its existence be prolonged one hour? Is it not evil, only evil, and that continually? What does its presence imply but the absence of all fear of God, all regard for man, on the part of the people of the United States? Heaven speed its eternal overthrow!

So profoundly ignorant of the nature of slavery are many persons, that they are stubbornly incredulous whenever they read or listen to any recital of the cruelties which are daily inflicted on its victims. They do not deny that the slaves are held as property; but that terrible fact seems to convey to their minds no idea of injustice, exposure to outrage, or savage barbarity. Tell them of cruel scourgings, of mutilations and brandings, of scenes of pollution and blood, of the banishment of all light and knowledge, and they affect to be greatly indignant at such enormous exaggerations, such wholesale misstatements, such abominable libels on the character of the southern planters! As if all these direful outrages were not the natural results of slavery! As if it were less cruel to reduce a human being to the condition of a thing, than to give him a severe flagellation, or to deprive him of necessary food and clothing! As if whips, chains, thumb-screws, paddles, blood-hounds, overseers, drivers, patrols, were not all indispensable to keep the slaves down, and to give protection to their ruthless oppressors! As if, when the marriage institution is abolished, concubinage, adultery, and incest, must not necessarily abound; when all the rights of humanity are annihilated, any barrier remains to protect the victim from the fury of the spoiler; when absolute power is assumed over life and liberty, it will not be wielded with destructive sway! Skeptics of this character abound in society. In some few instances, their incredulity arises from a want of reflection; but, generally, it indicates a hatred of the light, a desire to shield slavery from the assaults of its foes, a contempt of the colored race, whether bond or free. Such will try to discredit the shocking tales of slaveholding cruelty which are recorded in this truthful Narrative; but they will labor in vain. Mr. Douglass has frankly disclosed the place of his birth, the names of those who claimed ownership in his body and soul, and the names also of those who committed the crimes which he has alleged against them. His statements, therefore, may easily be disproved, if they are untrue.

In the course of his Narrative, he relates two instances of murderous cruelty,—in one of which a planter deliberately shot a slave belonging to a neighboring plantation, who had unintentionally gotten within his lordly domain in quest of fish; and in the other, an overseer blew out the brains of a slave who had fled to a stream of water to escape a bloody scourging. Mr. Douglass states that in neither of these instances was any thing done by way of legal arrest or judicial investigation. The Baltimore American, of March 17, 1845, relates a similar case of atrocity, perpetrated with similar impunity—as follows:—"*Shooting a slave.*—We learn, upon the authority of a letter from Charles county, Maryland, received by a gentleman of this city, that a young man, named Matthews, a nephew of General Matthews, and whose father, it is believed, holds an office at Washington, killed one of the slaves upon his father's farm by shooting him. The letter states that young Matthews had been left in charge of the farm; that he gave an order to the servant, which was disobeyed, when he proceeded to the house, *obtained a gun, and, returning, shot the servant.* He immediately, the letter continues, fled to his father's residence, where he still remains unmolested."—Let it never be forgotten, that no slaveholder or overseer can be convicted of any outrage perpetrated on the person of a slave, however diabolical it may be, on the testimony of colored witnesses, whether bond or free. By the slave code, they are adjudged to be as incompetent to testify against a white man, as though they were indeed a part of the brute creation. Hence, there is no legal protection in fact, whatever there may be in form, for the slave population; and any amount of cruelty may be inflicted on them with impunity. Is it possible for the human mind to conceive of a more horrible state of society?

The effect of a religious profession on the conduct of southern masters is vividly described in the following Narrative, and shown to be any thing but salutary. In the nature of the case, it must be in the highest degree pernicious. The testimony of Mr. Douglass, on this point, is sustained by a cloud of witnesses, whose veracity is unimpeachable. "A slaveholder's profession of Christianity is a palpable imposture. He is a felon of the highest grade. He is a man-stealer. It is of no importance what you put in the other scale."

Reader! are you with the man-stealers in sympathy and purpose, or on the side of their down-trodden victims? If with the former, then are you the foe of God and man. If with the latter, what are you prepared to do and dare in their behalf? Be faithful, be vigilant, be untiring in your efforts to break every yoke, and let the oppressed go free. Come what may— cost what it may—inscribe on the banner which you unfurl to the breeze, as your religious and political motto—"No Compromise with Slavery! No Union with Slaveholders!"

WM. LLOYD GARRISON
Boston, May 1, 1845.

LETTER
FROM WENDELL PHILLIPS, ESQ.

Boston, *April* 22, 1845.

My Dear Friend:

You remember the old fable of "The Man and the Lion," where the lion complained that he should not be so misrepresented "when the lions wrote history."

I am glad the time has come when the "lions write history." We have been left long enough to gather the character of slavery from the involuntary evidence of the masters. One might, indeed, rest sufficiently satisfied with what, it is evident, must be, in general, the results of such a relation, without seeking farther to find whether they have followed in every instance. Indeed, those who stare at the half-peck of corn a week, and love to count the lashes on the slave's back, are seldom the "stuff" out of which reformers and abolitionists are to be made. I remember that, in 1838, many were waiting for the results of the West India experiment, before they could come into our ranks. Those "results" have come long ago; but, alas! few of that number have come with them, as converts. A man must be disposed to judge of emancipation by other tests than whether it has increased the produce of sugar,—and to hate slavery for other reasons than because it starves men and whips women,—before he is ready to lay the first stone of his anti-slavery life.

I was glad to learn, in your story, how early the most neglected of God's children waken to a sense of their rights, and of the injustice done them. Experience is a keen teacher; and long before you had mastered your A B C, or knew where the "white sails" of the Chesapeake were bound, you began, I see, to gauge the wretchedness of the slave, not by his hunger and want, not by his lashes and toil, but by the cruel and blighting death which gathers over his soul.

In connection with this, there is one circumstance which makes your recollections peculiarly valuable, and renders your early insight the more remarkable. You come from that part of the country where we are told slavery appears with its fairest features. Let us hear, then, what it is at its best estate—gaze on its bright side, if it has one; and then imagination may task her powers to add dark lines to the picture, as she travels southward to that (for the colored man) Valley of the Shadow of Death, where the Mississippi sweeps along.

Again, we have known you long, and can put the most entire confidence in your truth, candor, and sincerity. Every one who has heard you speak has felt, and, I am confident, every one who reads your book will feel, persuaded that you give them a fair specimen of the whole truth. No one-sided portrait,—no wholesale complaints,—but strict justice done, whenever individual kindliness has neutralized, for a moment, the deadly system with which it was strangely allied. You have been with us, too, some years, and can fairly compare the twilight of rights, which your race enjoy at the North, with that "noon of night" under which they labor south of Mason and Dixon's line. Tell us whether, after all, the half-free colored man of Massachusetts is worse off than the pampered slave of the rice swamps!

In reading your life, no one can say that we have unfairly picked out some rare specimens of cruelty. We know that the bitter drops, which even you have drained from the cup, are no incidental aggravations, no individual ills, but such as must mingle always and necessarily in the lot of every slave. They are the essential ingredients, not the occasional results, of the system.

After all, I shall read your book with trembling for you. Some years ago, when you were beginning to tell me your real name and birthplace, you may remember I stopped you, and preferred to remain ignorant of all. With the exception of a vague description, so I continued, till the other day, when you read me your memoirs. I hardly knew, at the time, whether to thank you or not for the sight of them, when I reflected that it was still dangerous, in Massachusetts, for honest men to tell their names! They say the fathers, in 1776, signed the Declaration of Independence with the halter about their necks. You, too, publish your declaration of freedom with danger compassing you around. In all the broad lands which the Constitution of the United States overshadows, there is no single spot,—however narrow or desolate,—where a fugitive slave can plant himself and say, "I am safe." The whole armory of Northern Law has no shield for you. I am free to say that, in your place, I should throw the MS. into the fire.

You, perhaps, may tell your story in safety, endeared as you are to so many warm hearts by rare gifts, and a still rarer devotion of them to the service of others. But it will be owing only to your labors, and the fearless efforts of those who, trampling the laws and Constitution of the country under their feet, are determined that they will "hide the outcast," and that their hearths shall be, spite of the law, an asylum for the oppressed, if, some time or other, the humblest may stand in our streets, and bear witness in safety against the cruelties of which he has been the victim.

Yet it is sad to think, that these very throbbing hearts which welcome your story, and form your best safeguard in telling it, are all beating contrary to the "statute in such case made and provided." Go on, my dear friend, till you, and those who, like you, have been saved, so as by fire, from the dark prison-house, shall stereotype these free, illegal pulses into statutes; and New England, cutting loose from a blood-stained Union, shall glory in being the house of refuge for the oppressed,—till we no longer merely "*hide* the outcast," or make a merit of standing idly by while he is hunted in our midst; but, consecrating anew the soil of the Pilgrims as an asylum for the oppressed, proclaim our *welcome* to the slave so loudly, that the tones shall reach every hut in the Carolinas, and make the broken-hearted bondman leap up at the thought of old Massachusetts.

God speed the day!

Till then, and ever,

Yours truly,

WENDELL PHILLIPS.

Frederick Douglass.

NARRATIVE
OF THE LIFE OF
FREDERICK DOUGLASS

CHAPTER 1

I was born in Tuckahoe, near Hillsborough, and about twelve miles from Easton, in Talbot county, Maryland. I have no accurate knowledge of my age, never having seen any authentic record containing it. By far the larger part of the slaves know as little of their ages as horses know of theirs, and it is the wish of most masters within my knowledge to keep their slaves thus ignorant. I do not remember to have ever met a slave who could tell of his birthday. They seldom come nearer to it than planting-time, harvest-time, cherry-time, spring-time, or fall-time. A want of information concerning my own was a source of unhappiness to me even during childhood.

The white children could tell their ages. I could not tell why I ought to be deprived of the same privilege. I was not allowed to make any inquiries of my master concerning it. He deemed all such inquiries on the part of a slave improper and impertinent, and evidence of a restless spirit. The nearest estimate I can give makes me now between twenty-seven and twenty-eight years of age. I come to this, from hearing my master say, some time during 1835, I was about seventeen years old.

My mother was named Harriet Bailey. She was the daughter of Isaac and Betsey Bailey, both colored, and quite dark. My mother was of a darker complexion than either my grandmother or grandfather.

My father was a white man. He was admitted to be such by all I ever heard speak of my parentage. The opinion was also whispered that my master was my father; but of the correctness of this opinion, I know nothing; the means of knowing was withheld from me.

My mother and I were separated when I was but an infant—before I knew her as my mother. It is a common custom, in the part of Maryland from which I ran away, to part children from their mothers at a very early age. Frequently, before the child has reached its twelfth month, its mother is taken from it, and hired out on some farm a considerable distance off, and the child is placed under the care of an old woman, too old for field labor. For what this separation is done, I do not know, unless it be to hinder the development of the child's affection toward its mother, and to blunt and destroy the natural affection of the mother for the child. This is the inevitable result.

I never saw my mother, to know her as such, more than four or five times in my life; and each of these times was very short in duration, and at night. She was hired by a Mr. Stewart, who lived about twelve miles from my home. She made her journeys to see me in the night, travelling the whole distance on foot, after the performance of her day's work. She was a field hand, and a whipping is the penalty of not being in the field at sunrise, unless a slave has special permission from his or her master to the contrary—a permission which they seldom get, and one that gives to him that gives it the proud name of being a kind master. I do not recollect of ever seeing my mother by the light of day.

She was with me in the night. She would lie down with me, and get me to sleep, but long before I waked she was gone. Very little communication ever took place between us. Death soon ended what little we could have while she lived, and with it her hardships and suffering. She died when I was about seven years old, on one of my master's farms, near Lee's Mill. I was not allowed to be present during her illness, at her death, or burial. She was gone long before I knew any thing about it. Never having enjoyed, to any considerable extent, her soothing presence, her tender and watchful care, I received the tidings of her death with much the same emotions I should have probably felt at the death of a stranger.

Called thus suddenly away, she left me without the slightest intimation of who my father was. The whisper that my master was my father, may or may not be true; and, true or false, it is of but little consequence to my purpose whilst the fact remains, in all its glaring odiousness, that slaveholders have ordained, and by law established, that the children of slave women shall in all cases follow the condition of their mothers; and this is done too obviously to administer to their own lusts, and make a gratification of their wicked desires profitable as well as pleasurable; for by this cunning arrangement, the slaveholder, in cases not a few, sustains to his slaves the double relation of master and father.

I know of such cases; and it is worthy of remark that such slaves invariably suffer greater hardships, and have more to contend with, than others. They are, in the first place, a constant offence to their mistress. She is ever disposed to find fault with them; they can seldom do any thing to please her; she is never better pleased than when she sees them under the lash, especially when she suspects her husband of showing to his mulatto children favors which he withholds from his black slaves.

The master is frequently compelled to sell this class of his slaves, out of deference to the feelings of his white wife; and, cruel as the deed may strike any one to be, for a man to sell his own children to human flesh-mongers, it is often the dictate of humanity for him to do so; for, unless he does this, he must not only whip them himself, but must stand by and see one white son tie up his brother, of but few shades darker complexion than himself, and ply the gory lash to his naked back; and if he lisp one word of disapproval, it is set down to his parental partiality, and only makes a bad matter worse, both for himself and the slave whom he would protect and defend.

Every year brings with it multitudes of this class of slaves. It was doubtless in consequence of a knowledge of this fact, that one great statesman of the south predicted the downfall of slavery by the inevitable laws of population. Whether this prophecy is ever fulfilled or not, it is nevertheless plain that a very different-looking class of people are springing up at the south, and are now held in slavery, from those originally brought to this country from Africa; and if their increase do no other good, it will do away the force of the argument, that God cursed Ham, and therefore American slavery is right. If the lineal descendants of Ham are alone to be scripturally enslaved, it is certain that slavery at the south must soon become unscriptural; for thousands are ushered into the world, annually, who, like myself, owe their existence to white fathers, and those fathers most frequently their own masters.

I have had two masters. My first master's name was Anthony. I do not remember his first name. He was generally called Captain Anthony—a title which, I presume, he acquired by sailing a craft on the Chesapeake Bay. He was not considered a rich slaveholder. He owned two or three farms, and about thirty slaves.

His farms and slaves were under the care of an overseer. The overseer's name was Plummer. Mr. Plummer was a miserable drunkard, a profane swearer, and a savage monster. He always went armed with a cowskin and a heavy cudgel. I have known him to cut and slash the women's heads so horribly, that even master would be enraged at his cruelty, and would threaten to whip him if he did not mind himself.

Master, however, was not a humane slaveholder. It required extraordinary barbarity on the part of an overseer to affect him. He was a cruel man, hardened by a long life of slaveholding. He would at times seem to take great pleasure in whipping a slave. I have often been awakened at the dawn of day by the most heart-rending shrieks of an own aunt of mine, whom he used to tie up to a joist, and whip upon her naked back till she was literally covered with blood. No words, no tears, no prayers, from his gory victim, seemed to move his iron heart from its bloody purpose. The louder she screamed, the harder he whipped; and where the blood ran fastest, there he whipped longest. He would whip her to make her scream, and whip her to make her hush; and not until overcome by fatigue, would he cease to swing the blood-clotted cowskin. I remember the first time I ever witnessed this horrible exhibition. I was quite a child, but I well remember it. I never shall forget it whilst I remember any thing. It was the first of a long series of such outrages, of which I was doomed to be a witness and a participant. It struck me with awful force. It was the blood-stained gate, the entrance to the hell of slavery, through which I was about to pass. It was a most terrible spectacle. I wish I could commit to paper the feelings with which I beheld it.

This occurrence took place very soon after I went to live with my old master, and under the following circumstances. Aunt Hester went out one night,—where or for what I do not know,—and happened to be absent when my master desired her presence. He had ordered her not to go out evenings, and warned her that she must never let him catch her in company with a young man, who was paying attention to her belonging to Colonel Lloyd. The young man's name was Ned Roberts, generally called Lloyd's Ned. Why master was so careful of her, may be safely left to conjecture. She was a woman of noble form, and of graceful proportions, having very few equals, and fewer superiors, in personal appearance, among the colored or white women of our neighborhood.

Aunt Hester had not only disobeyed his orders in going out, but had been found in company with Lloyd's Ned; which circumstance, I found, from what he said while whipping her, was the chief offence. Had he been a man of pure morals himself, he might have been thought interested in protecting the innocence of my aunt; but those who knew him will not suspect him of any such virtue.

Before he commenced whipping Aunt Hester, he took her into the kitchen, and stripped her from neck to waist, leaving her neck, shoulders, and back, entirely naked. He then told her to cross her hands, calling her at the same time a d——d b——h. After crossing her hands, he tied them with a strong rope, and led her to a stool under a large hook in the joist, put in for the purpose. He made her get upon the stool, and tied her hands to the hook.

She now stood fair for his infernal purpose. Her arms were stretched up at their full length, so that she stood upon the ends of her toes. He then said to her, "Now, you d——d b——h, I'll learn you how to disobey my orders!" and after rolling up his sleeves, he commenced to lay on the heavy cowskin, and soon the warm, red blood (amid heart-rending shrieks from her, and horrid oaths from him) came dripping to the floor.

I was so terrified and horror-stricken at the sight, that I hid myself in a closet, and dared not venture out till long after the bloody transaction was over. I expected it would be my turn next. It was all new to me. I had never seen any thing like it before. I had always lived with my grandmother on the outskirts of the plantation, where she was put to raise the children of the younger women. I had therefore been, until now, out of the way of the bloody scenes that often occurred on the plantation.

CHAPTER 2

My master's family consisted of two sons, Andrew and Richard; one daughter, Lucretia, and her husband, Captain Thomas Auld. They lived in one house, upon the home plantation of Colonel Edward Lloyd. My master was Colonel Lloyd's clerk and superintendent. He was what might be called the overseer of the overseers. I spent two years of childhood on this plantation in my old master's family. It was here that I witnessed the bloody transaction recorded in the first chapter; and as I received my first impressions of slavery on this plantation, I will give some description of it, and of slavery as it there existed.

The plantation is about twelve miles north of Easton, in Talbot county, and is situated on the border of Miles River. The principal products raised upon it were tobacco, corn, and wheat. These were raised in great abundance; so that, with the products of this and the other farms belonging to him, he was able to keep in almost constant employment a large sloop, in carrying them to market at Baltimore. This sloop was named Sally Lloyd, in honor of one of the colonel's daughters. My master's son-in-law, Captain Auld, was master of the vessel; she was otherwise manned by the colonel's own slaves. Their names were Peter, Isaac, Rich, and Jake. These were esteemed very highly by the other slaves, and looked upon as the privileged ones of the plantation; for it was no small affair, in the eyes of the slaves, to be allowed to see Baltimore.

Colonel Lloyd kept from three to four hundred slaves on his home plantation, and owned a large number more on the neighboring farms belonging to him. The names of the farms nearest to the home plantation were Wye Town and New Design. "Wye Town" was under the overseership of a man named Noah Willis. New Design was under the overseership of a Mr. Townsend. The overseers of these, and all the rest of the farms, numbering over twenty, received advice and direction from the managers of the home plantation. This was the great business place. It was the seat of government for the whole twenty farms. All disputes among the overseers were settled here. If a slave was convicted of any high misdemeanor, became unmanageable, or evinced a determination to run away, he was brought immediately here, severely whipped, put on board the sloop, carried to Baltimore, and sold to Austin Woolfolk, or some other slave-trader, as a warning to the slaves remaining.

Here, too, the slaves of all the other farms received their monthly allowance of food, and their yearly clothing. The men and women slaves received, as their monthly allowance of food, eight pounds of pork, or its equivalent in fish, and one bushel of corn meal. Their yearly clothing consisted of two coarse linen shirts, one pair of linen trousers, like the shirts, one jacket, one pair of trousers for winter, made of coarse negro cloth, one pair of stockings, and one pair of shoes; the whole of which could not have cost more than seven dollars. The allowance of the slave children was given to their mothers, or the old women having the care of them. The children unable to work in the field had neither shoes, stockings, jackets, nor trousers, given to them; their clothing consisted of two coarse linen shirts per year. When these failed them, they went naked until the next allowance-day. Children from seven to ten years old, of both sexes, almost naked, might be seen at all seasons of the year.

There were no beds given the slaves, unless one coarse blanket be considered such, and none but the men and women had these. This, however, is not considered a very great privation. They find less difficulty from the want of beds, than from the want of time to sleep; for when their day's work in the field is done, the most of them having their washing, mending, and cooking to do, and having few or none of the ordinary facilities for doing either of these, very many of their sleeping hours are consumed in preparing for the field the coming day; and when this is done, old and young, male and female, married and single, drop down side by side, on one common bed,—the cold, damp floor,—each covering himself or herself with their miserable blankets; and here they sleep till they are summoned to the field by the driver's horn. At the sound of this, all must rise, and be off to the field. There must be no halting; every one must be at his or her post; and woe betides them who hear not this morning summons to the field; for if they are not awakened by the sense of hearing, they are by the sense of feeling: no age nor sex finds any favor. Mr. Severe, the overseer, used to stand by the door of the quarter, armed with a large hickory stick and heavy cowskin, ready to whip any one who was so unfortunate as not to hear, or, from any other cause, was prevented from being ready to start for the field at the sound of the horn.

Mr. Severe was rightly named: he was a cruel man. I have seen him whip a woman, causing the blood to run half an hour at the time; and this, too, in the midst of her crying children, pleading for their mother's release. He seemed to take pleasure in manifesting his fiendish barbarity. Added to his cruelty, he was a profane swearer. It was enough to chill the blood and stiffen the hair of an ordinary man to hear him talk. Scarce a sentence escaped him but that was commenced or concluded by some horrid oath. The field was the place to witness his cruelty and profanity. His presence made it both the field of blood and of blasphemy. From the rising till the going down of the sun, he was cursing, raving, cutting, and slashing among the slaves of the field, in the most frightful manner. His career was short. He died very soon after I went to Colonel Lloyd's; and he died as he lived, uttering, with his dying groans, bitter curses and horrid oaths. His death was regarded by the slaves as the result of a merciful providence.

Mr. Severe's place was filled by a Mr. Hopkins. He was a very different man. He was less cruel, less profane, and made less noise, than Mr. Severe. His course was characterized by no extraordinary demonstrations of cruelty. He whipped, but seemed to take no pleasure in it. He was called by the slaves a good overseer.

The home plantation of Colonel Lloyd wore the appearance of a country village. All the mechanical operations for all the farms were performed here. The shoemaking and mending, the blacksmithing, cartwrighting, coopering, weaving, and grain-grinding, were all performed by the slaves on the home plantation. The whole place wore a business-like aspect very unlike the neighboring farms. The number of houses, too, conspired to give it advantage over the neighboring farms. It was called by the slaves the *Great House Farm.*Few privileges were esteemed higher, by the slaves of the out-farms, than that of being selected to do errands at the Great House Farm. It was associated in their minds with greatness. A representative could not be prouder of his election to a seat in the American Congress, than a slave on one of the out-farms would be of his election to do errands at the Great House Farm. They regarded it as evidence of great confidence reposed in them by their overseers; and it was on this account, as well as a constant desire to be out of the field from under the driver's lash, that they esteemed it a high privilege, one worth careful living for. He was called the smartest and most trusty fellow, who had this honor conferred upon him the most frequently. The competitors for this office sought as diligently to please their overseers, as the office-seekers in the political parties seek to please and deceive the people. The same traits of character might be seen in Colonel Lloyd's slaves, as are seen in the slaves of the political parties.

The slaves selected to go to the Great House Farm, for the monthly allowance for themselves and their fellow-slaves, were peculiarly enthusiastic. While on their way, they would make the dense old woods, for miles around, reverberate with their wild songs, revealing at once the highest joy and the deepest sadness. They would compose and sing as they went along, consulting neither time nor tune. The thought that came up, came out—if not in the word, in the sound;—and as frequently in the one as in the other. They would sometimes sing the most pathetic sentiment in the most rapturous tone, and the most rapturous sentiment in the most pathetic tone. Into all of their songs they would manage to weave something of the Great House Farm. Especially would they do this, when leaving home. They would then sing most exultingly the following words:—

"I am going away to the Great House Farm!
O, yea! O, yea! O!"

This they would sing, as a chorus, to words which to many would seem unmeaning jargon, but which, nevertheless, were full of meaning to themselves. I have sometimes thought that the mere hearing of those songs would do more to impress some minds with the horrible character of slavery, than the reading of whole volumes of philosophy on the subject could do.

I did not, when a slave, understand the deep meaning of those rude and apparently incoherent songs. I was myself within the circle; so that I neither saw nor heard as those without might see and hear. They told a tale of woe which was then altogether beyond my feeble comprehension; they were tones loud, long, and deep; they breathed the prayer and complaint of souls boiling over with the bitterest anguish. Every tone was a testimony against slavery, and a prayer to God for deliverance from chains. The hearing of those wild notes always depressed my spirit, and filled me with ineffable sadness. I have frequently found myself in tears while hearing them. The mere recurrence to those songs, even now, afflicts me; and while I am writing these lines, an expression of feeling has already found its way down my cheek. To those songs I trace my first glimmering conception of the dehumanizing character of slavery. I can never get rid of that conception. Those songs still follow me, to deepen my hatred of slavery, and quicken my sympathies for my brethren in bonds. If any one wishes to be impressed with the soul-killing effects of slavery, let him go to Colonel Lloyd's plantation, and, on allowance-day, place himself in the deep pine woods, and there let him, in silence, analyze the sounds that shall pass through the chambers of his soul,—and if he is not thus impressed, it will only be because "there is no flesh in his obdurate heart."

I have often been utterly astonished, since I came to the north, to find persons who could speak of the singing, among slaves, as evidence of their contentment and happiness. It is impossible to conceive of a greater mistake. Slaves sing most when they are most unhappy. The songs of the slave represent the sorrows of his heart; and he is relieved by them, only as an aching heart is relieved by its tears. At least, such is my experience. I have often sung to drown my sorrow, but seldom to express my happiness. Crying for joy, and singing for joy, were alike uncommon to me while in the jaws of slavery. The singing of a man cast away upon a desolate island might be as appropriately considered as evidence of contentment and happiness, as the singing of a slave; the songs of the one and of the other are prompted by the same emotion.

CHAPTER 3

Colonel Lloyd kept a large and finely cultivated garden, which afforded almost constant employment for four men, besides the chief gardener, (Mr. M'Durmond.) This garden was probably the greatest attraction of the place. During the summer months, people came from far and near—from Baltimore, Easton, and Annapolis—to see it. It abounded in fruits of almost every description, from the hardy apple of the north to the delicate orange of the south. This garden was not the least source of trouble on the plantation. Its excellent fruit was quite a temptation to the hungry swarms of boys, as well as the older slaves, belonging to the colonel, few of whom had the virtue or the vice to resist it.

Scarcely a day passed, during the summer, but that some slave had to take the lash for stealing fruit. The colonel had to resort to all kinds of stratagems to keep his slaves out of the garden. The last and most successful one was that of tarring his fence all around; after which, if a slave was caught with any tar upon his person, it was deemed sufficient proof that he had either been into the garden, or had tried to get in. In either case, he was severely whipped by the chief gardener. This plan worked well; the slaves became as fearful of tar as of the lash. They seemed to realize the impossibility of touching *tar* without being defiled.

The colonel also kept a splendid riding equipage. His stable and carriage-house presented the appearance of some of our large city livery establishments. His horses were of the finest form and noblest blood. His carriage-house contained three splendid coaches, three or four gigs, besides dearborns and barouches of the most fashionable style.

This establishment was under the care of two slaves— old Barney and young Barney—father and son. To attend to this establishment was their sole work. But it was by no means an easy employment; for in nothing was Colonel Lloyd more particular than in the management of his horses. The slightest inattention to these was unpardonable, and was visited upon those, under whose care they were placed, with the severest punishment; no excuse could shield them, if the colonel only suspected any want of attention to his horses—a supposition which he frequently indulged, and one which, of course, made the office of old and young Barney a very trying one. They never knew when they were safe from punishment. They were frequently whipped when least deserving, and escaped whipping when most deserving it.

Every thing depended upon the looks of the horses, and the state of Colonel Lloyd's own mind when his horses were brought to him for use. If a horse did not move fast enough, or hold his head high enough, it was owing to some fault of his keepers. It was painful to stand near the stable-door, and hear the various complaints against the keepers when a horse was taken out for use. "This horse has not had proper attention. He has not been sufficiently rubbed and curried, or he has not been properly fed; his food was too wet or too dry; he got it too soon or too late; he was too hot or too cold; he had too much hay, and not enough of grain; or he had too much grain, and not enough of hay; instead of old Barney's attending to the horse, he had very improperly left it to his son." To all these complaints, no matter how unjust, the slave must answer never a word.

Colonel Lloyd could not brook any contradiction from a slave. When he spoke, a slave must stand, listen, and tremble; and such was literally the case. I have seen Colonel Lloyd make old Barney, a man between fifty and sixty years of age, uncover his bald head, kneel down upon the cold, damp ground, and receive upon his naked and toil-worn shoulders more than thirty lashes at the time.

Colonel Lloyd had three sons—Edward, Murray, and Daniel,—and three sons-in-law, Mr. Winder, Mr. Nicholson, and Mr. Lowndes. All of these lived at the Great House Farm, and enjoyed the luxury of whipping the servants when they pleased, from old Barney down to William Wilkes, the coach-driver. I have seen Winder make one of the house-servants stand off from him a suitable distance to be touched with the end of his whip, and at every stroke raise great ridges upon his back.

To describe the wealth of Colonel Lloyd would be almost equal to describing the riches of Job. He kept from ten to fifteen house-servants. He was said to own a thousand slaves, and I think this estimate quite within the truth. Colonel Lloyd owned so many that he did not know them when he saw them; nor did all the slaves of the out-farms know him. It is reported of him, that, while riding along the road one day, he met a colored man, and addressed him in the usual manner of speaking to colored people on the public highways of the south: "Well, boy, whom do you belong to?" "To Colonel Lloyd," replied the slave. "Well, does the colonel treat you well?" "No, sir," was the ready reply. "What, does he work you too hard?" "Yes, sir." "Well, don't he give you enough to eat?" "Yes, sir, he gives me enough, such as it is."

The colonel, after ascertaining where the slave belonged, rode on; the man also went on about his business, not dreaming that he had been conversing with his master. He thought, said, and heard nothing more of the matter, until two or three weeks afterwards. The poor man was then informed by his overseer that, for having found fault with his master, he was now to be sold to a Georgia trader. He was immediately chained and handcuffed; and thus, without a moment's warning, he was snatched away, and forever sundered, from his family and friends, by a hand more unrelenting than death. This is the penalty of telling the truth, of telling the simple truth, in answer to a series of plain questions.

It is partly in consequence of such facts, that slaves, when inquired of as to their condition and the character of their masters, almost universally say they are contented, and that their masters are kind. The slaveholders have been known to send in spies among their slaves, to ascertain their views and feelings in regard to their condition. The frequency of this has had the effect to establish among the slaves the maxim, that a still tongue makes a wise head. They suppress the truth rather than take the consequences of telling it, and in so doing prove themselves a part of the human family. If they have any thing to say of their masters, it is generally in their masters' favor, especially when speaking to an untried man. I have been frequently asked, when a slave, if I had a kind master, and do not remember ever to have given a negative answer; nor did I, in pursuing this course, consider myself as uttering what was absolutely false; for I always measured the kindness of my master by the standard of kindness set up among slaveholders around us. Moreover, slaves are like other people, and imbibe prejudices quite common to others. They think their own better than that of others. Many, under the influence of this prejudice, think their own masters are better than the masters of other slaves; and this, too, in some cases, when the very reverse is true. Indeed, it is not uncommon for slaves even to fall out and quarrel among themselves about the relative goodness of their masters, each contending for the superior goodness of his own over that of the others. At the very same time, they mutually execrate their masters when viewed separately.

It was so on our plantation. When Colonel Lloyd's slaves met the slaves of Jacob Jepson, they seldom parted without a quarrel about their masters; Colonel Lloyd's slaves contending that he was the richest, and Mr. Jepson's slaves that he was the smartest, and most of a man. Colonel Lloyd's slaves would boast his ability to buy and sell Jacob Jepson. Mr. Jepson's slaves would boast his ability to whip Colonel Lloyd. These quarrels would almost always end in a fight between the parties, and those that whipped were supposed to have gained the point at issue. They seemed to think that the greatness of their masters was transferable to themselves. It was considered as being bad enough to be a slave; but to be a poor man's slave was deemed a disgrace indeed!

CHAPTER 4

Mr. Hopkins remained but a short time in the office of overseer. Why his career was so short, I do not know, but suppose he lacked the necessary severity to suit Colonel Lloyd. Mr. Hopkins was succeeded by Mr. Austin Gore, a man possessing, in an eminent degree, all those traits of character indispensable to what is called a first-rate overseer. Mr. Gore had served Colonel Lloyd, in the capacity of overseer, upon one of the out-farms, and had shown himself worthy of the high station of overseer upon the home or Great House Farm.

Mr. Gore was proud, ambitious, and persevering. He was artful, cruel, and obdurate. He was just the man for such a place, and it was just the place for such a man. It afforded scope for the full exercise of all his powers, and he seemed to be perfectly at home in it. He was one of those who could torture the slightest look, word, or gesture, on the part of the slave, into impudence, and would treat it accordingly. There must be no answering back to him; no explanation was allowed a slave, showing himself to have been wrongfully accused. Mr. Gore acted fully up to the maxim laid down by slaveholders,—"It is better that a dozen slaves should suffer under the lash, than that the overseer should be convicted, in the presence of the slaves, of having been at fault."

No matter how innocent a slave might be—it availed him nothing, when accused by Mr. Gore of any misdemeanor. To be accused was to be convicted, and to be convicted was to be punished; the one always following the other with immutable certainty. To escape punishment was to escape accusation; and few slaves had the fortune to do either, under the overseership of Mr. Gore. He was just proud enough to demand the most debasing homage of the slave, and quite servile enough to crouch, himself, at the feet of the master.

He was ambitious enough to be contented with nothing short of the highest rank of overseers, and persevering enough to reach the height of his ambition. He was cruel enough to inflict the severest punishment, artful enough to descend to the lowest trickery, and obdurate enough to be insensible to the voice of a reproving conscience. He was, of all the overseers, the most dreaded by the slaves. His presence was painful; his eye flashed confusion; and seldom was his sharp, shrill voice heard, without producing horror and trembling in their ranks.

Mr. Gore was a grave man, and, though a young man, he indulged in no jokes, said no funny words, seldom smiled. His words were in perfect keeping with his looks, and his looks were in perfect keeping with his words. Overseers will sometimes indulge in a witty word, even with the slaves; not so with Mr. Gore. He spoke but to command, and commanded but to be obeyed; he dealt sparingly with his words, and bountifully with his whip, never using the former where the latter would answer as well. When he whipped, he seemed to do so from a sense of duty, and feared no consequences. He did nothing reluctantly, no matter how disagreeable; always at his post, never inconsistent. He never promised but to fulfil. He was, in a word, a man of the most inflexible firmness and stone-like coolness.

His savage barbarity was equalled only by the consummate coolness with which he committed the grossest and most savage deeds upon the slaves under his charge. Mr. Gore once undertook to whip one of Colonel Lloyd's slaves, by the name of Demby. He had given Demby but few stripes, when, to get rid of the scourging, he ran and plunged himself into a creek, and stood there at the depth of his shoulders, refusing to come out. Mr. Gore told him that he would give him three calls, and that, if he did not come out at the third call, he would shoot him. The first call was given. Demby made no response, but stood his ground. The second and third calls were given with the same result. Mr. Gore then, without consultation or deliberation with any one, not even giving Demby an additional call, raised his musket to his face, taking deadly aim at his standing victim, and in an instant poor Demby was no more. His mangled body sank out of sight, and blood and brains marked the water where he had stood.

A thrill of horror flashed through every soul upon the plantation, excepting Mr. Gore. He alone seemed cool and collected. He was asked by Colonel Lloyd and my old master, why he resorted to this extraordinary expedient. His reply was, (as well as I can remember,) that Demby had become unmanageable. He was setting a dangerous example to the other slaves,—one which, if suffered to pass without some such demonstration on his part, would finally lead to the total subversion of all rule and order upon the plantation. He argued that if one slave refused to be corrected, and escaped with his life, the other slaves would soon copy the example; the result of which would be, the freedom of the slaves, and the enslavement of the whites. Mr. Gore's defence was satisfactory. He was continued in his station as overseer upon the home plantation.

His fame as an overseer went abroad. His horrid crime was not even submitted to judicial investigation. It was committed in the presence of slaves, and they of course could neither institute a suit, nor testify against him; and thus the guilty perpetrator of one of the bloodiest and most foul murders goes unwhipped of justice, and uncensured by the community in which he lives.

Mr. Gore lived in St. Michael's, Talbot county, Maryland, when I left there; and if he is still alive, he very probably lives there now; and if so, he is now, as he was then, as highly esteemed and as much respected as though his guilty soul had not been stained with his brother's blood.

I speak advisedly when I say this,—that killing a slave, or any colored person, in Talbot county, Maryland, is not treated as a crime, either by the courts or the community. Mr. Thomas Lanman, of St. Michael's, killed two slaves, one of whom he killed with a hatchet, by knocking his brains out. He used to boast of the commission of the awful and bloody deed. I have heard him do so laughingly, saying, among other things, that he was the only benefactor of his country in the company, and that when others would do as much as he had done, we should be relieved of "the d——d niggers."

The wife of Mr. Giles Hicks, living but a short distance from where I used to live, murdered my wife's cousin, a young girl between fifteen and sixteen years of age, mangling her person in the most horrible manner, breaking her nose and breastbone with a stick, so that the poor girl expired in a few hours afterward. She was immediately buried, but had not been in her untimely grave but a few hours before she was taken up and examined by the coroner, who decided that she had come to her death by severe beating. The offence for which this girl was thus murdered was this:—She had been set that night to mind Mrs. Hicks's baby, and during the night she fell asleep, and the baby cried. She, having lost her rest for several nights previous, did not hear the crying.

They were both in the room with Mrs. Hicks. Mrs. Hicks, finding the girl slow to move, jumped from her bed, seized an oak stick of wood by the fireplace, and with it broke the girl's nose and breastbone, and thus ended her life. I will not say that this most horrid murder produced no sensation in the community. It did produce sensation, but not enough to bring the murderess to punishment. There was a warrant issued for her arrest, but it was never served. Thus she escaped not only punishment, but even the pain of being arraigned before a court for her horrid crime.

Whilst I am detailing bloody deeds which took place during my stay on Colonel Lloyd's plantation, I will briefly narrate another, which occurred about the same time as the murder of Demby by Mr. Gore.

Colonel Lloyd's slaves were in the habit of spending a part of their nights and Sundays in fishing for oysters, and in this way made up the deficiency of their scanty allowance. An old man belonging to Colonel Lloyd, while thus engaged, happened to get beyond the limits of Colonel Lloyd's, and on the premises of Mr. Beal Bondly. At this trespass, Mr. Bondly took offence, and with his musket came down to the shore, and blew its deadly contents into the poor old man.

Mr. Bondly came over to see Colonel Lloyd the next day, whether to pay him for his property, or to justify himself in what he had done, I know not. At any rate, this whole fiend-ish transaction was soon hushed up. There was very little said about it at all, and nothing done. It was a common saying, even among little white boys, that it was worth a half-cent to kill a "nigger," and a half-cent to bury one.

CHAPTER 5

As to my own treatment while I lived on Colonel Lloyd's plantation, it was very similar to that of the other slave children. I was not old enough to work in the field, and there being little else than field work to do, I had a great deal of leisure time. The most I had to do was to drive up the cows at evening, keep the fowls out of the garden, keep the front yard clean, and run of errands for my old master's daughter, Mrs. Lucretia Auld. The most of my leisure time I spent in helping Master Daniel Lloyd in finding his birds, after he had shot them. My connection with Master Daniel was of some advantage to me. He became quite attached to me, and was a sort of protector of me. He would not allow the older boys to impose upon me, and would divide his cakes with me.

I was seldom whipped by my old master, and suffered little from any thing else than hunger and cold. I suffered much from hunger, but much more from cold. In hottest summer and coldest winter, I was kept almost naked—no shoes, no stockings, no jacket, no trousers, nothing on but a coarse tow linen shirt, reaching only to my knees. I had no bed. I must have perished with cold, but that, the coldest nights, I used to steal a bag which was used for carrying corn to the mill. I would crawl into this bag, and there sleep on the cold, damp, clay floor, with my head in and feet out. My feet have been so cracked with the frost, that the pen with which I am writing might be laid in the gashes.

We were not regularly allowanced. Our food was coarse corn meal boiled. This was called *mush*. It was put into a large wooden tray or trough, and set down upon the ground. The children were then called, like so many pigs, and like so many pigs they would come and devour the mush; some with oyster-shells, others with pieces of shingle, some with naked hands, and none with spoons. He that ate fastest got most; he that was strongest secured the best place; and few left the trough satisfied.

I was probably between seven and eight years old when I left Colonel Lloyd's plantation. I left it with joy. I shall never forget the ecstasy with which I received the intelligence that my old master (Anthony) had determined to let me go to Baltimore, to live with Mr. Hugh Auld, brother to my old master's son-in-law, Captain Thomas Auld. I received this information about three days before my departure. They were three of the happiest days I ever enjoyed. I spent the most part of all these three days in the creek, washing off the plantation scurf, and preparing myself for my departure.

The pride of appearance which this would indicate was not my own. I spent the time in washing, not so much because I wished to, but because Mrs. Lucretia had told me I must get all the dead skin off my feet and knees before I could go to Baltimore; for the people in Baltimore were very cleanly, and would laugh at me if I looked dirty. Besides, she was going to give me a pair of trousers, which I should not put on unless I got all the dirt off me. The thought of owning a pair of trousers was great indeed! It was almost a sufficient motive, not only to make me take off what would be called by pig-drovers the mange, but the skin itself. I went at it in good earnest, working for the first time with the hope of reward.

The ties that ordinarily bind children to their homes were all suspended in my case. I found no severe trial in my departure. My home was charmless; it was not home to me; on parting from it, I could not feel that I was leaving any thing which I could have enjoyed by staying. My mother was dead, my grandmother lived far off, so that I seldom saw her. I had two sisters and one brother, that lived in the same house with me; but the early separation of us from our mother had well nigh blotted the fact of our relationship from our memories.

I looked for home elsewhere, and was confident of finding none which I should relish less than the one which I was leaving. If, however, I found in my new home hardship, hunger, whipping, and nakedness, I had the consolation that I should not have escaped any one of them by staying. Having already had more than a taste of them in the house of my old master, and having endured them there, I very naturally inferred my ability to endure them elsewhere, and especially at Baltimore; for I had something of the feeling about Baltimore that is expressed in the proverb, that "being hanged in England is preferable to dying a natural death in Ireland."

I had the strongest desire to see Baltimore. Cousin Tom, though not fluent in speech, had inspired me with that desire by his eloquent description of the place. I could never point out any thing at the Great House, no matter how beautiful or powerful, but that he had seen something at Baltimore far exceeding, both in beauty and strength, the object which I pointed out to him. Even the Great House itself, with all its pictures, was far inferior to many buildings in Baltimore. So strong was my desire, that I thought a gratification of it would fully compensate for whatever loss of comforts I should sustain by the exchange. I left without a regret, and with the highest hopes of future happiness.

We sailed out of Miles River for Baltimore on a Saturday morning. I remember only the day of the week, for at that time I had no knowledge of the days of the month, nor the months of the year. On setting sail, I walked aft, and gave to Colonel Lloyd's plantation what I hoped would be the last look. I then placed myself in the bows of the sloop, and there spent the remainder of the day in looking ahead, interesting myself in what was in the distance rather than in things near by or behind.

In the afternoon of that day, we reached Annapolis, the capital of the State. We stopped but a few moments, so that I had no time to go on shore. It was the first large town that I had ever seen, and though it would look small compared with some of our New England factory villages, I thought it a wonderful place for its size—more imposing even than the Great House Farm!

We arrived at Baltimore early on Sunday morning, landing at Smith's Wharf, not far from Bowley's Wharf. We had on board the sloop a large flock of sheep; and after aiding in driving them to the slaughterhouse of Mr. Curtis on Louden Slater's Hill, I was conducted by Rich, one of the hands belonging on board of the sloop, to my new home in Alliciana Street, near Mr. Gardner's ship-yard, on Fells Point.

Mr. and Mrs. Auld were both at home, and met me at the door with their little son Thomas, to take care of whom I had been given. And here I saw what I had never seen before; it was a white face beaming with the most kindly emotions; it was the face of my new mistress, Sophia Auld. I wish I could describe the rapture that flashed through my soul as I beheld it. It was a new and strange sight to me, brightening up my pathway with the light of happiness. Little Thomas was told, there was his Freddy,—and I was told to take care of little Thomas; and thus I entered upon the duties of my new home with the most cheering prospect ahead.

I look upon my departure from Colonel Lloyd's plantation as one of the most interesting events of my life. It is possible, and even quite probable, that but for the mere circumstance of being removed from that plantation to Baltimore, I should have to-day, instead of being here seated by my own table, in the enjoyment of freedom and the happiness of home, writing this Narrative, been confined in the galling chains of slavery.

Going to live at Baltimore laid the foundation, and opened the gateway, to all my subsequent prosperity. I have ever regarded it as the first plain manifestation of that kind providence which has ever since attended me, and marked my life with so many favors. I regarded the selection of myself as being somewhat remarkable. There were a number of slave children that might have been sent from the plantation to Baltimore. There were those younger, those older, and those of the same age. I was chosen from among them all, and was the first, last, and only choice.

I may be deemed superstitious, and even egotistical, in regarding this event as a special interposition of divine Providence in my favor. But I should be false to the earliest sentiments of my soul, if I suppressed the opinion. I prefer to be true to myself, even at the hazard of incurring the ridicule of others, rather than to be false, and incur my own abhorrence. From my earliest recollection, I date the entertainment of a deep conviction that slavery would not always be able to hold me within its foul embrace; and in the darkest hours of my career in slavery, this living word of faith and spirit of hope departed not from me, but remained like ministering angels to cheer me through the gloom. This good spirit was from God, and to him I offer thanksgiving and praise.

CHAPTER 6

My new mistress proved to be all she appeared when I first met her at the door,—a woman of the kindest heart and finest feelings. She had never had a slave under her control previously to myself, and prior to her marriage she had been dependent upon her own industry for a living. She was by trade a weaver; and by constant application to her business, she had been in a good degree preserved from the blighting and dehumanizing effects of slavery.

I was utterly astonished at her goodness. I scarcely knew how to behave towards her. She was entirely unlike any other white woman I had ever seen. I could not approach her as I was accustomed to approach other white ladies. My early instruction was all out of place. The crouching servility, usually so acceptable a quality in a slave, did not answer when manifested toward her. Her favor was not gained by it; she seemed to be disturbed by it. She did not deem it impudent or unmannerly for a slave to look her in the face. The meanest slave was put fully at ease in her presence, and none left without feeling better for having seen her. Her face was made of heavenly smiles, and her voice of tranquil music.

But, alas! this kind heart had but a short time to remain such. The fatal poison of irresponsible power was already in her hands, and soon commenced its infernal work. That cheerful eye, under the influence of slavery, soon became red with rage; that voice, made all of sweet accord, changed to one of harsh and horrid discord; and that angelic face gave place to that of a demon.

Very soon after I went to live with Mr. and Mrs. Auld, she very kindly commenced to teach me the A, B, C. After I had learned this, she assisted me in learning to spell words of three or four letters. Just at this point of my progress, Mr. Auld found out what was going on, and at once forbade Mrs. Auld to instruct me further, telling her, among other things, that it was unlawful, as well as unsafe, to teach a slave to read. To use his own words, further, he said, "If you give a nigger an inch, he will take an ell. A nigger should know nothing but to obey his master—to do as he is told to do. Learning would *spoil* the best nigger in the world. Now," said he, "if you teach that nigger (speaking of myself) how to read, there would be no keeping him. It would forever unfit him to be a slave. He would at once become unmanageable, and of no value to his master. As to himself, it could do him no good, but a great deal of harm. It would make him discontented and unhappy."

These words sank deep into my heart, stirred up sentiments within that lay slumbering, and called into existence an entirely new train of thought. It was a new and special revelation, explaining dark and mysterious things, with which my youthful understanding had struggled, but struggled in vain. I now understood what had been to me a most perplexing difficulty—to wit, the white man's power to enslave the black man. It was a grand achievement, and I prized it highly. From that moment, I understood the pathway from slavery to freedom. It was just what I wanted, and I got it at a time when I the least expected it.

Whilst I was saddened by the thought of losing the aid of my kind mistress, I was gladdened by the invaluable instruction which, by the merest accident, I had gained from my master. Though conscious of the difficulty of learning without a teacher, I set out with high hope, and a fixed purpose, at whatever cost of trouble, to learn how to read.

The very decided manner with which he spoke, and strove to impress his wife with the evil consequences of giving me instruction, served to convince me that he was deeply sensible of the truths he was uttering. It gave me the best assurance that I might rely with the utmost confidence on the results which, he said, would flow from teaching me to read. What he most dreaded, that I most desired.

What he most loved, that I most hated. That which to him was a great evil, to be carefully shunned, was to me a great good, to be diligently sought; and the argument which he so warmly urged, against my learning to read, only served to inspire me with a desire and determination to learn. In learning to read, I owe almost as much to the bitter opposition of my master, as to the kindly aid of my mistress. I acknowledge the benefit of both.

I had resided but a short time in Baltimore before I observed a marked difference, in the treatment of slaves, from that which I had witnessed in the country. A city slave is almost a freeman, compared with a slave on the plantation. He is much better fed and clothed, and enjoys privileges altogether unknown to the slave on the plantation. There is a vestige of decency, a sense of shame, that does much to curb and check those outbreaks of atrocious cruelty so commonly enacted upon the plantation. He is a desperate slaveholder, who will shock the humanity of his non-slaveholding neighbors with the cries of his lacerated slave. Few are willing to incur the odium attaching to the reputation of being a cruel master; and above all things, they would not be known as not giving a slave enough to eat. Every city slaveholder is anxious to have it known of him, that he feeds his slaves well; and it is due to them to say, that most of them do give their slaves enough to eat.

There are, however, some painful exceptions to this rule. Directly opposite to us, on Philpot Street, lived Mr. Thomas Hamilton. He owned two slaves. Their names were Henrietta and Mary. Henrietta was about twenty-two years of age, Mary was about fourteen; and of all the mangled and emaciated creatures I ever looked upon, these two were the most so. His heart must be harder than stone, that could look upon these unmoved. The head, neck, and shoulders of Mary were literally cut to pieces. I have frequently felt her head, and found it nearly covered with festering sores, caused by the lash of her cruel mistress. I do not know that her master ever whipped her, but I have been an eye-witness to the cruelty of Mrs. Hamilton.

I used to be in Mr. Hamilton's house nearly every day. Mrs. Hamilton used to sit in a large chair in the middle of the room, with a heavy cowskin always by her side, and scarce an hour passed during the day but was marked by the blood of one of these slaves. The girls seldom passed her without her saying, "Move faster, you *black gip!*" at the same time giving them a blow with the cowskin over the head or shoulders, often drawing the blood. She would then say, "Take that, you *black gip!*" continuing, "If you don't move faster, I'll move you!" Added to the cruel lashings to which these slaves were subjected, they were kept nearly half-starved. They seldom knew what it was to eat a full meal. I have seen Mary contending with the pigs for the offal thrown into the street. So much was Mary kicked and cut to pieces, that she was oftener called "*pecked*" than by her name.

CHAPTER 7

I lived in Master Hugh's family about seven years. During this time, I succeeded in learning to read and write. In accomplishing this, I was compelled to resort to various stratagems. I had no regular teacher. My mistress, who had kindly commenced to instruct me, had, in compliance with the advice and direction of her husband, not only ceased to instruct, but had set her face against my being instructed by any one else. It is due, however, to my mistress to say of her, that she did not adopt this course of treatment immediately. She at first lacked the depravity indispensable to shutting me up in mental darkness. It was at least necessary for her to have some training in the exercise of irresponsible power, to make her equal to the task of treating me as though I were a brute.

My mistress was, as I have said, a kind and tender-hearted woman; and in the simplicity of her soul she commenced, when I first went to live with her, to treat me as she supposed one human being ought to treat another. In entering upon the duties of a slaveholder, she did not seem to perceive that I sustained to her the relation of a mere chattel, and that for her to treat me as a human being was not only wrong, but dangerously so. Slavery proved as injurious to her as it did to me. When I went there, she was a pious, warm, and tender-hearted woman. There was no sorrow or suffering for which she had not a tear. She had bread for the hungry, clothes for the naked, and comfort for every mourner that came within her reach.

Slavery soon proved its ability to divest her of these heavenly qualities. Under its influence, the tender heart became stone, and the lamblike disposition gave way to one of tiger-like fierceness. The first step in her downward course was in her ceasing to instruct me. She now commenced to practise her husband's precepts. She finally became even more violent in her opposition than her husband himself. She was not satisfied with simply doing as well as he had commanded; she seemed anxious to do better. Nothing seemed to make her more angry than to see me with a newspaper. She seemed to think that here lay the danger. I have had her rush at me with a face made all up of fury, and snatch from me a newspaper, in a manner that fully revealed her apprehension. She was an apt woman; and a little experience soon demonstrated, to her satisfaction, that education and slavery were incompatible with each other.

From this time I was most narrowly watched. If I was in a separate room any considerable length of time, I was sure to be suspected of having a book, and was at once called to give an account of myself. All this, however, was too late. The first step had been taken. Mistress, in teaching me the alphabet, had given me the *inch*, and no precaution could prevent me from taking the *ell*.

The plan which I adopted, and the one by which I was most successful, was that of making friends of all the little white boys whom I met in the street. As many of these as I could, I converted into teachers. With their kindly aid, obtained at different times and in different places, I finally succeeded in learning to read. When I was sent of errands, I always took my book with me, and by going one part of my errand quickly, I found time to get a lesson before my return.

I used also to carry bread with me, enough of which was always in the house, and to which I was always welcome; for I was much better off in this regard than many of the poor white children in our neighborhood. This bread I used to bestow upon the hungry little urchins, who, in return, would give me that more valuable bread of knowledge.

I am strongly tempted to give the names of two or three of those little boys, as a testimonial of the gratitude and affection I bear them; but prudence forbids;—not that it would injure me, but it might embarrass them; for it is almost an unpardonable offence to teach slaves to read in this Christian country. It is enough to say of the dear little fellows, that they lived on Philpot Street, very near Durgin and Bailey's shipyard. I used to talk this matter of slavery over with them. I would sometimes say to them, I wished I could be as free as they would be when they got to be men. "You will be free as soon as you are twenty-one, *but I am a slave for life!* Have not I as good a right to be free as you have?" These words used to trouble them; they would express for me the liveliest sympathy, and console me with the hope that something would occur by which I might be free.

I was now about twelve years old, and the thought of being *a slave for life* began to bear heavily upon my heart. Just about this time, I got hold of a book entitled "The Columbian Orator." Every opportunity I got, I used to read this book. Among much of other interesting matter, I found in it a dialogue between a master and his slave. The slave was represented as having run away from his master three times. The dialogue represented the conversation which took place between them, when the slave was retaken the third time. In this dialogue, the whole argument in behalf of slavery was brought forward by the master, all of which was disposed of by the slave. The slave was made to say some very smart as well as impressive things in reply to his master—things which had the desired though unexpected effect; for the conversation resulted in the voluntary emancipation of the slave on the part of the master.

In the same book, I met with one of Sheridan's mighty speeches on and in behalf of Catholic emancipation. These were choice documents to me. I read them over and over again with unabated interest. They gave tongue to interesting thoughts of my own soul, which had frequently flashed through my mind, and died away for want of utterance. The moral which I gained from the dialogue was the power of truth over the conscience of even a slaveholder. What I got from Sheridan was a bold denunciation of slavery, and a powerful vindication of human rights. The reading of these documents enabled me to utter my thoughts, and to meet the arguments brought forward to sustain slavery; but while they relieved me of one difficulty, they brought on another even more painful than the one of which I was relieved. The more I read, the more I was led to abhor and detest my enslavers. I could regard them in no other light than a band of successful robbers, who had left their homes, and gone to Africa, and stolen us from our homes, and in a strange land reduced us to slavery. I loathed them as being the meanest as well as the most wicked of men.

As I read and contemplated the subject, behold! that very discontentment which Master Hugh had predicted would follow my learning to read had already come, to torment and sting my soul to unutterable anguish. As I writhed under it, I would at times feel that learning to read had been a curse rather than a blessing. It had given me a view of my wretched condition, without the remedy. It opened my eyes to the horrible pit, but to no ladder upon which to get out. In moments of agony, I envied my fellow-slaves for their stupidity.

I have often wished myself a beast. I preferred the condition of the meanest reptile to my own. Any thing, no matter what, to get rid of thinking! It was this everlasting thinking of my condition that tormented me. There was no getting rid of it. It was pressed upon me by every object within sight or hearing, animate or inanimate. The silver trump of freedom had roused my soul to eternal wakefulness. Freedom now appeared, to disappear no more forever. It was heard in every sound, and seen in every thing. It was ever present to torment me with a sense of my wretched condition. I saw nothing without seeing it, I heard nothing without hearing it, and felt nothing without feeling it. It looked from every star, it smiled in every calm, breathed in every wind, and moved in every storm.

I often found myself regretting my own existence, and wishing myself dead; and but for the hope of being free, I have no doubt but that I should have killed myself, or done something for which I should have been killed. While in this state of mind, I was eager to hear any one speak of slavery. I was a ready listener. Every little while, I could hear something about the abolitionists. It was some time before I found what the word meant. It was always used in such connections as to make it an interesting word to me.

If a slave ran away and succeeded in getting clear, or if a slave killed his master, set fire to a barn, or did any thing very wrong in the mind of a slaveholder, it was spoken of as the fruit of *abolition*. Hearing the word in this connection very often, I set about learning what it meant. The dictionary afforded me little or no help. I found it was "the act of abolishing;" but then I did not know what was to be abolished. Here I was perplexed. I did not dare to ask any one about its meaning, for I was satisfied that it was something they wanted me to know very little about. After a patient waiting, I got one of our city papers, containing an account of the number of petitions from the north, praying for the abolition of slavery in the District of Columbia, and of the slave trade between the States.

From this time I understood the words *abolition* and *abolitionist*, and always drew near when that word was spoken, expecting to hear something of importance to myself and fellow-slaves. The light broke in upon me by degrees. I went one day down on the wharf of Mr. Waters; and seeing two Irishmen unloading a scow of stone, I went, unasked, and helped them. When we had finished, one of them came to me and asked me if I were a slave. I told him I was. He asked, "Are ye a slave for life?" I told him that I was. The good Irishman seemed to be deeply affected by the statement. He said to the other that it was a pity so fine a little fellow as myself should be a slave for life. He said it was a shame to hold me. They both advised me to run away to the north; that I should find friends there, and that I should be free.

I pretended not to be interested in what they said, and treated them as if I did not understand them; for I feared they might be treacherous. White men have been known to encourage slaves to escape, and then, to get the reward, catch them and return them to their masters. I was afraid that these seemingly good men might use me so; but I nevertheless remembered their advice, and from that time I resolved to run away. I looked forward to a time at which it would be safe for me to escape. I was too young to think of doing so immediately; besides, I wished to learn how to write, as I might have occasion to write my own pass. I consoled myself with the hope that I should one day find a good chance. Meanwhile, I would learn to write.

The idea as to how I might learn to write was suggested to me by being in Durgin and Bailey's ship-yard, and frequently seeing the ship carpenters, after hewing, and getting a piece of timber ready for use, write on the timber the name of that part of the ship for which it was intended. When a piece of timber was intended for the larboard side, it would be marked thus—"L." When a piece was for the starboard side, it would be marked thus—"S." A piece for the larboard side forward, would be marked thus—"L. F." When a piece was for starboard side forward, it would be marked thus—"S. F."

For larboard aft, it would be marked thus—"L. A." For starboard aft, it would be marked thus—"S. A." I soon learned the names of these letters, and for what they were intended when placed upon a piece of timber in the ship-yard. I immediately commenced copying them, and in a short time was able to make the four letters named.

After that, when I met with any boy who I knew could write, I would tell him I could write as well as he. The next word would be, "I don't believe you. Let me see you try it." I would then make the letters which I had been so fortunate as to learn, and ask him to beat that. In this way I got a good many lessons in writing, which it is quite possible I should never have gotten in any other way.

During this time, my copy-book was the board fence, brick wall, and pavement; my pen and ink was a lump of chalk. With these, I learned mainly how to write. I then commenced and continued copying the Italics in Webster's Spelling Book, until I could make them all without looking on the book. By this time, my little Master Thomas had gone to school, and learned how to write, and had written over a number of copy-books. These had been brought home, and shown to some of our near neighbors, and then laid aside.

My mistress used to go to class meeting at the Wilk Street meetinghouse every Monday afternoon, and leave me to take care of the house. When left thus, I used to spend the time in writing in the spaces left in Master Thomas's copy-book, copying what he had written. I continued to do this until I could write a hand very similar to that of Master Thomas. Thus, after a long, tedious effort for years, I finally succeeded in learning how to write.

CHAPTER 8

In a very short time after I went to live at Baltimore, my old master's youngest son Richard died; and in about three years and six months after his death, my old master, Captain Anthony, died, leaving only his son, Andrew, and daughter, Lucretia, to share his estate. He died while on a visit to see his daughter at Hillsborough. Cut off thus unexpectedly, he left no will as to the disposal of his property. It was therefore necessary to have a valuation of the property, that it might be equally divided between Mrs. Lucretia and Master Andrew. I was immediately sent for, to be valued with the other property.

Here again my feelings rose up in detestation of slavery. I had now a new conception of my degraded condition. Prior to this, I had become, if not insensible to my lot, at least partly so. I left Baltimore with a young heart overborne with sadness, and a soul full of apprehension. I took passage with Captain Rowe, in the schooner Wild Cat, and, after a sail of about twenty-four hours, I found myself near the place of my birth. I had now been absent from it almost, if not quite, five years. I, however, remembered the place very well. I was only about five years old when I left it, to go and live with my old master on Colonel Lloyd's plantation; so that I was now between ten and eleven years old.

We were all ranked together at the valuation. Men and women, old and young, married and single, were ranked with horses, sheep, and swine. There were horses and men, cattle and women, pigs and children, all holding the same rank in the scale of being, and were all subjected to the same narrow examination. Silvery-headed age and sprightly youth, maids and matrons, had to undergo the same indelicate inspection. At this moment, I saw more clearly than ever the brutalizing effects of slavery upon both slave and slaveholder.

After the valuation, then came the division. I have no language to express the high excitement and deep anxiety which were felt among us poor slaves during this time. Our fate for life was now to be decided. We had no more voice in that decision than the brutes among whom we were ranked. A single word from the white men was enough—against all our wishes, prayers, and entreaties—to sunder forever the dearest friends, dearest kindred, and strongest ties known to human beings.

In addition to the pain of separation, there was the horrid dread of falling into the hands of Master Andrew. He was known to us all as being a most cruel wretch,—a common drunkard, who had, by his reckless mismanagement and profligate dissipation, already wasted a large portion of his father's property. We all felt that we might as well be sold at once to the Georgia traders, as to pass into his hands; for we knew that that would be our inevitable condition,—a condition held by us all in the utmost horror and dread.

I suffered more anxiety than most of my fellow-slaves. I had known what it was to be kindly treated; they had known nothing of the kind. They had seen little or nothing of the world. They were in very deed men and women of sorrow, and acquainted with grief. Their backs had been made familiar with the bloody lash, so that they had become callous; mine was yet tender; for while at Baltimore I got few whippings, and few slaves could boast of a kinder master and mistress than myself; and the thought of passing out of their hands into those of Master Andrew—a man who, but a few days before, to give me a sample of his bloody disposition, took my little brother by the throat, threw him on the ground, and with the heel of his boot stamped upon his head till the blood gushed from his nose and ears—was well calculated to make me anxious as to my fate. After he had committed this savage outrage upon my brother, he turned to me, and said that was the way he meant to serve me one of these days,— meaning, I suppose, when I came into his possession.

Thanks to a kind Providence, I fell to the portion of Mrs. Lucretia, and was sent immediately back to Baltimore, to live again in the family of Master Hugh. Their joy at my return equalled their sorrow at my departure. It was a glad day to me. I had escaped a worse than lion's jaws. I was absent from Baltimore, for the purpose of valuation and division, just about one month, and it seemed to have been six.

Very soon after my return to Baltimore, my mistress, Lucretia, died, leaving her husband and one child, Amanda;

and in a very short time after her death, Master Andrew died. Now all the property of my old master, slaves included, was in the hands of strangers,—strangers who had had nothing to do with accumulating it. Not a slave was left free. All remained slaves, from the youngest to the oldest. If any one thing in my experience, more than another, served to deepen my conviction of the infernal character of slavery, and to fill me with unutterable loathing of slaveholders, it was their base ingratitude to my poor old grandmother.

She had served my old master faithfully from youth to old age. She had been the source of all his wealth; she had peopled his plantation with slaves; she had become a great grandmother in his service. She had rocked him in infancy, attended him in childhood, served him through life, and at his death wiped from his icy brow the cold death-sweat, and closed his eyes forever.

She was nevertheless left a slave—a slave for life—a slave in the hands of strangers; and in their hands she saw her children, her grandchildren, and her great-grandchildren, divided, like so many sheep, without being gratified with the small privilege of a single word, as to their or her own destiny. And, to cap the climax of their base ingratitude and fiendish barbarity, my grandmother, who was now very old, having outlived my old master and all his children, having seen the beginning and end of all of them, and her present owners finding she was of but little value, her frame already racked with the pains of old age, and complete helplessness fast stealing over her once active limbs, they took her to the woods, built her a little hut, put up a little mud-chimney, and then made her welcome to the privilege of supporting herself there in perfect loneliness; thus virtually turning her out to die! If my poor old grandmother now lives, she lives to suffer in utter loneliness; she lives to remember and mourn over the loss of children, the loss of grandchildren, and the loss of great-grandchildren. They are, in the language of the slave's poet, Whittier,—

"Gone, gone, sold and gone
　　To the rice swamp dank and lone,
　　Where the slave-whip ceaseless swings,
　　Where the noisome insect stings,
　　Where the fever-demon strews
　　Poison with the falling dews,
　　Where the sickly sunbeams glare
　　Through the hot and misty air:—
　　　　Gone, gone, sold and gone
　　　　To the rice swamp dank and lone,
　　　　From Virginia hills and waters—
　　　　Woe is me, my stolen daughters!"

The hearth is desolate. The children, the unconscious children, who once sang and danced in her presence, are gone. She gropes her way, in the darkness of age, for a drink of water. Instead of the voices of her children, she hears by day the moans of the dove, and by night the screams of the hideous owl. All is gloom. The grave is at the door. And now, when weighed down by the pains and aches of old age, when the head inclines to the feet, when the beginning and ending of human existence meet, and helpless infancy and painful old age combine together—at this time, this most needful time, the time for the exercise of that tenderness and affection which children only can exercise towards a declining parent—my poor old grandmother, the devoted mother of twelve children, is left all alone, in yonder little hut, before a few dim embers. She stands—she sits—she staggers—she falls—she groans—she dies—and there are none of her children or grandchildren present, to wipe from her wrinkled brow the cold sweat of death, or to place beneath the sod her fallen remains. Will not a righteous God visit for these things?

In about two years after the death of Mrs. Lucretia, Master Thomas married his second wife. Her name was Rowena Hamilton. She was the eldest daughter of Mr. William Hamilton. Master now lived in St. Michael's. Not long after his marriage, a misunderstanding took place between himself and Master Hugh; and as a means of punishing his brother, he took me from him to live with himself at St. Michael's.

Here I underwent another most painful separation. It, however, was not so severe as the one I dreaded at the division of property; for, during this interval, a great change had taken place in Master Hugh and his once kind and affectionate wife. The influence of brandy upon him, and of slavery upon her, had effected a disastrous change in the characters of both; so that, as far as they were concerned, I thought I had little to lose by the change.

But it was not to them that I was attached. It was to those little Baltimore boys that I felt the strongest attachment. I had received many good lessons from them, and was still receiving them, and the thought of leaving them was painful indeed. I was leaving, too, without the hope of ever being allowed to return. Master Thomas had said he would never let me return again. The barrier betwixt himself and brother he considered impassable.

I then had to regret that I did not at least make the attempt to carry out my resolution to run away; for the chances of success are tenfold greater from the city than from the country.

I sailed from Baltimore for St. Michael's in the sloop Amanda, Captain Edward Dodson. On my passage, I paid particular attention to the direction which the steamboats took to go to Philadelphia. I found, instead of going down, on reaching North Point they went up the bay, in a north-easterly direction. I deemed this knowledge of the utmost importance. My determination to run away was again revived. I resolved to wait only so long as the offering of a favorable opportunity. When that came, I was determined to be off.

CHAPTER 9

I have now reached a period of my life when I can give dates. I left Baltimore, and went to live with Master Thomas Auld, at St. Michael's, in March, 1832. It was now more than seven years since I lived with him in the family of my old master, on Colonel Lloyd's plantation. We of course were now almost entire strangers to each other. He was to me a new master, and I to him a new slave. I was ignorant of his temper and disposition; he was equally so of mine. A very short time, however, brought us into full acquaintance with each other. I was made acquainted with his wife not less than with himself. They were well matched, being equally mean and cruel.

I was now, for the first time during a space of more than seven years, made to feel the painful gnawings of hunger—a something which I had not experienced before since I left Colonel Lloyd's plantation. It went hard enough with me then, when I could look back to no period at which I had enjoyed a sufficiency. It was tenfold harder after living in Master Hugh's family, where I had always had enough to eat, and of that which was good. I have said Master Thomas was a mean man. He was so. Not to give a slave enough to eat, is regarded as the most aggravated development of meanness even among slaveholders. The rule is, no matter how coarse the food, only let there be enough of it. This is the theory; and in the part of Maryland from which I came, it is the general practice,—though there are many exceptions. Master Thomas gave us enough of neither coarse nor fine food.

There were four slaves of us in the kitchen—my sister Eliza, my aunt Priscilla, Henny, and myself; and we were allowed less than a half of a bushel of corn-meal per week, and very little else, either in the shape of meat or vegetables. It was not enough for us to subsist upon. We were therefore reduced to the wretched necessity of living at the expense of our neighbors. This we did by begging and stealing, whichever came handy in the time of need, the one being considered as legitimate as the other. A great many times have we poor creatures been nearly perishing with hunger, when food in abundance lay mouldering in the safe and smoke-house, and our pious mistress was aware of the fact; and yet that mistress and her husband would kneel every morning, and pray that God would bless them in basket and store!

Bad as all slaveholders are, we seldom meet one destitute of every element of character commanding respect. My master was one of this rare sort. I do not know of one single noble act ever performed by him. The leading trait in his character was meanness; and if there were any other element in his nature, it was made subject to this. He was mean; and, like most other mean men, he lacked the ability to conceal his meanness. Captain Auld was not born a slaveholder. He had been a poor man, master only of a Bay craft. He came into possession of all his slaves by marriage; and of all men, adopted slaveholders are the worst. He was cruel, but cowardly. He commanded without firmness. In the enforcement of his rules, he was at times rigid, and at times lax. At times, he spoke to his slaves with the firmness of Napoleon and the fury of a demon; at other times, he might well be mistaken for an inquirer who had lost his way.

He did nothing of himself. He might have passed for a lion, but for his ears. In all things noble which he attempted, his own meanness shone most conspicuous. His airs, words, and actions, were the airs, words, and actions of born slaveholders, and, being assumed, were awkward enough. He was not even a good imitator. He possessed all the disposition to deceive, but wanted the power.

Having no resources within himself, he was compelled to be the copyist of many, and being such, he was forever the victim of inconsistency; and of consequence he was an object of contempt, and was held as such even by his slaves. The luxury of having slaves of his own to wait upon him was something new and unprepared for. He was a slaveholder without the ability to hold slaves. He found himself incapable of managing his slaves either by force, fear, or fraud.

We seldom called him "master;" we generally called him "Captain Auld," and were hardly disposed to title him at all. I doubt not that our conduct had much to do with making him appear awkward, and of consequence fretful. Our want of reverence for him must have perplexed him greatly. He wished to have us call him master, but lacked the firmness necessary to command us to do so. His wife used to insist upon our calling him so, but to no purpose. In August, 1832, my master attended a Methodist camp-meeting held in the Bay-side, Talbot county, and there experienced religion. I indulged a faint hope that his conversion would lead him to emancipate his slaves, and that, if he did not do this, it would, at any rate, make him more kind and humane.

I was disappointed in both these respects. It neither made him to be humane to his slaves, nor to emancipate them. If it had any effect on his character, it made him more cruel and hateful in all his ways; for I believe him to have been a much worse man after his conversion than before. Prior to his conversion, he relied upon his own depravity to shield and sustain him in his savage barbarity; but after his conversion, he found religious sanction and support for his slaveholding cruelty. He made the greatest pretensions to piety.

His house was the house of prayer. He prayed morning, noon, and night. He very soon distinguished himself among his brethren, and was soon made a class-leader and exhorter. His activity in revivals was great, and he proved himself an instrument in the hands of the church in converting many souls. His house was the preachers' home. They used to take great pleasure in coming there to put up; for while he starved us, he stuffed them. We have had three or four preachers there at a time.

The names of those who used to come most frequently while I lived there, were Mr. Storks, Mr. Ewery, Mr. Humphry, and Mr. Hickey. I have also seen Mr. George Cookman at our house. We slaves loved Mr. Cookman. We believed him to be a good man. We thought him instrumental in getting Mr. Samuel Harrison, a very rich slaveholder, to emancipate his slaves; and by some means got the impression that he was laboring to effect the emancipation of all the slaves. When he was at our house, we were sure to be called in to prayers. When the others were there, we were sometimes called in and sometimes not. Mr. Cookman took more notice of us than either of the other ministers. He could not come among us without betraying his sympathy for us, and, stupid as we were, we had the sagacity to see it.

While I lived with my master in St. Michael's, there was a white young man, a Mr. Wilson, who proposed to keep a Sabbath school for the instruction of such slaves as might be disposed to learn to read the New Testament. We met but three times, when Mr. West and Mr. Fairbanks, both class-leaders, with many others, came upon us with sticks and other missiles, drove us off, and forbade us to meet again. Thus ended our little Sabbath school in the pious town of St. Michael's.

I have said my master found religious sanction for his cruelty. As an example, I will state one of many facts going to prove the charge. I have seen him tie up a lame young woman, and whip her with a heavy cowskin upon her naked shoulders, causing the warm red blood to drip; and, in justi-fication of the bloody deed, he would quote this passage of Scripture—"He that knoweth his master's will, and doeth it not, shall be beaten with many stripes."

Master would keep this lacerated young woman tied up in this horrid situation four or five hours at a time. I have known him to tie her up early in the morning, and whip her before breakfast; leave her, go to his store, return at dinner, and whip her again, cutting her in the places already made raw with his cruel lash. The secret of master's cruelty toward "Henny" is found in the fact of her being almost helpless. When quite a child, she fell into the fire, and burned herself horribly. Her hands were so burnt that she never got the use of them. She could do very little but bear heavy burdens. She was to master a bill of expense; and as he was a mean man, she was a constant offence to him. He seemed desirous of getting the poor girl out of existence. He gave her away once to his sister; but, being a poor gift, she was not disposed to keep her. Finally, my benevolent master, to use his own words, "set her adrift to take care of herself." Here was a recently-converted man, holding on upon the mother, and at the same time turning out her helpless child, to starve and die! Master Thomas was one of the many pious slaveholders who hold slaves for the very charitable purpose of taking care of them.

My master and myself had quite a number of differences. He found me unsuitable to his purpose. My city life, he said, had had a very pernicious effect upon me. It had almost ruined me for every good purpose, and fitted me for every thing which was bad. One of my greatest faults was that of letting his horse run away, and go down to his father-inlaw's farm, which was about five miles from St. Michael's. I would then have to go after it.

My reason for this kind of carelessness, or carefulness, was, that I could always get something to eat when I went there. Master William Hamilton, my master's father-in-law, always gave his slaves enough to eat. I never left there hungry, no matter how great the need of my speedy return. Master Thomas at length said he would stand it no longer. I had lived with him nine months, during which time he had given me a number of severe whippings, all to no good purpose. He resolved to put me out, as he said, to be broken; and, for this purpose, he let me for one year to a man named Edward Covey.

Mr. Covey was a poor man, a farm-renter. He rented the place upon which he lived, as also the hands with which he tilled it. Mr. Covey had acquired a very high reputation for breaking young slaves, and this reputation was of immense value to him. It enabled him to get his farm tilled with much less expense to himself than he could have had it done without such a reputation. Some slaveholders thought it not much loss to allow Mr. Covey to have their slaves one year, for the sake of the training to which they were subjected, without any other compensation. He could hire young help with great ease, in consequence of this reputation.

Added to the natural good qualities of Mr. Covey, he was a professor of religion—a pious soul—a member and a class-leader in the Methodist church. All of this added weight to his reputation as a "nigger-breaker." I was aware of all the facts, having been made acquainted with them by a young man who had lived there. I nevertheless made the change gladly; for I was sure of getting enough to eat, which is not the smallest consideration to a hungry man.

CHAPTER 10

I had left Master Thomas's house, and went to live with Mr. Covey, on the 1st of January, 1833. I was now, for the first time in my life, a field hand. In my new employment, I found myself even more awkward than a country boy appeared to be in a large city. I had been at my new home but one week before Mr. Covey gave me a very severe whipping, cutting my back, causing the blood to run, and raising ridges on my flesh as large as my little finger.

The details of this affair are as follows: Mr. Covey sent me, very early in the morning of one of our coldest days in the month of January, to the woods, to get a load of wood. He gave me a team of unbroken oxen. He told me which was the in-hand ox, and which the off-hand one. He then tied the end of a large rope around the horns of the in-hand ox, and gave me the other end of it, and told me, if the oxen started to run, that I must hold on upon the rope. I had never driven oxen before, and of course I was very awkward. I, however, succeeded in getting to the edge of the woods with little difficulty; but I had got a very few rods into the woods, when the oxen took fright, and started full tilt, carrying the cart against trees, and over stumps, in the most frightful manner. I expected every moment that my brains would be dashed out against the trees.

After running thus for a considerable distance, they finally upset the cart, dashing it with great force against a tree, and threw themselves into a dense thicket. How I escaped death, I do not know. There I was, entirely alone, in a thick wood, in a place new to me. My cart was upset and shattered, my oxen were entangled among the young trees, and there was none to help me. After a long spell of effort, I succeeded in getting my cart righted, my oxen disentangled, and again yoked to the cart.

I now proceeded with my team to the place where I had, the day before, been chopping wood, and loaded my cart pretty heavily, thinking in this way to tame my oxen. I then proceeded on my way home. I had now consumed one half of the day. I got out of the woods safely, and now felt out of danger.

I stopped my oxen to open the woods gate; and just as I did so, before I could get hold of my ox-rope, the oxen again started, rushed through the gate, catching it between the wheel and the body of the cart, tearing it to pieces, and coming within a few inches of crushing me against the gate-post. Thus twice, in one short day, I escaped death by the merest chance.

On my return, I told Mr. Covey what had happened, and how it happened. He ordered me to return to the woods again immediately. I did so, and he followed on after me. Just as I got into the woods, he came up and told me to stop my cart, and that he would teach me how to trifle away my time, and break gates. He then went to a large gum-tree, and with his axe cut three large switches, and, after trimming them up neatly with his pocketknife, he ordered me to take off my clothes. I made him no answer, but stood with my clothes on. He repeated his order. I still made him no answer, nor did I move to strip myself. Upon this he rushed at me with the fierceness of a tiger, tore off my clothes, and lashed me till he had worn out his switches, cutting me so savagely as to leave the marks visible for a long time after. This whipping was the first of a number just like it, and for similar offences.

I lived with Mr. Covey one year. During the first six months, of that year, scarce a week passed without his whipping me. I was seldom free from a sore back. My awkwardness was almost always his excuse for whipping me. We were worked fully up to the point of endurance. Long before day we were up, our horses fed, and by the first approach of day we were off to the field with our hoes and ploughing teams. Mr. Covey gave us enough to eat, but scarce time to eat it. We were often less than five minutes taking our meals. We were often in the field from the first approach of day till its last lingering ray had left us; and at saving-fodder time, midnight often caught us in the field binding blades.

Covey would be out with us. The way he used to stand it, was this. He would spend the most of his afternoons in bed. He would then come out fresh in the evening, ready to urge us on with his words, example, and frequently with the whip. Mr. Covey was one of the few slaveholders who could and did work with his hands. He was a hard-working man. He knew by himself just what a man or a boy could do. There was no deceiving him. His work went on in his absence almost as well as in his presence; and he had the faculty of making us feel that he was ever present with us. This he did by surprising us. He seldom approached the spot where we were at work openly, if he could do it secretly. He always aimed at taking us by surprise. Such was his cunning, that we used to call him, among ourselves, "the snake." When we were at work in the cornfield, he would sometimes crawl on his hands and knees to avoid detection, and all at once he would rise nearly in our midst, and scream out, "Ha, ha! Come, come! Dash on, dash on!" This being his mode of attack, it was never safe to stop a single minute.

His comings were like a thief in the night. He appeared to us as being ever at hand. He was under every tree, behind every stump, in every bush, and at every window, on the plantation. He would sometimes mount his horse, as if bound to St. Michael's, a distance of seven miles, and in half an hour afterwards you would see him coiled up in the corner of the wood-fence, watching every motion of the slaves. He would, for this purpose, leave his horse tied up in the woods. Again, he would sometimes walk up to us, and give us orders as though he was upon the point of starting on a long journey, turn his back upon us, and make as though he was going to the house to get ready; and, before he would get half way thither, he would turn short and crawl into a fence-corner, or behind some tree, and there watch us till the going down of the sun.

Mr. Covey's *forte* consisted in his power to deceive. His life was devoted to planning and perpetrating the grossest deceptions. Every thing he possessed in the shape of learning or religion, he made conform to his disposition to deceive. He seemed to think himself equal to deceiving the Almighty. He would make a short prayer in the morning, and a long prayer at night; and, strange as it may seem, few men would at times appear more devotional than he. The exercises of his family devotions were always commenced with singing; and, as he was a very poor singer himself, the duty of raising the hymn generally came upon me. He would read his hymn, and nod at me to commence. I would at times do so; at others, I would not. My non-compliance would almost always produce much confusion. To show himself independent of me, he would start and stagger through with his hymn in the most discordant manner. In this state of mind, he prayed with more than ordinary spirit. Poor man! such was his disposition, and success at deceiving, I do verily believe that he sometimes deceived himself into the solemn belief, that he was a sincere worshipper of the most high God; and this, too, at a time when he may be said to have been guilty of compelling his woman slave to commit the sin of adultery.

The facts in the case are these: Mr. Covey was a poor man; he was just commencing in life; he was only able to buy one slave; and, shocking as is the fact, he bought her, as he said, for *a breeder*. This woman was named Caroline. Mr. Covey bought her from Mr. Thomas Lowe, about six miles from St. Michael's. She was a large, able-bodied woman, about twenty years old. She had already given birth to one child, which proved her to be just what he wanted. After buying her, he hired a married man of Mr. Samuel Harrison, to live with him one year; and him he used to fasten up with her every night! The result was, that, at the end of the year, the miserable woman gave birth to twins.

At this result Mr. Covey seemed to be highly pleased, both with the man and the wretched woman. Such was his joy, and that of his wife, that nothing they could do for Caroline during her confinement was too good, or too hard, to be done. The children were regarded as being quite an addition to his wealth.

If at any one time of my life more than another, I was made to drink the bitterest dregs of slavery, that time was during the first six months of my stay with Mr. Covey. We were worked in all weathers. It was never too hot or too cold; it could never rain, blow, hail, or snow, too hard for us to work in the field. Work, work, work, was scarcely more the order of the day than of the night. The longest days were too short for him, and the shortest nights too long for him. I was somewhat unmanageable when I first went there, but a few months of this discipline tamed me. Mr. Covey succeeded in breaking me. I was broken in body, soul, and spirit. My natural elasticity was crushed, my intellect languished, the disposition to read departed, the cheerful spark that lingered about my eye died; the dark night of slavery closed in upon me; and behold a man transformed into a brute!

Sunday was my only leisure time. I spent this in a sort of beast-like stupor, between sleep and wake, under some large tree. At times I would rise up, a flash of energetic freedom would dart through my soul, accompanied with a faint beam of hope, that flickered for a moment, and then vanished. I sank down again, mourning over my wretched condition. I was sometimes prompted to take my life, and that of Covey, but was prevented by a combination of hope and fear. My sufferings on this plantation seem now like a dream rather than a stern reality.

Our house stood within a few rods of the Chesapeake Bay, whose broad bosom was ever white with sails from every quarter of the habitable globe. Those beautiful vessels, robed in purest white, so delightful to the eye of freemen, were to me so many shrouded ghosts, to terrify and torment me with thoughts of my wretched condition. I have often, in the deep stillness of a summer's Sabbath, stood all alone upon the lofty banks of that noble bay, and traced, with saddened heart and tearful eye, the countless number of sails moving off to the mighty ocean. The sight of these always affected me powerfully. My thoughts would compel utterance; and there, with no audience but the Almighty, I would pour out my soul's complaint, in my rude way, with an apostrophe to the moving multitude of ships:—

"You are loosed from your moorings, and are free; I am fast in my chains, and am a slave! You move merrily before the gentle gale, and I sadly before the bloody whip! You are freedom's swift-winged angels, that fly round the world; I am confined in bands of iron! O that I were free! O, that I were on one of your gallant decks, and under your protecting wing! Alas! betwixt me and you, the turbid waters roll. Go on, go on. O that I could also go! Could I but swim! If I could fly! O, why was I born a man, of whom to make a brute! The glad ship is gone; she hides in the dim distance. I am left in the hottest hell of unending slavery. O God, save me! God, deliver me! Let me be free! Is there any God? Why am I a slave? I will run away. I will not stand it. Get caught, or get clear, I'll try it. I had as well die with ague as the fever. I have only one life to lose. I had as well be killed running as die standing. Only think of it; one hundred miles straight north, and I am free! Try it? Yes! God helping me, I will. It cannot be that I shall live and die a slave. I will take to the water. This very bay shall yet bear me into freedom. The steamboats steered in a north-east course from North Point. I will do the same; and when I get to the head of the bay, I will turn my canoe adrift, and walk straight through Delaware into Pennsylvania. When I get there, I shall not be required to have a pass; I can travel without being disturbed. Let but the first opportunity offer, and, come what will, I am off. Meanwhile, I will try to bear up under the yoke. I am not the only slave in the world. Why should I fret? I can bear as much as any of them. Besides, I am but a boy, and all boys are bound to some one. It may be that my misery in slavery will only increase my happiness when I get free. There is a better day coming."

Thus I used to think, and thus I used to speak to myself; goaded almost to madness at one moment, and at the next reconciling myself to my wretched lot.

I have already intimated that my condition was much worse, during the first six months of my stay at Mr. Covey's, than in the last six. The circumstances leading to the change in Mr. Covey's course toward me form an epoch in my humble history. You have seen how a man was made a slave; you shall see how a slave was made a man.

On one of the hottest days of the month of August, 1833, Bill Smith, William Hughes, a slave named Eli, and myself, were engaged in fanning wheat. Hughes was clearing the fanned wheat from before the fan. Eli was turning, Smith was feeding, and I was carrying wheat to the fan. The work was simple, requiring strength rather than intellect; yet, to one entirely unused to such work, it came very hard. About three o'clock of that day, I broke down; my strength failed me; I was seized with a violent aching of the head, attended with extreme dizziness; I trembled in every limb. Finding what was coming, I nerved myself up, feeling it would never do to stop work. I stood as long as I could stagger to the hopper with grain. When I could stand no longer, I fell, and felt as if held down by an immense weight. The fan of course stopped; every one had his own work to do; and no one could do the work of the other, and have his own go on at the same time.

Mr. Covey was at the house, about one hundred yards from the treading-yard where we were fanning. On hearing the fan stop, he left immediately, and came to the spot where we were. He hastily inquired what the matter was. Bill answered that I was sick, and there was no one to bring wheat to the fan. I had by this time crawled away under the side of the post and rail-fence by which the yard was enclosed, hoping to find relief by getting out of the sun. He then asked where I was. He was told by one of the hands.

He came to the spot, and, after looking at me awhile, asked me what was the matter. I told him as well as I could, for I scarce had strength to speak. He then gave me a savage kick in the side, and told me to get up. I tried to do so, but fell back in the attempt. He gave me another kick, and again told me to rise. I again tried, and succeeded in gaining my feet; but, stooping to get the tub with which I was feeding the fan, I again staggered and fell.

While down in this situation, Mr. Covey took up the hickory slat with which Hughes had been striking off the half-bushel measure, and with it gave me a heavy blow upon the head, making a large wound, and the blood ran freely; and with this again told me to get up. I made no effort to comply, having now made up my mind to let him do his worst. In a short time after receiving this blow, my head grew better. Mr. Covey had now left me to my fate.

At this moment I resolved, for the first time, to go to my master, enter a complaint, and ask his protection. In order to do this, I must that afternoon walk seven miles; and this, under the circumstances, was truly a severe undertaking. I was exceedingly feeble; made so as much by the kicks and blows which I received, as by the severe fit of sickness to which I had been subjected.

I, however, watched my chance, while Covey was looking in an opposite direction, and started for St. Michael's. I succeeded in getting a considerable distance on my way to the woods, when Covey discovered me, and called after me to come back, threatening what he would do if I did not come. I disregarded both his calls and his threats, and made my way to the woods as fast as my feeble state would allow; and thinking I might be overhauled by him if I kept the road, I walked through the woods, keeping far enough from the road to avoid detection, and near enough to prevent losing my way.

I had not gone far before my little strength again failed me. I could go no farther. I fell down, and lay for a considerable time. The blood was yet oozing from the wound on my head. For a time I thought I should bleed to death; and think now that I should have done so, but that the blood so matted my hair as to stop the wound.

After lying there about three quarters of an hour, I nerved myself up again, and started on my way, through bogs and briers, barefooted and bareheaded, tearing my feet sometimes at nearly every step; and after a journey of about seven miles, occupying some five hours to perform it, I arrived at master's store. I then presented an appearance enough to affect any but a heart of iron.

From the crown of my head to my feet, I was covered with blood. My hair was all clotted with dust and blood; my shirt was stiff with blood. I suppose I looked like a man who had escaped a den of wild beasts, and barely escaped them. In this state I appeared before my master, humbly entreating him to interpose his authority for my protection. I told him all the circumstances as well as I could, and it seemed, as I spoke, at times to affect him. He would then walk the floor, and seek to justify Covey by saying he expected I deserved it.

He asked me what I wanted. I told him, to let me get a new home; that as sure as I lived with Mr. Covey again, I should live with but to die with him; that Covey would surely kill me; he was in a fair way for it. Master Thomas ridiculed the idea that there was any danger of Mr. Covey's killing me, and said that he knew Mr. Covey; that he was a good man, and that he could not think of taking me from him; that, should he do so, he would lose the whole year's wages; that I belonged to Mr. Covey for one year, and that I must go back to him, come what might; and that I must not trouble him with any more stories, or that he would himself *get hold of me.*

After threatening me thus, he gave me a very large dose of salts, telling me that I might remain in St. Michael's that night, (it being quite late,) but that I must be off back to Mr. Covey's early in the morning; and that if I did not, he would *get hold of me*, which meant that he would whip me. I remained all night, and, according to his orders, I started off to Covey's in the morning, (Saturday morning,) wearied in body and broken in spirit. I got no supper that night, or breakfast that morning. I reached Covey's about nine o'clock; and just as I was getting over the fence that divided Mrs. Kemp's fields from ours, out ran Covey with his cowskin, to give me another whipping.

Before he could reach me, I succeeded in getting to the cornfield; and as the corn was very high, it afforded me the means of hiding. He seemed very angry, and searched for me a long time. My behavior was altogether unaccountable. He finally gave up the chase, thinking, I suppose, that I must come home for something to eat; he would give himself no further trouble in looking for me. I spent that day mostly in the woods, having the alternative before me,—to go home and be whipped to death, or stay in the woods and be starved to death.

That night, I fell in with Sandy Jenkins, a slave with whom I was somewhat acquainted. Sandy had a free wife who lived about four miles from Mr. Covey's; and it being Saturday, he was on his way to see her. I told him my circumstances, and he very kindly invited me to go home with him. I went home with him, and talked this whole matter over, and got his advice as to what course it was best for me to pursue. I found Sandy an old adviser. He told me, with great solemnity, I must go back to Covey; but that before I went, I must go with him into another part of the woods, where there was a certain *root*, which, if I would take some of it with me, carrying it *always on my right side*, would render it impossible for Mr. Covey, or any other white man, to whip me.

He said he had carried it for years; and since he had done so, he had never received a blow, and never expected to while he carried it. I at first rejected the idea, that the simple carrying of a root in my pocket would have any such effect as he had said, and was not disposed to take it; but Sandy impressed the necessity with much earnestness, telling me it could do no harm, if it did no good. To please him, I at length took the root, and, according to his direction, carried it upon my right side. This was Sunday morning. I immediately started for home; and upon entering the yard gate, out came Mr. Covey on his way to meeting. He spoke to me very kindly, bade me drive the pigs from a lot near by, and passed on towards the church. Now, this singular conduct of Mr. Covey really made me begin to think that there was something in the *root* which Sandy had given me; and had it been on any other day than Sunday, I could have attributed the conduct to no other cause than the influence of that root; and as it was, I was half inclined to think the *root* to be something more than I at first had taken it to be.

All went well till Monday morning. On this morning, the virtue of the *root* was fully tested. Long before daylight, I was called to go and rub, curry, and feed, the horses. I obeyed, and was glad to obey. But whilst thus engaged, whilst in the act of throwing down some blades from the loft, Mr. Covey entered the stable with a long rope; and just as I was half out of the loft, he caught hold of my legs, and was about tying me. As soon as I found what he was up to, I gave a sudden spring, and as I did so, he holding to my legs, I was brought sprawling on the stable floor.

Mr. Covey seemed now to think he had me, and could do what he pleased; but at this moment—from whence came the spirit I don't know—I resolved to fight; and, suiting my action to the resolution, I seized Covey hard by the throat; and as I did so, I rose. He held on to me, and I to him. My resistance was so entirely unexpected that Covey seemed taken all aback. He trembled like a leaf. This gave me assurance, and I held him uneasy, causing the blood to run where I touched him with the ends of my fingers.

Mr. Covey soon called out to Hughes for help. Hughes came, and, while Covey held me, attempted to tie my right hand. While he was in the act of doing so, I watched my chance, and gave him a heavy kick close under the ribs. This kick fairly sickened Hughes, so that he left me in the hands of Mr. Covey. This kick had the effect of not only weakening Hughes, but Covey also.

When he saw Hughes bending over with pain, his courage quailed. He asked me if I meant to persist in my resistance. I told him I did, come what might; that he had used me like a brute for six months, and that I was determined to be used so no longer. With that, he strove to drag me to a stick that was lying just out of the stable door. He meant to knock me down. But just as he was leaning over to get the stick, I seized him with both hands by his collar, and brought him by a sudden snatch to the ground.

By this time, Bill came. Covey called upon him for assistance. Bill wanted to know what he could do. Covey said, "Take hold of him, take hold of him!" Bill said his master hired him out to work, and not to help to whip me; so he left Covey and myself to fight our own battle out. We were at it for nearly two hours. Covey at length let me go, puffing and blowing at a great rate, saying that if I had not resisted, he would not have whipped me half so much.

The truth was, that he had not whipped me at all. I considered him as getting entirely the worst end of the bargain; for he had drawn no blood from me, but I had from him. The whole six months afterwards, that I spent with Mr. Covey, he never laid the weight of his finger upon me in anger. He would occasionally say, he didn't want to get hold of me again. "No," thought I, "you need not; for you will come off worse than you did before."

This battle with Mr. Covey was the turning-point in my career as a slave. It rekindled the few expiring embers of freedom, and revived within me a sense of my own manhood. It recalled the departed self-confidence, and inspired me again with a determination to be free. The gratification afforded by the triumph was a full compensation for whatever else might follow, even death itself. He only can understand the deep satisfaction which I experienced, who has himself repelled by force the bloody arm of slavery. I felt as I never felt before.

It was a glorious resurrection, from the tomb of slavery, to the heaven of freedom. My long-crushed spirit rose, cowardice departed, bold defiance took its place; and I now resolved that, however long I might remain a slave in form, the day had passed forever when I could be a slave in fact. I did not hesitate to let it be known of me, that the white man who expected to succeed in whipping, must also succeed in killing me.

From this time I was never again what might be called fairly whipped, though I remained a slave four years afterwards. I had several fights, but was never whipped.

It was for a long time a matter of surprise to me why Mr. Covey did not immediately have me taken by the constable to the whipping-post, and there regularly whipped for the crime of raising my hand against a white man in defence of myself. And the only explanation I can now think of does not entirely satisfy me; but such as it is, I will give it. Mr. Covey enjoyed the most unbounded reputation for being a first-rate overseer and negro-breaker. It was of considerable importance to him. That reputation was at stake; and had he sent me—a boy about sixteen years old—to the public whipping-post, his reputation would have been lost; so, to save his reputation, he suffered me to go unpunished.

My term of actual service to Mr. Edward Covey ended on Christmas day, 1833. The days between Christmas and New Year's day are allowed as holidays; and, accordingly, we were not required to perform any labor, more than to feed and take care of the stock. This time we regarded as our own, by the grace of our masters; and we therefore used or abused it nearly as we pleased. Those of us who had families at a distance, were generally allowed to spend the whole six days in their society.

This time, however, was spent in various ways. The staid, sober, thinking and industrious ones of our number would employ themselves in making corn-brooms, mats, horse-collars, and baskets; and another class of us would spend the time in hunting opossums, hares, and coons. But by far the larger part engaged in such sports and merriments as playing ball, wrestling, running foot-races, fiddling, dancing, and drinking whisky; and this latter mode of spending the time was by far the most agreeable to the feelings of our masters.

A slave who would work during the holidays was considered by our masters as scarcely deserving them. He was regarded as one who rejected the favor of his master. It was deemed a disgrace not to get drunk at Christmas; and he was regarded as lazy indeed, who had not provided himself with the necessary means, during the year, to get whisky enough to last him through Christmas.

From what I know of the effect of these holidays upon the slave, I believe them to be among the most effective means in the hands of the slaveholder in keeping down the spirit of insurrection. Were the slaveholders at once to abandon this practice, I have not the slightest doubt it would lead to an immediate insurrection among the slaves. These holidays serve as conductors, or safety-valves, to carry off the rebellious spirit of enslaved humanity. But for these, the slave would be forced up to the wildest desperation; and woe betide the slaveholder, the day he ventures to remove or hinder the operation of those conductors! I warn him that, in such an event, a spirit will go forth in their midst, more to be dreaded than the most appalling earthquake.

The holidays are part and parcel of the gross fraud, wrong, and inhumanity of slavery. They are professedly a custom established by the benevolence of the slaveholders; but I undertake to say, it is the result of selfishness, and one of the grossest frauds committed upon the down-trodden slave. They do not give the slaves this time because they would not like to have their work during its continuance, but because they know it would be unsafe to deprive them of it.

This will be seen by the fact, that the slaveholders like to have their slaves spend those days just in such a manner as to make them as glad of their ending as of their beginning. Their object seems to be, to disgust their slaves with freedom, by plunging them into the lowest depths of dissipation. For instance, the slaveholders not only like to see the slave drink of his own accord, but will adopt various plans to make him drunk.

One plan is, to make bets on their slaves, as to who can drink the most whisky without getting drunk; and in this way they succeed in getting whole multitudes to drink to excess. Thus, when the slave asks for virtuous freedom, the cunning slaveholder, knowing his ignorance, cheats him with a dose of vicious dissipation, artfully labelled with the name of liberty. The most of us used to drink it down, and the result was just what might be supposed; many of us were led to think that there was little to choose between liberty and slavery. We felt, and very properly too, that we had almost as well be slaves to man as to rum. So, when the holidays ended, we staggered up from the filth of our wallowing, took a long breath, and marched to the field,—feeling, upon the whole, rather glad to go, from what our master had deceived us into a belief was freedom, back to the arms of slavery.

I have said that this mode of treatment is a part of the whole system of fraud and inhumanity of slavery. It is so. The mode here adopted to disgust the slave with freedom, by allowing him to see only the abuse of it, is carried out in other things. For instance, a slave loves molasses; he steals some. His master, in many cases, goes off to town, and buys a large quantity; he returns, takes his whip, and commands the slave to eat the molasses, until the poor fellow is made sick at the very mention of it. The same mode is sometimes adopted to make the slaves refrain from asking for more food than their regular allowance. A slave runs through his allowance, and applies for more. His master is enraged at him; but, not willing to send him off without food, gives him more than is necessary, and compels him to eat it within a given time.

Then, if he complains that he cannot eat it, he is said to be satisfied neither full nor fasting, and is whipped for being hard to please! I have an abundance of such illustrations of the same principle, drawn from my own observation, but think the cases I have cited sufficient. The practice is a very common one.

On the first of January, 1834, I left Mr. Covey, and went to live with Mr. William Freeland, who lived about three miles from St. Michael's. I soon found Mr. Freeland a very different man from Mr. Covey. Though not rich, he was what would be called an educated southern gentleman. Mr. Covey, as I have shown, was a well-trained negro-breaker and slave-driver. The former (slaveholder though he was) seemed to possess some regard for honor, some reverence for justice, and some respect for humanity. The latter seemed totally insensible to all such sentiments. Mr. Freeland had many of the faults peculiar to slaveholders, such as being very passionate and fretful; but I must do him the justice to say, that he was exceedingly free from those degrading vices to which Mr.

Covey was constantly addicted. The one was open and frank, and we always knew where to find him. The other was a most artful deceiver, and could be understood only by such as were skilful enough to detect his cunningly-devised frauds.

Another advantage I gained in my new master was, he made no pretensions to, or profession of, religion; and this, in my opinion, was truly a great advantage. I assert most unhesitatingly, that the religion of the south is a mere covering for the most horrid crimes,—a justifier of the most appalling barbarity,—a sanctifier of the most hateful frauds,—and a dark shelter under, which the darkest, foulest, grossest, and most infernal deeds of slaveholders find the strongest protection.

Were I to be again reduced to the chains of slavery, next to that enslavement, I should regard being the slave of a religious master the greatest calamity that could befall me. For of all slaveholders with whom I have ever met, religious slaveholders are the worst. I have ever found them the meanest and basest, the most cruel and cowardly, of all others. It was my unhappy lot not only to belong to a religious slaveholder, but to live in a community of such religionists. Very near Mr. Freeland lived the Rev. Daniel Weeden, and in the same neighborhood lived the Rev. Rigby Hopkins. These were members and ministers in the Reformed Methodist Church. Mr. Weeden owned, among others, a woman slave, whose name I have forgotten. This woman's back, for weeks, was kept literally raw, made so by the lash of this merciless, *religious* wretch. He used to hire hands. His maxim was, Behave well or behave ill, it is the duty of a master occasionally to whip a slave, to remind him of his master's authority. Such was his theory, and such his practice.

Mr. Hopkins was even worse than Mr. Weeden. His chief boast was his ability to manage slaves. The peculiar feature of his government was that of whipping slaves in advance of deserving it. He always managed to have one or more of his slaves to whip every Monday morning. He did this to alarm their fears, and strike terror into those who escaped. His plan was to whip for the smallest offences, to prevent the commission of large ones.

Mr. Hopkins could always find some excuse for whipping a slave. It would astonish one, unaccustomed to a slaveholding life, to see with what wonderful ease a slaveholder can find things, of which to make occasion to whip a slave. A mere look, word, or motion,—a mistake, accident, or want of power,—are all matters for which a slave may be whipped at any time. Does a slave look dissatisfied? It is said, he has the devil in him, and it must be whipped out. Does he speak loudly when spoken to by his master? Then he is getting high-minded, and should be taken down a button-hole lower. Does he forget to pull off his hat at the approach of a white person? Then he is wanting in reverence, and should be whipped for it. Does he ever venture to vindicate his conduct, when censured for it? Then he is guilty of impudence,—one of the greatest crimes of which a slave can be guilty. Does he ever venture to suggest a different mode of doing things from that pointed out by his master? He is indeed presumptuous, and getting above himself; and nothing less than a flogging will do for him. Does he, while ploughing, break a plough,—or, while hoeing, break a hoe? It is owing to his carelessness, and for it a slave must always be whipped.

Mr. Hopkins could always find something of this sort to justify the use of the lash, and he seldom failed to embrace such opportunities. There was not a man in the whole county, with whom the slaves who had the getting their own home, would not prefer to live, rather than with this Rev. Mr. Hopkins. And yet there was not a man any where round, who made higher professions of religion, or was more active in revivals,—more attentive to the class, love-feast, prayer and preaching meetings, or more devotional in his family,—that prayed earlier, later, louder, and longer,—than this same reverend slave-driver, Rigby Hopkins.

But to return to Mr. Freeland, and to my experience while in his employment. He, like Mr. Covey, gave us enough to eat; but, unlike Mr. Covey, he also gave us sufficient time to take our meals. He worked us hard, but always between sunrise and sunset. He required a good deal of work to be done, but gave us good tools with which to work. His farm was large, but he employed hands enough to work it, and with ease, compared with many of his neighbors. My treatment, while in his employment, was heavenly, compared with what I experienced at the hands of Mr. Edward Covey.

Mr. Freeland was himself the owner of but two slaves. Their names were Henry Harris and John Harris. The rest of his hands he hired. These consisted of myself, Sandy Jenkins,[1] and Handy Caldwell. Henry and John were quite intel-

---

[1] This is the same man who gave me the roots to prevent my being whipped by Mr. Covey. He was "a clever soul." We used frequently to talk about the fight with Covey, and as often as we did so, he would claim my success as the result of the roots which he gave me. This superstition is very common among the more ignorant slaves. A slave seldom dies but that his death is attributed to trickery.

ligent, and in a very little while after I went there, I succeeded in creating in them a strong desire to learn how to read.

This desire soon sprang up in the others also. They very soon mustered up some old spelling-books, and nothing would do but that I must keep a Sabbath school. I agreed to do so, and accordingly devoted my Sundays to teaching these my loved fellow-slaves how to read. Neither of them knew his letters when I went there. Some of the slaves of the neighboring farms found what was going on, and also availed themselves of this little opportunity to learn to read. It was understood, among all who came, that there must be as little display about it as possible. It was necessary to keep our religious masters at St. Michael's unacquainted with the fact, that, instead of spending the Sabbath in wrestling, boxing, and drinking whisky, we were trying to learn how to read the will of God; for they had much rather see us engaged in those degrading sports, than to see us behaving like intellectual, moral, and accountable beings.

My blood boils as I think of the bloody manner in which Messrs. Wright Fairbanks and Garrison West, both class-leaders, in connection with many others, rushed in upon us with sticks and stones, and broke up our virtuous little Sabbath school, at St. Michael's—all calling themselves Christians! humble followers of the Lord Jesus Christ! But I am again digressing.

I held my Sabbath school at the house of a free colored man, whose name I deem it imprudent to mention; for should it be known, it might embarrass him greatly, though the crime of holding the school was committed ten years ago. I had at one time over forty scholars, and those of the right sort, ardently desiring to learn. They were of all ages, though mostly men and women. I look back to those Sundays with an amount of pleasure not to be expressed. They were great days to my soul.

The work of instructing my dear fellow-slaves was the sweetest engagement with which I was ever blessed. We loved each other, and to leave them at the close of the Sabbath was a severe cross indeed. When I think that these precious souls are to-day shut up in the prison-house of slavery, my feelings overcome me, and I am almost ready to ask, "Does a righteous God govern the universe? and for what does he hold the thunders in his right hand, if not to smite the oppressor, and deliver the spoiled out of the hand of the spoiler?"

These dear souls came not to Sabbath school because it was popular to do so, nor did I teach them because it was reputable to be thus engaged. Every moment they spent in that school, they were liable to be taken up, and given thirty-nine lashes. They came because they wished to learn. Their minds had been starved by their cruel masters. They had been shut up in mental darkness. I taught them, because it was the delight of my soul to be doing something that looked like bettering the condition of my race. I kept up my school nearly the whole year I lived with Mr. Freeland; and, beside my Sabbath school, I devoted three evenings in the week, during the winter, to teaching the slaves at home. And I have the happiness to know, that several of those who came to Sabbath school learned how to read; and that one, at least, is now free through my agency.

The year passed off smoothly. It seemed only about half as long as the year which preceded it. I went through it without receiving a single blow. I will give Mr. Freeland the credit of being the best master I ever had, *till I became my own master.* For the ease with which I passed the year, I was, however, somewhat indebted to the society of my fellow-slaves. They were noble souls; they not only possessed loving hearts, but brave ones. We were linked and interlinked with each other.

I loved them with a love stronger than any thing I have experienced since. It is sometimes said that we slaves do not love and confide in each other. In answer to this assertion, I can say, I never loved any or confided in any people more than my fellow-slaves, and especially those with whom I lived at Mr. Freeland's. I believe we would have died for each other. We never undertook to do any thing, of any importance, without a mutual consultation. We never moved separately. We were one; and as much so by our tempers and dispositions, as by the mutual hardships to which we were necessarily subjected by our condition as slaves.

At the close of the year 1834, Mr. Freeland again hired me of my master, for the year 1835. But, by this time, I began to want to live *upon free land* as well as *with Freeland;* and I was no longer content, therefore, to live with him or any other slaveholder. I began, with the commencement of the year, to prepare myself for a final struggle, which should decide my fate one way or the other. My tendency was upward. I was fast approaching manhood, and year after year had passed, and I was still a slave.

These thoughts roused me—I must do something. I therefore resolved that 1835 should not pass without witnessing an attempt, on my part, to secure my liberty. But I was not willing to cherish this determination alone. My fellow-slaves were dear to me. I was anxious to have them participate with me in this, my life-giving determination. I therefore, though with great prudence, commenced early to ascertain their views and feelings in regard to their condition, and to imbue their minds with thoughts of freedom. I bent myself to devising ways and means for our escape, and meanwhile strove, on all fitting occasions, to impress them with the gross fraud and inhumanity of slavery.

I went first to Henry, next to John, then to the others. I found, in them all, warm hearts and noble spirits. They were ready to hear, and ready to act when a feasible plan should be proposed. This was what I wanted. I talked to them of our want of manhood, if we submitted to our enslavement without at least one noble effort to be free. We met often, and consulted frequently, and told our hopes and fears, recounted the difficulties, real and imagined, which we should be called on to meet. At times we were almost disposed to give up, and try to content ourselves with our wretched lot; at others, we were firm and unbending in our determination to go.

Whenever we suggested any plan, there was shrinking—the odds were fearful. Our path was beset with the greatest obstacles; and if we succeeded in gaining the end of it, our right to be free was yet questionable—we were yet liable to be returned to bondage. We could see no spot, this side of the ocean, where we could be free. We knew nothing about Canada. Our knowledge of the north did not extend farther than New York; and to go there, and be forever harassed with the frightful liability of being returned to slavery—with the certainty of being treated tenfold worse than before—the thought was truly a horrible one, and one which it was not easy to overcome.

The case sometimes stood thus: At every gate through which we were to pass, we saw a watchman—at every ferry a guard—on every bridge a sentinel—and in every wood a patrol. We were hemmed in upon every side. Here were the difficulties, real or imagined—the good to be sought, and the evil to be shunned. On the one hand, there stood slavery, a stern reality, glaring frightfully upon us,—its robes already crimsoned with the blood of millions, and even now feasting itself greedily upon our own flesh.

On the other hand, away back in the dim distance, under the flickering light of the north star, behind some craggy hill or snow-covered mountain, stood a doubtful freedom—half frozen—beckoning us to come and share its hospitality. This in itself was sometimes enough to stagger us; but when we permitted ourselves to survey the road, we were frequently appalled. Upon either side we saw grim death, assuming the most horrid shapes.

Now it was starvation, causing us to eat our own flesh;—now we were contending with the waves, and were drowned;—now we were overtaken, and torn to pieces by the fangs of the terrible bloodhound. We were stung by scorpions, chased by wild beasts, bitten by snakes, and finally, after having nearly reached the desired spot,—after swimming rivers, encountering wild beasts, sleeping in the woods, suffering hunger and nakedness,—we were overtaken by our pursuers, and, in our resistance, we were shot dead upon the spot! I say, this picture sometimes appalled us, and made us

"rather bear those ills we had,
Than fly to others, that we knew not of."

In coming to a fixed determination to run away, we did more than Patrick Henry, when he resolved upon liberty or death. With us it was a doubtful liberty at most, and almost certain death if we failed. For my part, I should prefer death to hopeless bondage.

Sandy, one of our number, gave up the notion, but still encouraged us. Our company then consisted of Henry Harris, John Harris, Henry Bailey, Charles Roberts, and myself. Henry Bailey was my uncle, and belonged to my master. Charles married my aunt: he belonged to my master's father-in-law, Mr. William Hamilton.

The plan we finally concluded upon was, to get a large canoe belonging to Mr. Hamilton, and upon the Saturday night previous to Easter holidays, paddle directly up the Chesapeake Bay. On our arrival at the head of the bay, a distance of seventy or eighty miles from where we lived, it was our purpose to turn our canoe adrift, and follow the guidance of the north star till we got beyond the limits of Maryland. Our reason for taking the water route was, that we were less liable to be suspected as runaways; we hoped to be regarded as fishermen; whereas, if we should take the land route, we should be subjected to interruptions of almost every kind. Any one having a white face, and being so disposed, could stop us, and subject us to examination.

The week before our intended start, I wrote several protections, one for each of us. As well as I can remember, they were in the following words, to wit:—

"This is to certify that I, the undersigned, have given the bearer, my servant, full liberty to go to Baltimore, and spend the Easter holidays.

Written with mine own hand, &c., 1835.

"WILLIAM HAMILTON,

"Near St. Michael's, in Talbot county, Maryland."

We were not going to Baltimore; but, in going up the bay, we went toward Baltimore, and these protections were only intended to protect us while on the bay.

As the time drew near for our departure, our anxiety became more and more intense. It was truly a matter of life and death with us. The strength of our determination was about to be fully tested. At this time, I was very active in explaining every difficulty, removing every doubt, dispelling every fear, and inspiring all with the firmness indispensable to success in our undertaking; assuring them that half was gained the instant we made the move; we had talked long enough; we were now ready to move; if not now, we never should be; and if we did not intend to move now, we had as well fold our arms, sit down, and acknowledge ourselves fit only to be slaves. This, none of us were prepared to acknowledge. Every man stood firm; and at our last meeting, we pledged ourselves afresh, in the most solemn manner, that, at the time appointed, we would certainly start in pursuit of freedom. This was in the middle of the week, at the end of which we were to be off. We went, as usual, to our several fields of labor, but with bosoms highly agitated with thoughts of our truly hazardous under-taking. We tried to conceal our feelings as much as possible; and I think we succeeded very well.

After a painful waiting, the Saturday morning, whose night was to witness our departure, came. I hailed it with joy, bring what of sadness it might. Friday night was a sleepless one for me. I probably felt more anxious than the rest, because I was, by common consent, at the head of the whole affair. The responsibility of success or failure lay heavily upon me. The glory of the one, and the confusion of the other, were alike mine. The first two hours of that morning were such as I never experienced before, and hope never to again. Early in the morning, we went, as usual, to the field. We were spreading manure; and all at once, while thus engaged, I was overwhelmed with an indescribable feeling, in the fulness of which I turned to Sandy, who was near by, and said, "We are betrayed!" "Well," said he, "that thought has this moment struck me." We said no more. I was never more certain of any thing.

The horn was blown as usual, and we went up from the field to the house for breakfast. I went for the form, more than for want of any thing to eat that morning. Just as I got to the house, in looking out at the lane gate, I saw four white men, with two colored men. The white men were on horseback, and the colored ones were walking behind, as if tied. I watched them a few moments till they got up to our lane gate. Here they halted, and tied the colored men to the gate-post. I was not yet certain as to what the matter was. In a few moments, in rode Mr. Hamilton, with a speed betokening great excitement. He came to the door, and inquired if Master William was in. He was told he was at the barn. Mr. Hamilton, without dismounting, rode up to the barn with extraordinary speed. In a few moments, he and Mr. Freeland returned to the house.

By this time, the three constables rode up, and in great haste dismounted, tied their horses, and met Master William and Mr. Hamilton returning from the barn; and after talking awhile, they all walked up to the kitchen door. There was no one in the kitchen but myself and John. Henry and Sandy were up at the barn. Mr. Freeland put his head in at the door, and called me by name, saying, there were some gentlemen at the door who wished to see me. I stepped to the door, and inquired what they wanted.

They at once seized me, and, without giving me any satisfaction, tied me—lashing my hands closely together. I insisted upon knowing what the matter was. They at length said, that they had learned I had been in a "scrape," and that I was to be examined before my master; and if their information proved false, I should not be hurt.

In a few moments, they succeeded in tying John. They then turned to Henry, who had by this time returned, and commanded him to cross his hands. "I won't!" said Henry, in a firm tone, indicating his readiness to meet the consequences of his refusal. "Won't you?" said Tom Graham, the constable. "No, I won't!" said Henry, in a still stronger tone. With this, two of the constables pulled out their shining pistols, and swore, by their Creator, that they would make him cross his hands or kill him. Each cocked his pistol, and, with fingers on the trigger, walked up to Henry, saying, at the same time, if he did not cross his hands, they would blow his damned heart out. "Shoot me, shoot me!" said Henry; "you can't kill me but once. Shoot, shoot,—and be damned! *I won't be tied!*" This he said in a tone of loud defiance; and at the same time, with a motion as quick as lightning, he with one single stroke dashed the pistols from the hand of each constable. As he did this, all hands fell upon him, and, after beating him some time, they finally overpowered him, and got him tied.

During the scuffle, I managed, I know not how, to get my pass out, and, without being discovered, put it into the fire. We were all now tied; and just as we were to leave for Easton jail, Betsy Freeland, mother of William Freeland, came to the door with her hands full of biscuits, and divided them between Henry and John. She then delivered herself of a speech, to the following effect:—addressing herself to me, she said, *"You devil! You yellow devil!* it was you that put it into the heads of Henry and John to run away. But for you, you long-legged mulatto devil! Henry nor John would never have thought of such a thing." I made no reply, and was immediately hurried off towards St. Michael's. Just a moment previous to the scuffle with Henry, Mr. Hamilton suggested the propriety of making a search for the protections which he had understood Frederick had written for himself and the rest. But, just at the moment he was about carrying his proposal into effect, his aid was needed in helping to tie Henry; and the excitement attending the scuffle caused them either to forget, or to deem it unsafe, under the circumstances, to search. So we were not yet convicted of the intention to run away.

When we got about half way to St. Michael's, while the constables having us in charge were looking ahead, Henry inquired of me what he should do with his pass. I told him to eat it with his biscuit, and own nothing; and we passed the word around, *"Own nothing;"* and *"Own nothing!"* said we all. Our confidence in each other was unshaken. We were resolved to succeed or fail together, after the calamity had befallen us as much as before.

We were now prepared for any thing. We were to be dragged that morning fifteen miles behind horses, and then to be placed in the Easton jail. When we reached St. Michael's, we underwent a sort of examination. We all denied that we ever intended to run away. We did this more to bring out the evidence against us, than from any hope of getting clear of being sold; for, as I have said, we were ready for that.

The fact was, we cared but little where we went, so we went together. Our greatest concern was about separation. We dreaded that more than any thing this side of death. We found the evidence against us to be the testimony of one person; our master would not tell who it was; but we came to a unanimous decision among ourselves as to who their informant was.

We were sent off to the jail at Easton. When we got there, we were delivered up to the sheriff, Mr. Joseph Graham, and by him placed in jail. Henry, John, and myself, were placed in one room together—Charles, and Henry Bailey, in another. Their object in separating us was to hinder concert.

We had been in jail scarcely twenty minutes, when a swarm of slave traders, and agents for slave traders, flocked into jail to look at us, and to ascertain if we were for sale. Such a set of beings I never saw before! I felt myself surrounded by so many fiends from perdition. A band of pirates never looked more like their father, the devil. They laughed and grinned over us, saying, "Ah, my boys! we have got you, haven't we?" And after taunting us in various ways, they one by one went into an examination of us, with intent to ascertain our value. They would impudently ask us if we would not like to have them for our masters. We would make them no answer, and leave them to find out as best they could. Then they would curse and swear at us, telling us that they could take the devil out of us in a very little while, if we were only in their hands.

While in jail, we found ourselves in much more comfortable quarters than we expected when we went there. We did not get much to eat, nor that which was very good; but we had a good clean room, from the windows of which we could see what was going on in the street, which was very much better than though we had been placed in one of the dark, damp cells. Upon the whole, we got along very well, so far as the jail and its keeper were concerned.

Immediately after the holidays were over, contrary to all our expectations, Mr. Hamilton and Mr. Freeland came up to Easton, and took Charles, the two Henrys, and John, out of jail, and carried them home, leaving me alone. I regarded this separation as a final one. It caused me more pain than any thing else in the whole transaction. I was ready for any thing rather than separation.

I supposed that they had consulted together, and had decided that, as I was the whole cause of the intention of the others to run away, it was hard to make the innocent suffer with the guilty; and that they had, therefore, concluded to take the others home, and sell me, as a warning to the others that remained. It is due to the noble Henry to say, he seemed almost as reluctant at leaving the prison as at leaving home to come to the prison. But we knew we should, in all probability, be separated, if we were sold; and since he was in their hands, he concluded to go peaceably home.

I was now left to my fate. I was all alone, and within the walls of a stone prison. But a few days before, and I was full of hope. I expected to have been safe in a land of freedom; but now I was covered with gloom, sunk down to the utmost despair. I thought the possibility of freedom was gone. I was kept in this way about one week, at the end of which, Captain Auld, my master, to my surprise and utter astonishment, came up, and took me out, with the intention of sending me, with a gentleman of his acquaintance, into Alabama. But, from some cause or other, he did not send me to Alabama, but concluded to send me back to Baltimore, to live again with his brother Hugh, and to learn a trade.

Thus, after an absence of three years and one month, I was once more permitted to return to my old home at Baltimore. My master sent me away, because there existed against me a very great prejudice in the community, and he feared I might be killed.

In a few weeks after I went to Baltimore, Master Hugh hired me to Mr. William Gardner, an extensive ship-builder, on Fell's Point. I was put there to learn how to calk. It, however, proved a very unfavorable place for the accomplishment of this object. Mr. Gardner was engaged that spring in building two large man-of-war brigs, professedly for the Mexican government. The vessels were to be launched in the July of that year, and in failure thereof, Mr. Gardner was to lose a considerable sum; so that when I entered, all was hurry. There was no time to learn any thing. Every man had to do that which he knew how to do.

In entering the shipyard, my orders from Mr. Gardner were, to do whatever the carpenters commanded me to do. This was placing me at the beck and call of about seventy-five men. I was to regard all these as masters. Their word was to be my law. My situation was a most trying one. At times I needed a dozen pair of hands.

I was called a dozen ways in the space of a single minute. Three or four voices would strike my ear at the same moment. It was—"Fred., come help me to cant this timber here."—"Fred., come carry this timber yonder."—"Fred., bring that roller here."—"Fred., go get a fresh can of water."—"Fred., come help saw off the end of this timber."—"Fred., go quick, and get the crowbar."—"Fred., hold on the end of this fall."—"Fred., go to the blacksmith's shop, and get a new punch."—"Hurra, Fred! run and bring me a cold chisel."—"I say, Fred., bear a hand, and get up a fire as quick as lightning under that steam-box."—"Halloo, nigger! come, turn this grindstone."—"Come, come! move, move! and *bowse* this timber forward."—"I say, darky, blast your eyes, why don't you heat up some pitch?"—"Halloo! halloo! halloo!" (Three voices at the same time.) "Come here!—Go there!—Hold on where you are! Damn you, if you move, I'll knock your brains out!"

This was my school for eight months; and I might have remained there longer, but for a most horrid fight I had with four of the white apprentices, in which my left eye was nearly knocked out, and I was horribly mangled in other respects. The facts in the case were these: Until a very little while after I went there, white and black ship-carpenters worked side by side, and no one seemed to see any impropriety in it. All hands seemed to be very well satisfied. Many of the black carpenters were freemen. Things seemed to be going on very well.

All at once, the white carpenters knocked off, and said they would not work with free colored workmen. Their reason for this, as alleged, was, that if free colored carpenters were encouraged, they would soon take the trade into their own hands, and poor white men would be thrown out of employment. They therefore felt called upon at once to put a stop to it. And, taking advantage of Mr. Gardner's necessities, they broke off, swearing they would work no longer, unless he would discharge his black carpenters.

Now, though this did not extend to me in form, it did reach me in fact. My fellow-apprentices very soon began to feel it degrading to them to work with me. They began to put on airs, and talk about the "niggers" taking the country, saying we all ought to be killed; and, being encouraged by the journeymen, they commenced making my condition as hard as they could, by hectoring me around, and sometimes striking me. I, of course, kept the vow I made after the fight with Mr. Covey, and struck back again, regardless of consequences; and while I kept them from combining, I succeeded very well; for I could whip the whole of them, taking them separately. They, however, at length combined, and came upon me, armed with sticks, stones, and heavy handspikes. One came in front with a half brick. There was one at each side of me, and one behind me.

While I was attending to those in front, and on either side, the one behind ran up with the handspike, and struck me a heavy blow upon the head. It stunned me. I fell, and with this they all ran upon me, and fell to beating me with their fists. I let them lay on for a while, gathering strength. In an instant, I gave a sudden surge, and rose to my hands and knees. Just as I did that, one of their number gave me, with his heavy boot, a powerful kick in the left eye. My eyeball seemed to have burst.

When they saw my eye closed, and badly swollen, they left me. With this I seized the handspike, and for a time pursued them. But here the carpenters interfered, and I thought I might as well give it up. It was impossible to stand my hand against so many. All this took place in sight of not less than fifty white ship-carpenters, and not one interposed a friendly word; but some cried, "Kill the damned nigger! Kill him! kill him! He struck a white person." I found my only chance for life was in flight. I succeeded in getting away without an additional blow, and barely so; for to strike a white man is death by Lynch law,—and that was the law in Mr. Gardner's ship-yard; nor is there much of any other out of Mr. Gardner's ship-yard.

I went directly home, and told the story of my wrongs to Master Hugh; and I am happy to say of him, irreligious as he was, his conduct was heavenly, compared with that of his brother Thomas under similar circumstances. He listened attentively to my narration of the circumstances leading to the savage outrage, and gave many proofs of his strong indignation at it. The heart of my once overkind mistress was again melted into pity. My puffed-out eye and blood-covered face moved her to tears. She took a chair by me, washed the blood from my face, and, with a mother's tenderness, bound up my head, covering the wounded eye with a lean piece of fresh beef. It was almost compensation for my suffering to witness, once more, a manifestation of kindness from this, my once affectionate old mistress.

Master Hugh was very much enraged. He gave expression to his feelings by pouring out curses upon the heads of those who did the deed. As soon as I got a little the better of my bruises, he took me with him to Esquire Watson's, on Bond Street, to see what could be done about the matter. Mr. Watson inquired who saw the assault committed. Master Hugh told him it was done in Mr. Gardner's ship-yard at midday, where there were a large company of men at work. "As to that," he said, "the deed was done, and there was no question as to who did it." His answer was, he could do nothing in the case, unless some white man would come forward and testify. He could issue no warrant on my word. If I had been killed in the presence of a thousand colored people, their testimony combined would have been insufficient to have arrested one of the murderers.

Master Hugh, for once, was compelled to say this state of things was too bad. Of course, it was impossible to get any white man to volunteer his testimony in my behalf, and against the white young men. Even those who may have sympathized with me were not prepared to do this. It required a degree of courage unknown to them to do so; for just at that time, the slightest manifestation of humanity toward a colored person was denounced as abolitionism, and that name subjected its bearer to frightful liabilities. The watchwords of the bloody-minded in that region, and in those days, were, "Damn the abolitionists!" and "Damn the niggers!" There was nothing done, and probably nothing would have been done if I had been killed. Such was, and such remains, the state of things in the Christian city of Baltimore.

Master Hugh, finding he could get no redress, refused to let me go back again to Mr. Gardner. He kept me himself, and his wife dressed my wound till I was again restored to health. He then took me into the ship-yard of which he was foreman, in the employment of Mr. Walter Price. There I was immediately set to calking, and very soon learned the art of using my mallet and irons.

In the course of one year from the time I left Mr. Gardner's, I was able to command the highest wages given to the most experienced calkers. I was now of some importance to my master. I was bringing him from six to seven dollars per week. I sometimes brought him nine dollars per week: my wages were a dollar and a half a day.

After learning how to calk, I sought my own employment, made my own contracts, and collected the money which I earned. My pathway became much more smooth than before; my condition was now much more comfortable. When I could get no calking to do, I did nothing. During these leisure times, those old notions about freedom would steal over me again.

When in Mr. Gardner's employment, I was kept in such a perpetual whirl of excitement, I could think of nothing, scarcely, but my life; and in thinking of my life, I almost forgot my liberty. I have observed this in my experience of slavery,—that whenever my condition was improved, instead of its increasing my contentment, it only increased my desire to be free, and set me to thinking of plans to gain my freedom.

I have found that, to make a contented slave, it is necessary to make a thoughtless one. It is necessary to darken his moral and mental vision, and, as far as possible, to annihilate the power of reason. He must be able to detect no inconsistencies in slavery; he must be made to feel that slavery is right; and he can be brought to that only when he ceases to be a man.

I was now getting, as I have said, one dollar and fifty cents per day. I contracted for it; I earned it; it was paid to me; it was rightfully my own; yet, upon each returning Saturday night, I was compelled to deliver every cent of that money to Master Hugh. And why? Not because he earned it,—not because he had any hand in earning it,—not because I owed it to him,—nor because he possessed the slightest shadow of a right to it; but solely because he had the power to compel me to give it up. The right of the grim-visaged pirate upon the high seas is exactly the same.

CHAPTER 11

I now come to that part of my life during which I planned, and finally succeeded in making, my escape from slavery. But before narrating any of the peculiar circumstances, I deem it proper to make known my intention not to state all the facts connected with the transaction. My reasons for pursuing this course may be understood from the following: First, were I to give a minute statement of all the facts, it is not only possible, but quite probable, that others would thereby be involved in the most embarrassing difficulties. Secondly, such a statement would most undoubtedly induce greater vigilance on the part of slaveholders than has existed heretofore among them; which would, of course, be the means of guarding a door whereby some dear brother bondman might escape his galling chains.

I deeply regret the necessity that impels me to suppress any thing of importance connected with my experience in slavery. It would afford me great pleasure indeed, as well as materially add to the interest of my narrative, were I at liberty to gratify a curiosity, which I know exists in the minds of many, by an accurate statement of all the facts pertaining to my most fortunate escape. But I must deprive myself of this pleasure, and the curious of the gratification which such a statement would afford. I would allow myself to suffer under the greatest imputations which evil-minded men might suggest, rather than exculpate myself, and thereby run the hazard of closing the slightest avenue by which a brother slave might clear himself of the chains and fetters of slavery.

I have never approved of the very public manner in which some of our western friends have conducted what they call the *underground railroad*, but which I think, by their open declarations, has been made most emphatically the *upper-ground railroad*. I honor those good men and women for their noble daring, and applaud them for willingly subjecting themselves to bloody persecution, by openly avowing their participation in the escape of slaves. I, however, can see very little good resulting from such a course, either to themselves or the slaves escaping; while, upon the other hand, I see and feel assured that those open declarations are a positive evil to the slaves remaining, who are seeking to escape.

They do nothing towards enlightening the slave, whilst they do much towards enlightening the master. They stimulate him to greater watchfulness, and enhance his power to capture his slave. We owe something to the slave south of the line as well as to those north of it; and in aiding the latter on their way to freedom, we should be careful to do nothing which would be likely to hinder the former from escaping from slavery. I would keep the merciless slaveholder profoundly ignorant of the means of flight adopted by the slave. I would leave him to imagine himself surrounded by myriads of invisible tormentors, ever ready to snatch from his infernal grasp his trembling prey.

Let him be left to feel his way in the dark; let darkness commensurate with his crime hover over him; and let him feel that at every step he takes, in pursuit of the flying bond-man, he is running the frightful risk of having his hot brains dashed out by an invisible agency. Let us render the tyrant no aid; let us not hold the light by which he can trace the foot-prints of our flying brother. But enough of this. I will now proceed to the statement of those facts, connected with my escape, for which I am alone responsible, and for which no one can be made to suffer but myself.

In the early part of the year 1838, I became quite restless. I could see no reason why I should, at the end of each week, pour the reward of my toil into the purse of my master. When I carried to him my weekly wages, he would, after counting the money, look me in the face with a robber-like fierceness, and ask, "Is this all?" He was satisfied with nothing less than the last cent. He would, however, when I made him six dollars, sometimes give me six cents, to encourage me.

It had the opposite effect. I regarded it as a sort of admission of my right to the whole. The fact that he gave me any part of my wages was proof, to my mind, that he believed me entitled to the whole of them. I always felt worse for having received any thing; for I feared that the giving me a few cents would ease his conscience, and make him feel himself to be a pretty honorable sort of robber. My discontent grew upon me. I was ever on the look-out for means of escape; and, finding no direct means, I determined to try to hire my time, with a view of getting money with which to make my escape.

In the spring of 1838, when Master Thomas came to Baltimore to purchase his spring goods, I got an opportunity, and applied to him to allow me to hire my time. He unhesitatingly refused my request, and told me this was another stratagem by which to escape. He told me I could go nowhere but that he could get me; and that, in the event of my running away, he should spare no pains in his efforts to catch me. He exhorted me to content myself, and be obedient. He told me, if I would be happy, I must lay out no plans for the future. He said, if I behaved myself properly, he would take care of me.

Indeed, he advised me to complete thoughtlessness of the future, and taught me to depend solely upon him for happiness. He seemed to see fully the pressing necessity of setting aside my intellectual nature, in order to contentment in slavery. But in spite of him, and even in spite of myself, I continued to think, and to think about the injustice of my enslavement, and the means of escape.

About two months after this, I applied to Master Hugh for the privilege of hiring my time. He was not acquainted with the fact that I had applied to Master Thomas, and had been refused. He too, at first, seemed disposed to refuse; but, after some reflection, he granted me the privilege, and proposed the following terms: I was to be allowed all my time, make all contracts with those for whom I worked, and find my own employment; and, in return for this liberty, I was to pay him three dollars at the end of each week; find myself in calking tools, and in board and clothing.

My board was two dollars and a half per week. This, with the wear and tear of clothing and calking tools, made my regular expenses about six dollars per week. This amount I was compelled to make up, or relinquish the privilege of hiring my time. Rain or shine, work or no work, at the end of each week the money must be forthcoming, or I must give up my privilege.

This arrangement, it will be perceived, was decidedly in my master's favor. It relieved him of all need of looking after me. His money was sure. He received all the benefits of slave-holding without its evils; while I endured all the evils of a slave, and suffered all the care and anxiety of a freeman. I found it a hard bargain. But, hard as it was, I thought it better than the old mode of getting along. It was a step towards freedom to be allowed to bear the responsibilities of a freeman, and I was determined to hold on upon it.

I bent myself to the work of making money. I was ready to work at night as well as day, and by the most untiring perseverance and industry, I made enough to meet my expenses, and lay up a little money every week. I went on thus from May till August.

Master Hugh then refused to allow me to hire my time longer. The ground for his refusal was a failure on my part, one Saturday night, to pay him for my week's time. This failure was occasioned by my attending a camp meeting about ten miles from Baltimore. During the week, I had entered into an engagement with a number of young friends to start from Baltimore to the camp ground early Saturday evening; and being detained by my employer, I was unable to get down to Master Hugh's without disappointing the company. I knew that Master Hugh was in no special need of the money that night. I therefore decided to go to camp meeting, and upon my return pay him the three dollars. I staid at the camp meeting one day longer than I intended when I left.

But as soon as I returned, I called upon him to pay him what he considered his due. I found him very angry; he could scarce restrain his wrath. He said he had a great mind to give me a severe whipping. He wished to know how I dared go out of the city without asking his permission. I told him I hired my time and while I paid him the price which he asked for it, I did not know that I was bound to ask him when and where I should go. This reply troubled him; and, after reflecting a few moments, he turned to me, and said I should hire my time no longer; that the next thing he should know of, I would be running away.

Upon the same plea, he told me to bring my tools and clothing home forthwith. I did so; but instead of seeking work, as I had been accustomed to do previously to hiring my time, I spent the whole week without the performance of a single stroke of work. I did this in retaliation. Saturday night, he called upon me as usual for my week's wages. I told him I had no wages; I had done no work that week. Here we were upon the point of coming to blows. He raved, and swore his determination to get hold of me. I did not allow myself a single word; but was resolved, if he laid the weight of his hand upon me, it should be blow for blow. He did not strike me, but told me that he would find me in constant employment in future. I thought the matter over during the next day, Sunday, and finally resolved upon the third day of September, as the day upon which I would make a second attempt to secure my freedom.

I now had three weeks during which to prepare for my journey. Early on Monday morning, before Master Hugh had time to make any engagement for me, I went out and got employment of Mr. Butler, at his ship-yard near the draw-bridge, upon what is called the City Block, thus making it unnecessary for him to seek employment for me. At the end of the week, I brought him between eight and nine dollars. He seemed very well pleased, and asked why I did not do the same the week before. He little knew what my plans were.

My object in working steadily was to remove any suspicion he might entertain of my intent to run away; and in this I succeeded admirably. I suppose he thought I was never better satisfied with my condition than at the very time during which I was planning my escape. The second week passed, and again I carried him my full wages; and so well pleased was he, that he gave me twenty-five cents, (quite a large sum for a slaveholder to give a slave,) and bade me to make a good use of it. I told him I would.

Things went on without very smoothly indeed, but within there was trouble. It is impossible for me to describe my feelings as the time of my contemplated start drew near. I had a number of warmhearted friends in Baltimore,—friends that I loved almost as I did my life,—and the thought of being separated from them forever was painful beyond expression.

It is my opinion that thousands would escape from slavery, who now remain, but for the strong cords of affection that bind them to their friends. The thought of leaving my friends was decidedly the most painful thought with which I had to contend. The love of them was my tender point, and shook my decision more than all things else. Besides the pain of separation, the dread and apprehension of a failure exceeded what I had experienced at my first attempt.

The appalling defeat I then sustained returned to torment me. I felt assured that, if I failed in this attempt, my case would be a hopeless one—it would seal my fate as a slave forever. I could not hope to get off with any thing less than the severest punishment, and being placed beyond the means of escape. It required no very vivid imagination to depict the most frightful scenes through which I should have to pass, in case I failed.

The wretchedness of slavery, and the blessedness of freedom, were perpetually before me. It was life and death with me. But I remained firm, and, according to my resolution, on the third day of September, 1838, I left my chains, and succeeded in reaching New York without the slightest interruption of any kind. How I did so,—what means I adopted,—what direction I travelled, and by what mode of conveyance,—I must leave unexplained, for the reasons before mentioned.

I have been frequently asked how I felt when I found myself in a free State. I have never been able to answer the question with any satisfaction to myself. It was a moment of the highest excitement I ever experienced. I suppose I felt as one may imagine the unarmed mariner to feel when he is rescued by a friendly man-of-war from the pursuit of a pirate. In writing to a dear friend, immediately after my arrival at New York, I said I felt like one who had escaped a den of hungry lions.

This state of mind, however, very soon subsided; and I was again seized with a feeling of great insecurity and loneliness. I was yet liable to be taken back, and subjected to all the tortures of slavery. This in itself was enough to damp the ardor of my enthusiasm. But the loneliness overcame me. There I was in the midst of thousands, and yet a perfect stranger; without home and without friends, in the midst of thousands of my own brethren—children of a common Father, and yet I dared not to unfold to any one of them my sad condition. I was afraid to speak to any one for fear of speaking to the wrong one, and thereby falling into the hands of money-loving kidnappers, whose business it was to lie in wait for the panting fugitive, as the ferocious beasts of the forest lie in wait for their prey.

The motto which I adopted when I started from slavery was this—"Trust no man!" I saw in every white man an enemy, and in almost every colored man cause for distrust. It was a most painful situation; and, to understand it, one must needs experience it, or imagine himself in similar circumstances.

Let him be a fugitive slave in a strange land—a land given up to be the hunting-ground for slaveholders—whose inhabitants are legalized kidnappers—where he is every moment subjected to the terrible liability of being seized upon by his fellowmen, as the hideous crocodile seizes upon his prey!—I say, let him place himself in my situation—without home or friends—without money or credit—wanting shelter, and no one to give it—wanting bread, and no money to buy it,—and at the same time let him feel that he is pursued by merciless men-hunters, and in total darkness as to what to do, where to go, or where to stay,—perfectly helpless both as to the means of defence and means of escape,—in the midst of plenty, yet suffering the terrible gnawings of hunger,—in the midst of houses, yet having no home,—among fellow-men, yet feeling as if in the midst of wild beasts, whose greediness to swallow up the trembling and half-famished fugitive is only equalled by that with which the monsters of the deep swallow up the helpless fish upon which they subsist,—I say, let him be placed in this most trying situation,—the situation in which I was placed,—then, and not till then, will he fully appreciate the hardships of, and know how to sympathize with, the toil-worn and whip-scarred fugitive slave.

Thank Heaven, I remained but a short time in this distressed situation. I was relieved from it by the humane hand of Mr. David Ruggles, whose vigilance, kindness, and perseverance, I shall never forget. I am glad of an opportunity to express, as far as words can, the love and gratitude I bear him. Mr. Ruggles is now afflicted with blindness, and is himself in need of the same kind offices which he was once so forward in the performance of toward others.

I had been in New York but a few days, when Mr. Ruggles sought me out, and very kindly took me to his boarding-house at the corner of Church and Lespenard Streets. Mr. Ruggles was then very deeply engaged in the memorable *Darg* case, as well as attending to a number of other fugitive slaves, devising ways and means for their successful escape; and, though watched and hemmed in on almost every side, he seemed to be more than a match for his enemies.

Very soon after I went to Mr. Ruggles, he wished to know of me where I wanted to go; as he deemed it unsafe for me to remain in New York. I told him I was a calker, and should like to go where I could get work. I thought of going to Canada; but he decided against it, and in favor of my going to New Bedford, thinking I should be able to get work there at my trade.

At this time, Anna,[1] my intended wife, came on; for I wrote to her immediately after my arrival at New York, (notwithstanding my homeless, houseless, and helpless condition,) informing her of my successful flight, and wishing her to come on forthwith. In a few days after her arrival, Mr. Ruggles called in the Rev. J. W. C. Pennington, who, in the presence of Mr. Ruggles, Mrs. Michaels, and two or three others, performed the marriage ceremony, and gave us a certificate, of which the following is an exact copy:—

"This may certify, that I joined together in holy matrimony Frederick Johnson[2] and Anna Murray, as man and wife, in the presence of Mr. David Ruggles and Mrs. Michaels.
"JAMES W. C. PENNINGTON
"*New York, Sept. 15, 1838*"

Upon receiving this certificate, and a five-dollar bill from Mr. Ruggles, I shouldered one part of our baggage, and Anna took up the other, and we set out forthwith to take passage on board of the steamboat John W. Richmond for Newport, on our way to New Bedford. Mr. Ruggles gave me a letter to a Mr. Shaw in Newport, and told me, in case my money did not serve me to New Bedford, to stop in Newport and obtain further assistance; but upon our arrival at Newport, we were

[1] She was free.

[2] I had changed my name from Frederick *Bailey* to that of *Johnson*.

so anxious to get to a place of safety, that, notwithstanding we lacked the necessary money to pay our fare, we decided to take seats in the stage, and promise to pay when we got to New Bedford.

We were encouraged to do this by two excellent gentlemen, residents of New Bedford, whose names I afterward ascertained to be Joseph Ricketson and William C. Taber. They seemed at once to understand our circumstances, and gave us such assurance of their friendliness as put us fully at ease in their presence. It was good indeed to meet with such friends, at such a time.

Upon reaching New Bedford, we were directed to the house of Mr. Nathan Johnson, by whom we were kindly received, and hospitably provided for. Both Mr. and Mrs. Johnson took a deep and lively interest in our welfare. They proved themselves quite worthy of the name of abolitionists. When the stage-driver found us unable to pay our fare, he held on upon our baggage as security for the debt. I had but to mention the fact to Mr. Johnson, and he forthwith advanced the money.

We now began to feel a degree of safety, and to prepare ourselves for the duties and responsibilities of a life of freedom. On the morning after our arrival at New Bedford, while at the breakfast-table, the question arose as to what name I should be called by. The name given me by my mother was, "Frederick Augustus Washington Bailey." I, however, had dispensed with the two middle names long before I left Maryland so that I was generally known by the name of "Frederick Bailey." I started from Baltimore bearing the name of "Stanley." When I got to New York, I again changed my name to "Frederick Johnson," and thought that would be the last change.

But when I got to New Bedford, I found it necessary again to change my name. The reason of this necessity was, that there were so many Johnsons in New Bedford, it was already quite difficult to distinguish between them. I gave Mr. Johnson the privilege of choosing me a name, but told him he must not take from me the name of "Frederick." I must hold on to that, to preserve a sense of my identity.

Mr. Johnson had just been reading the "Lady of the Lake," and at once suggested that my name be "Douglass." From that time until now I have been called "Frederick Douglass;" and as I am more widely known by that name than by either of the others, I shall continue to use it as my own.

I was quite disappointed at the general appearance of things in New Bedford. The impression which I had received respecting the character and condition of the people of the north, I found to be singularly erroneous. I had very strangely supposed, while in slavery, that few of the comforts, and scarcely any of the luxuries, of life were enjoyed at the north, compared with what were enjoyed by the slaveholders of the south. I probably came to this conclusion from the fact that northern people owned no slaves.

I supposed that they were about upon a level with the non-slaveholding population of the south. I knew *they* were exceedingly poor, and I had been accustomed to regard their poverty as the necessary consequence of their being non-slaveholders. I had somehow imbibed the opinion that, in the absence of slaves, there could be no wealth, and very little refinement.

And upon coming to the north, I expected to meet with a rough, hard-handed, and uncultivated population, living in the most Spartan-like simplicity, knowing nothing of the ease, luxury, pomp, and grandeur of southern slaveholders. Such being my conjectures, any one acquainted with the appearance of New Bedford may very readily infer how palpably I must have seen my mistake.

In the afternoon of the day when I reached New Bedford, I visited the wharves, to take a view of the shipping. Here I found myself surrounded with the strongest proofs of wealth. Lying at the wharves, and riding in the stream, I saw many ships of the finest model, in the best order, and of the largest size.

Upon the right and left, I was walled in by granite warehouses of the widest dimensions, stowed to their utmost capacity with the necessaries and comforts of life. Added to this, almost every body seemed to be at work, but noiselessly so, compared with what I had been accustomed to in Baltimore. There were no loud songs heard from those engaged in loading and unloading ships. I heard no deep oaths or horrid curses on the laborer. I saw no whipping of men; but all seemed to go smoothly on. Every man appeared to understand his work, and went at it with a sober, yet cheerful earnestness, which betokened the deep interest which he felt in what he was doing, as well as a sense of his own dignity as a man. To me this looked exceedingly strange.

From the wharves I strolled around and over the town, gazing with wonder and admiration at the splendid churches, beautiful dwellings, and finely-cultivated gardens; evincing an amount of wealth, comfort, taste, and refinement, such as I had never seen in any part of slaveholding Maryland.

Every thing looked clean, new, and beautiful. I saw few or no dilapidated houses, with poverty-stricken inmates; no half-naked children and barefooted women, such as I had been accustomed to see in Hillsborough, Easton, St. Michael's, and Baltimore. The people looked more able, stronger, healthier, and happier, than those of Maryland. I was for once made glad by a view of extreme wealth, without being saddened by seeing extreme poverty.

But the most astonishing as well as the most interesting thing to me was the condition of the colored people, a great many of whom, like myself, had escaped thither as a refuge from the hunters of men. I found many, who had not been seven years out of their chains, living in finer houses, and evidently enjoying more of the comforts of life, than the average of slaveholders in Maryland. I will venture to assert, that my friend Mr. Nathan Johnson (of whom I can say with a grateful heart, "I was hungry, and he gave me meat; I was thirsty, and he gave me drink; I was a stranger, and he took me in") lived in a neater house; dined at a better table; took, paid for, and read, more newspapers; better understood the moral, religious, and political character of the nation,—than nine tenths of the slaveholders in Talbot county Maryland.

Yet Mr. Johnson was a working man. His hands were hardened by toil, and not his alone, but those also of Mrs. Johnson. I found the colored people much more spirited than I had supposed they would be. I found among them a determination to protect each other from the blood-thirsty kidnapper, at all hazards.

Soon after my arrival, I was told of a circumstance which illustrated their spirit. A colored man and a fugitive slave were on unfriendly terms. The former was heard to threaten the latter with informing his master of his whereabouts. Straightway a meeting was called among the colored people, under the stereotyped notice, "Business of importance!"

The betrayer was invited to attend. The people came at the appointed hour, and organized the meeting by appointing a very religious old gentleman as president, who, I believe, made a prayer, after which he addressed the meeting as follows: *"Friends, we have got him here, and I would recommend that you young men just take him outside the door, and kill him!"* With this, a number of them bolted at him; but they were intercepted by some more timid than themselves, and the betrayer escaped their vengeance, and has not been seen in New Bedford since. I believe there have been no more such threats, and should there be hereafter, I doubt not that death would be the consequence.

I found employment, the third day after my arrival, in stowing a sloop with a load of oil. It was new, dirty, and hard work for me; but I went at it with a glad heart and a willing hand. I was now my own master. It was a happy moment, the rapture of which can be understood only by those who have been slaves. It was the first work, the reward of which was to be entirely my own. There was no Master Hugh standing ready, the moment I earned the money, to rob me of it. I worked that day with a pleasure I had never before experienced.

I was at work for myself and newly-married wife. It was to me the starting-point of a new existence. When I got through with that job, I went in pursuit of a job of calking; but such was the strength of prejudice against color, among the white calkers, that they refused to work with me, and of course I could get no employment.[3] Finding my trade of no immediate benefit, I threw off my calking habiliments, and prepared myself to do any kind of work I could get to do.

Mr. Johnson kindly let me have his wood-horse and saw, and I very soon found myself a plenty of work. There was no work too hard—none too dirty. I was ready to saw wood, shovel coal, carry wood, sweep the chimney, or roll oil casks,—all of which I did for nearly three years in New Bedford, before I became known to the anti-slavery world.

In about four months after I went to New Bedford, there came a young man to me, and inquired if I did not wish to take the "Liberator." I told him I did; but, just having made my escape from slavery, I remarked that I was unable to pay for it then. I, however, finally became a subscriber to it. The paper came, and I read it from week to week with such feelings as it would be quite idle for me to attempt to describe.

The paper became my meat and my drink. My soul was set all on fire. Its sympathy for my brethren in bonds—its scathing denunciations of slaveholders—its faithful exposures of slavery—and its powerful attacks upon the upholders of the institution—sent a thrill of joy through my soul, such as I had never felt before!

I had not long been a reader of the "Liberator," before I got a pretty correct idea of the principles, measures and spirit

---

[3] I am told that colored persons can now get employment at calking in New Bedford; a result of anti-slavery effort.

of the anti-slavery reform. I took right hold of the cause. I could do but little; but what I could, I did with a joyful heart, and never felt happier than when in an anti-slavery meeting. I seldom had much to say at the meetings, because what I wanted to say was said so much better by others.

But, while attending an anti-slavery convention at Nantucket, on the 11th of August, 1841, I felt strongly moved to speak, and was at the same time much urged to do so by Mr. William C. Coffin, a gentleman who had heard me speak in the colored people's meeting at New Bedford. It was a severe cross, and I took it up reluctantly.

The truth was, I felt myself a slave, and the idea of speaking to white people weighed me down. I spoke but a few moments, when I felt a degree of freedom, and said what I desired with considerable ease. From that time until now, I have been engaged in pleading the cause of my brethren—with what success, and with what devotion, I leave those acquainted with my labors to decide.

APPENDIX

I find, since reading over the foregoing Narrative, that I have, in several instances, spoken in such a tone and manner, respecting religion, as may possibly lead those unacquainted with my religious views to suppose me an opponent of all religion. To remove the liability of such misapprehension, I deem it proper to append the following brief explanation. What I have said respecting and against religion, I mean strictly to apply to the *slaveholding religion* of this land, and with no possible reference to Christianity proper; for, between the Christianity of this land, and the Christianity of Christ, I recognize the widest possible difference—so wide, that to receive the one as good, pure, and holy, is of necessity to reject the other as bad, corrupt, and wicked. To be the friend of the one, is of necessity to be the enemy of the other. I love the pure, peaceable, and impartial Christianity of Christ: I therefore hate the corrupt, slaveholding, women-whipping, cradle-plundering, partial and hypocritical Christianity of this land. Indeed, I can see no reason, but the most deceitful one, for calling the religion of this land Christianity. I look upon it as the climax of all misnomers, the boldest of all frauds, and the grossest of all libels. Never was there a clearer case of "stealing the livery of the court of heaven to serve the devil in." I am filled with unutterable loathing when I contemplate the religious pomp and show, together with the horrible inconsistencies, which every where surround me. We have men-stealers for ministers, women-whippers for missionaries, and cradle-plunderers for church members. The man who wields the blood-clotted cowskin during the week fills the pulpit on Sunday, and claims to be a minister of the meek and lowly Jesus. The man who robs me of my earnings at the end of each week meets me as a class-leader on Sunday morning, to show me the way of life, and the path of salvation. He who sells my sister, for purposes of prostitution, stands forth as the pious advocate of purity. He who proclaims it a religious duty to read the Bible denies me the right of learning to read the name of the God who made me. He who is the religious advocate of marriage robs whole millions of its sacred influence, and leaves them to the ravages of wholesale pollution. The warm defender of the sacredness of the family relation is the same that scatters whole families,—sundering husbands and wives, parents and children, sisters and brothers,—leaving the hut vacant, and the hearth desolate. We see the thief preaching against theft, and the adulterer against adultery. We have men sold to build churches, women sold to support the gospel, and babes sold to purchase Bibles for the *Poor Heathen!* *All For The Glory Of God And The Good Of Souls!* The slave auctioneer's bell and the church-going bell chime in with each other, and the bitter cries of the heart-broken slave are drowned in the religious shouts of his pious master. Revivals of religion and revivals in the slave-trade go hand in hand together.

The slave prison and the church stand near each other. The clanking of fetters and the rattling of chains in the prison, and the pious psalm and solemn prayer in the church, may be heard at the same time. The dealers in the bodies and souls of men erect their stand in the presence of the pulpit, and they mutually help each other. The dealer gives his blood-stained gold to support the pulpit, and the pulpit, in return, covers his infernal business with the garb of Christianity. Here we have religion and robbery the allies of each other—devils dressed in angels' robes, and hell presenting the semblance of paradise.

> "Just God! and these are they,
>   Who minister at thine altar, God of right!
> Men who their hands, with prayer and blessing, lay
>   On Israel's ark of light.
>
> "What! preach, and kidnap men?
>   Give thanks, and rob thy own afflicted poor?
> Talk of thy glorious liberty, and then
>   Bolt hard the captive's door?
>
> "What! servants of thy own
>   Merciful Son, who came to seek and save
> The homeless and the outcast, fettering down
>   The tasked and plundered slave!

"Pilate and Herod friends!
   Chief priests and rulers, as of old, combine!
Just God and holy! is that church which lends
   Strength to the spoiler thine?"

The Christianity of America is a Christianity, of whose votaries it may be as truly said, as it was of the ancient scribes and Pharisees, "They bind heavy burdens, and grievous to be borne, and lay them on men's shoulders, but they themselves will not move them with one of their fingers. All their works they do for to be seen of men.—They love the uppermost rooms at feasts, and the chief seats in the synagogues, ... and to be called of men, Rabbi, Rabbi.— But woe unto you, scribes and Pharisees, hypocrites! for ye shut up the kingdom of heaven against men; for ye neither go in yourselves, neither suffer ye them that are entering to go in. Ye devour widows' houses, and for a pretence make long prayers; therefore ye shall receive the greater damnation. Ye compass sea and land to make one proselyte, and when he is made, ye make him twofold more the child of hell than yourselves.—Woe unto you, scribes and Pharisees, hypocrites! for ye pay tithe of mint, and anise, and cumin, and have omitted the weightier matters of the law, judgment, mercy, and faith; these ought ye to have done, and not to leave the other undone. Ye blind guides! which strain at a gnat, and swallow a camel. Woe unto you, scribes and Pharisees, hypocrites! for ye make clean the outside of the cup and of the platter; but within, they are full of extortion and excess.—Woe unto you, scribes and Pharisees, hypocrites! for ye are like unto whited sepulchres, which indeed appear beautiful outward, but are within full of dead men's bones, and of all uncleanness. Even so ye also outwardly appear righteous unto men, but within ye are full of hypocrisy and iniquity."

Dark and terrible as is this picture, I hold it to be strictly true of the overwhelming mass of professed Christians in America. They strain at a gnat, and swallow a camel. Could any thing be more true of our churches? They would be shocked at the proposition of fellowshipping a *sheep*-stealer; and at the same time they hug to their communion a *man*-stealer, and brand me with being an infidel, if I find fault with them for it. They attend with Pharisaical strictness to the outward forms of religion, and at the same time neglect the weightier matters of the law, judgment, mercy, and faith. They are always ready to sacrifice, but seldom to show mercy. They are they who are represented as professing to love God whom they have not seen, whilst they hate their brother whom they have seen. They love the heathen on the other side of the globe. They can pray for him, pay money to have the Bible put into his hand, and missionaries to instruct him; while they despise and totally neglect the heathen at their own doors.

Such is, very briefly, my view of the religion of this land; and to avoid any misunderstanding, growing out of the use of general terms, I mean by the religion of this land, that which is revealed in the words, deeds, and actions, of those bodies, north and south, calling themselves Christian churches, and yet in union with slaveholders. It is against religion, as presented by these bodies, that I have felt it my duty to testify.

I conclude these remarks by copying the following portrait of the religion of the south, (which is, by communion and fellowship, the religion of the north,) which I soberly affirm is "true to the life," and without caricature or the slightest exaggeration. It is said to have been drawn, several years before the present anti-slavery agitation began, by a northern Methodist preacher, who, while residing at the south, had an opportunity to see slaveholding morals, manners, and piety, with his own eyes. "Shall I not visit for these things? saith the Lord. Shall not my soul be avenged on such a nation as this?"

A PARODY

"Come, saints and sinners, hear me tell
How pious priests whip Jack and Nell,
And women buy and children sell,
And preach all sinners down to hell,
   And sing of heavenly union.

"They'll bleat and baa, dona like goats,
Gorge down black sheep, and strain at motes,
Array their backs in fine black coats,
Then seize their negroes by their throats,
   And choke, for heavenly union.

"They'll church you if you sip a dram,
And damn you if you steal a lamb;
Yet rob old Tony, Doll, and Sam,
Of human rights, and bread and ham;
   Kidnapper's heavenly union.

"They'll loudly talk of Christ's reward,
And bind his image with a cord,
And scold, and swing the lash abhorred,
And sell their brother in the Lord
   To handcuffed heavenly union.

"They'll read and sing a sacred song,
And make a prayer both loud and long,
And teach the right and do the wrong,
Hailing the brother, sister throng,
   With words of heavenly union.

"We wonder how such saints can sing,
Or praise the Lord upon the wing,
Who roar, and scold, and whip, and sting,
And to their slaves and mammon cling,
   In guilty conscience union.

"They'll raise tobacco, corn, and rye,
And drive, and thieve, and cheat, and lie,
And lay up treasures in the sky,
By making switch and cowskin fly,
   In hope of heavenly union.

"They'll crack old Tony on the skull,
And preach and roar like Bashan bull,
Or braying ass, of mischief full,
Then seize old Jacob by the wool,
   And pull for heavenly union.

"A roaring, ranting, sleek man-thief,
Who lived on mutton, veal, and beef,
Yet never would afford relief
To needy, sable sons of grief,
    Was big with heavenly union.

"'Love not the world,' the preacher said,
And winked his eye, and shook his head;
He seized on Tom, and Dick, and Ned,
Cut short their meat, and clothes, and bread,
    Yet still loved heavenly union.

"Another preacher whining spoke
Of One whose heart for sinners broke:
He tied old Nanny to an oak,
And drew the blood at every stroke,
    And prayed for heavenly union.

"Two others oped their iron jaws,
And waved their children-stealing paws;
There sat their children in gewgaws;
By stinting negroes' backs and maws,
    They kept up heavenly union.

"All good from Jack another takes,
And entertains their flirts and rakes,
Who dress as sleek as glossy snakes,
And cram their mouths with sweetened cakes;
    And this goes down for union."

Sincerely and earnestly hoping that this little book may do something toward throwing light on the American slave system, and hastening the glad day of deliverance to the millions of my brethren in bonds—faithfully relying upon the power of truth, love, and justice, for success in my humble efforts—and solemnly pledging my self anew to the sacred cause,—I subscribe myself,

FREDERICK DOUGLASS.
LYNN, Mass., April 28, 1845.

THE END

ABOUT THE AUTHOR

Frederick Douglass was born in slavery as Frederick Augustus Washington Bailey near Easton in Talbot County, Maryland. He was not sure of the exact year of his birth, but he knew that it was 1817 or 1818. As a young boy he was sent to Baltimore, to be a house servant, where he learned to read and write, with the assistance of his master's wife. In 1838 he escaped from slavery and went to New York City, where he married Anna Murray, a free slave woman whom he had met in Baltimore. Soon thereafter he changed his name to Frederick Douglass. In 1841 he addressed a convention of the Massachusetts Anti-Slavery Society in Nantucket and so greatly impressed the group that they immediately employed him as an agent. He was such an impressive orator that numerous persons doubted if he had ever been a slave, so he wrote *The Narrative of The Life of Frederick Douglass*. During the Civil War he assisted in the recruiting of African American men for the 54th and 55th Massachusetts Regiments and consistently argued for the emancipation of slaves. After the war he was active in securing and protecting the rights of the freemen. In his later years, at different times, he was secretary of the Santo Domingo Commission, Marshall and Recorder of Deeds of the District of Columbia, and United States Minister to Haiti. His other autobiographical works are *My Bondage and My Freedom* and *Life and Times of Frederick Douglass*, published in 1855 and 1881 respectively. He died in 1895.

In 2017, The United States Congress passed the Frederick Douglass Bicentennial Commission Act to form a committee of 16 members to plan, develop and carry out programs and activities to honor Douglass on the occasion of the bicentennial anniversary of his birth.

INDEX

CAREFUL WHAT YOU WISH FOR

LEIGHANN DOBBS
LISA FENWICK

1

Harper Sullivan clutched the GoPro hidden inside her tote bag as she darted off the elevator and stepped into the dim basement. It was eerily quiet, and the silence gave her the creeps. The elevator doors whooshed shut behind her, causing her to jump a little and move quickly to the doorway a few feet away.

As she pushed open the heavy, old wooden door leading into the giant storage area her heart raced. She switched the lights on quickly while telling herself to calm down. The overhead fluorescent lightbulbs slowly came to life, each one creating a low humming sound as it went on, the lights soft at first then intensifying as they warmed up. As her eyes adjusted to the brightness she stepped further into the room and surveyed the transformation that had taken place over the last few weeks.

What was once a large storage room with smaller rooms off to each side had now become a staging area for one of O'Rourke's Signature Events most ground-breaking affairs, a fashion show debuting a clothing line for wheelchair-bound people.

Created by Draconia Fashions, with key input from Gertie O'Rourke herself, this line was sure to garner a ton of attention from the press, so it was beyond critical everything went smoothly. The entire staff here at O'Rourke's had been working extremely long hours prepping and staging the basement area, and Harper was happy with how it had all come along so far. As the newly promoted Assistant to the Events Manager she wanted to make sure this was a huge success, especially since her new boss, Veronica, hadn't seemed exactly thrilled when Gertie announced Harper's promotion.

She walked slowly towards her destination, looking over the changes made so far. Most of the smaller storage rooms located off the giant main storage area had been turned into makeshift dressing rooms. Each one furnished with a giant mirror, along with an area for makeup and hair. Harper had also added some personal touches like placing plants in each room along with a few colorful contemporary floor vases.

Since the basement was the only part of the vast mill building that hadn't been modernized during the renovation, Harper had felt it was important to make the rooms seem as beautiful as the rest of the building upstairs, even if they were only being used for the models to get changed. The rooms looked somewhat shabby chic now, with their exposed brick walls and old, wood floors. Veronica had even complimented Harper on them, which was rare. Veronica wasn't big on handing out compliments.

The actual runway for the show had been staged in the wide-open main storage area. It was monumental and intimidating, and after seeing how much work went into constructing it, Harper had a whole new sense of respect for the people involved in these fashion shows. The runway had to be a certain height, with lighting strategically placed all around as well as above it. As the models for this show were in wheel-chairs, this runway had been built wider than standard ones, and the end was also in a U-shape instead of the normal square type. This was so the models would have enough room to circle around.

Because it was nonstandard, they'd set up the runway inside to test it out and work out any kinks before they set up the final version outdoors for the actual show.

As she continued to walk towards one of the storage rooms in the rear of the open area, she heard a noise behind her. She stopped short and turned to look behind her, clutching the bag with the GoPro inside to her chest.

"Hello?" She was unsure she'd heard anything, maybe she was just being paranoid.

Ugh. She didn't like being down here alone! It was so big, and even with the lights on, it still made her jumpy for some reason. She picked up her pace and practically jogged down to the room.

Turning the doorknob slowly, she pushed open the door and entered, then switched the overhead lights on. It was one of the larger storage rooms, probably big enough to hold fifty people or so, but since it was in the basement it would never be used for an event and was perfect for holding all the huge lights needed for the show.

The lighting was lined up on the floor in long rows, each one having a note in front of it designating where it belonged on the runway. The lighting designer had spent hours with the lights, placing each one inside a metal holder that attached to different areas of the runway. As a key part of the fashion show, everything depended on the lighting being as perfect as possible. There were even a few giant spotlights to light up the sky over the river during the show. It had been repeatedly said by Edward Kenney, the owner of Draconia Fashions, how important the lighting for the show was and how critical it was they "don't screw it up." After all, if people couldn't see the runway models then what good was a fashion show?

Looking around the room, Harper tried to figure out the best location to place the GoPro. What could someone do to ruin the lights anyway? Smash the bulbs? Cut the cords? Her Uncle Tanner had said if he were going to screw things up he would ruin the lighting. He should know since he'd tried to sabotage Gertie's last event and had enlisted Harper's help to do so. Thank God he'd had a change of heart at the last minute and hadn't gone through with what he'd intended.

She gave up on thinking about all the different scenarios someone might use to ruin the lights and settled on a corner to hide the device, setting it up strategically behind some papers then creating an opening for the lens. When she was satisfied it would record a large section of the room, she turned and snuck out quietly.

She glanced at her watch quickly as she walked

away. There were a few minutes left before she was supposed to meet Uncle Tanner at his restaurant for lunch, so she headed towards the loading dock at the other end of the building. There had been a small black and gray tabby cat hanging around there the last few times she'd signed for deliveries, and before leaving for work that day, she'd grabbed a can of tuna from her kitchen for it. She knew she probably shouldn't encourage the cat to hang around by feeding it, but she also felt sorry for it. Besides, one can of tuna wasn't going to hurt.

Stepping outside onto the loading dock, she peeled the cover off the tuna can and set it down on the cool concrete ground, calling out for the cat as she looked around. She heard a faint "meow" come from an overgrown area beyond the chain-link fence that ran along the property. The black and gray tabby darted out from between the tall green and yellow weeds and ran over to the can of food. She reached down and patted it as it eagerly ate the tuna, its tail swishing in the air.

The cat seemed well fed for a stray, she—or he— wasn't all skin and bone and its fur was shiny. Maybe she was wrong, and it wasn't a stray after all. Maybe it just liked to hang around here. She looked past the chain-link fence to the abandoned mill behind it. Maybe it lived in there? The building looked like it hadn't been active in years. Harper gave the tabby one last pat on the head and left, heading back towards the lobby.

Once inside the building she hesitated as she walked to the elevator giving one last glance towards the storage area where she'd set the camera up. She knew she was doing the right thing by trying to find out who was screwing with Gertie's company, but at the same time it felt weird spying on the people she worked with. It felt like she was invading their privacy. Especially since she'd been the one who had caused issues with the last event. Kind of hypocritical making it her mission to catch this person.

At least she hadn't done anything horrible. She hadn't ever let it get that far. Common sense prevailed, and she'd put her foot down and refused to go along with Uncle Tanner's plan. In the end everything had worked out fine. The event had been a huge success. Uncle Tanner had confessed and righted all the wrongs he'd instigated.

She stepped onto the elevator and pushed the button for the lobby, determined not to let her anxiety take over. She knew Gertie trusted her. If she didn't, then she wouldn't have promoted her. The old woman could be hard to please at times, but Gertie really was an amazing woman. She reminded Harper of her dear

Aunt Emily, with her sassiness and never-give-up attitude. Harper had learned so much from Gertie over the few months she'd worked there and was very grateful for the continued opportunities and the trust Gertie had placed in her.

As she walked into the lobby she held her head up high. She was determined to stop whoever was trying to sabotage Gertie; no matter what.

LOGAN CARTER EASED BACK in the cushy, fabric banquet chair and closed his eyes, enjoying the silence in the basement. He liked it down here, it was a good place to escape the hectic office upstairs, even if it was only for a few minutes. Hardly anyone came down here and he could usually grab a few minutes of alone time when he needed. Not that this new job was crazy compared to being a cop, but he was used to being on his own, or with a partner, in a car as opposed to having an office full of people buzzing around him constantly. Unfortunately, the fashion show setup had meant more people in the basement to ready the dressing rooms and tend to the staging, but they usually were done before noon.

Hearing footsteps approaching made him jolt

upright and he bolted behind a huge wooden beam to avoid being seen by whoever was down there. He watched in silence as Harper scurried out of the room housing the fashion show lighting. She looked on edge, glancing around as if to make sure no one was watching her before shutting the door and bolting away towards the shipping area.

He waited until the echo of her footsteps died down before stepping out from behind the wooden beam. He'd assumed the person Gertie hired him to catch would try to screw up the lighting, but hadn't pegged that cute redhead, Harper, as the perp.

He didn't know her well, but she seemed like a sweet girl. Kind of timid. Not the kind of girl who went around sabotaging fashion shows. She didn't talk too much and hustled around a lot making sure things got done. Maybe she was in the room for another reason, after all, her job did require her to come down here. Or did it?

He glanced around to make sure no one else was around. The last thing he wanted was for someone to see him and ask why the new head of IT was skulking around in the basement. Not that he wouldn't be able to give a good answer, as a former cop he had the ability to think fast on his feet, and he could always come up with something believable. He was also pretty good at sneaking around, which was probably one of the reasons Gertie had hired him.

She'd called him after getting his contact information from a mutual friend, asking him to catch whoever was trying to ruin her business. At the time, Logan had thought the old woman was crazy. Who would want to mess with an event planning business?

When he'd asked Gertie why she thought someone was trying to ruin her business, her reply had been it was up to him to get her the answers if he wanted the job. After mulling it over for a few days he'd accepted, coming on board undercover as the IT Manager.

He'd still thought Gertie was probably being paranoid, but figured worse case, he'd stick around and keep an eye on things to reassure her everything was okay. After being here for a week though, he was starting to think Gertie was right. She wasn't a crazy old lady at all, in fact she was pretty damn smart. And he had to admit, he'd developed a fondness for her. He wanted to make sure her suspicions weren't correct.

Gertie was also extremely insightful, almost to the point she made him feel she could see right into him, and that scared him. The one question that kept popping into his head was why she'd never asked him about the circumstances that had forced him to quit the police force. Not that he would have answered her, that was a subject he didn't talk about at all. Ever. Still, it was funny she accepted he would do a good job with no questions asked about his former failures.

He walked towards the lighting room and entered it slowly, flicking on the overhead lights. The large lights were all lined up in a row and he could see some wires sticking out from behind several of them. He reached out and grasped one inspecting it closely. It had definitely been mucked around with. Almost to the point of being cut in half. The way it was now, the light would still work, but after a few minutes of being turned on it had a high chance of sparking and causing a fire.

These weren't average light bulbs, they were high intensity. And the metal holders they were in consisted of a lens and a reflector. If the break in the wire didn't start a fire, the jolting electricity could cause a bulb to blow and that could cause the glass lens to burst. Lots of potential for disaster here. Just like Gertie was afraid of.

He walked slowly down the row, checking each light. Almost half of them had the same problem. Whoever did this knew what they were doing. An amateur would have fully cut the wires to render the lights useless. Whoever did this, wanted these lights to be used. They wanted them to think nothing was wrong until it was too late. They wanted to cause harm to the fashion show or, worse, to cause harm to someone involved in the show. The wires could easily cause a shock to whoever plugged them in, never mind a fire.

Maybe that cute redhead wasn't as innocent as he thought. He left the room, making a mental note to contact the lighting specialist and have the bad lights replaced as soon as possible, it was too risky even to have them rewired.

He paused as he shut the lights off, rubbing the day-old stubble on his chin. Should he tell Gertie about this? He didn't want to jump to any conclusions, and he wasn't positive Harper was responsible for cutting the wires. She hadn't been inside the room very long and cutting the wires the way they were required a little time and patience. Unless she knew exactly what she was doing, she wouldn't have had time to cut them. Maybe running a complete background check on her was the next step before mentioning this to Gertie.

On the way back to his office he took a detour, walking to the loading dock located at the opposite end of the storage area. On his first day at work he'd fed some of his tuna sandwich to a black and gray tabby cat that had shown up as he sat alone on the brick wall next to the loading dock. It had sat with him for a while after devouring what Logan fed to him, so he'd bought some cat treats that night but had forgotten to bring them into work, until today.

As he stepped outside onto the loading dock he noticed an empty can of tuna on the ground, licked clean. Someone else must be feeding the cat as well.

Meow!

The tabby came trotting over from between a gap in the nearby chain-link fence. Logan crouched down and reached into his pocket, grabbing a few of the treats. He held one out to the purring cat and it rubbed up against his leg then gently took the treat from between his fingers.

As he crouched down to pat the cat, his eyes wandered to the overgrown area it had come from. The gap in the chain-link fence separating the two properties needed to be repaired, it was big. While the building that housed O'Rourke's Signature Events had been completely renovated by Gertie and was now a gorgeous trendy mill on the waterfront, the abandoned mill next to it was the complete opposite. Gertie had set her space up so all the function rooms faced the water and not the old mill, but that didn't eliminate the fact that vagrants liked to frequent the mill.

The cat meowed loudly for another treat, rubbing its head impatiently against his hand. He reached for another and scanned the empty building. It had been a grain mill over a hundred years ago and had a huge waterwheel in it. The wheel probably hadn't moved in a hundred years, but it was still mostly intact, although the iron cogs were all rusty and a few of the giant wooden paddles were missing or cracked. The water powering the wheel was still inside the mill, and over the years had become a murky black mess. More than once the police had pulled out the body of some drunk or drugged-out vagrant who had stumbled into it. Logan knew because he'd been there on those calls.

His thoughts were interrupted when he saw someone approaching via the alley out of the corner of his eye. As they walked closer the tabby got spooked, jumped down off the loading dock and ran back through the chain-link fence. It paused briefly to look back at him as if to say thank you before it disappeared under the fence.

"Hey, Logan, umm you have, I mean, looks like you made a new friend, huh?"

It was Ben, one of Gertie's maintenance guys. Logan had talked to him a few times since he'd started working there. He seemed kind of nervous. Why was he skulking around in the alley and stumbling around with his words?

"Yeah, what can I say. I'm a sucker for animals. What were you doing in the alley, anything good down there?" Logan asked him nonchalantly. He didn't want to come off as suspicious but was curious why Ben would be in the alley.

"Oh, just taking a quick smoke break. Gertie hates smoking so I walk over to the alley to do it, so she won't see me. Umm, you won't rat me out, will you?"

"Your secret is safe with me. I'm just the IT guy, it's none of my business what goes on otherwise." Logan faked a smile.

"Okay, thanks. I wouldn't want Gertie to be disappointed in me, about smoking. You know how she is. Anyway, I better get back. See ya." Ben walked past him and headed inside amidst the scent of aftershave and peppermint candy.

Logan watched Ben disappear into the building, catching him quickly turn his head to glance back at Logan before vanishing.

2

Harper strolled through the sunlit lobby on her way to meet Uncle Tanner for lunch. The smell of the fresh cut flowers, always on the reception desk, perfumed the air as she looked through the wall of glass stretching the entire length of the spacious area to the sunny day outside. She stopped in front of Myrtle, the receptionist, and bent down to pick up several pieces of paper that had spilled over the top of her reception desk onto the polished wide pine floor.

"What's going on?" Harper asked her, as the obviously overwhelmed Myrtle grabbed the papers from her hand and placed them on top of one of several large piles she'd lined up across the top of the desk.

Myrtle brushed a chunk of her short cranberry red spiky hair out of her eyes. "I'm putting together all the

Press Releases and programs for the fashion show, and good Lord it's a lot of paper!"

The frames of the hot pink cat's-eye glasses perched on Myrtle's nose glinted in the sunlight and contrasted with the garish pink, orange, and green beaded chain that dangled from the ends and around the back of Myrtles neck. Myrtle made the chains herself, Harper knew as she'd complimented them many times because they were usually startling, sometimes in a good way and sometimes not. Either way they were always an attention getter.

"Here, let me help you." Harper helped her sort the papers into the piles as Myrtle moved over to make room for her behind the large desk.

"Thanks. There's so many damn papers!" Myrtle grabbed another stack from a box. "So, have you seen the new guy?" she asked Harper casually, a grin on her face and her eyebrows waggling as she continued to collate the mountain of papers.

"Hmm. Nope, I don't think so." Harper grabbed another stack from the never-ending pile. There were new people joining the company almost daily and it was hard to keep track. Besides, she'd been far too busy lately to really notice a new employee.

"Well, he is really hot. Tall, dark hair, kind of has

that rugged look. And single from what I've heard. You two would make such a cute couple!"

Harper frowned and shook her head. She'd been engaged once and the wedding had been called off mere days before it was supposed to happen. It hadn't exactly left the best taste in her mouth for relationships. She'd only been out on one date since then and it had been a complete fiasco, from spilling wine on herself to her date choking on a piece of food and insisting they go to the ER afterwards to make sure he was okay. She'd ended up calling an Uber and left after half an hour in the waiting room with him, where he'd whined about a sore throat as well as the restaurant not giving them their meals for free.

"No thanks. Been there, done that. I am perfectly happy being single."

"Oh, be careful what you wish for, dearie! You don't want to end up an old maid like me, do you?" Myrtle teased her as she handed over the last of the papers.

Myrtle was sixty-two and had never been married, but she had a better social life than most women half her age. She always had great stories on Monday mornings about what she'd done over her weekend. Dating, horseback riding, day trips to the mountains, weekends at the beach. She was always busy, and Harper lived vicariously through her.

They finished sorting the last pile of papers and Harper left for her lunch date at her Uncle Tanner's restaurant. As she walked along the busy sidewalk she thought about her love life, or really the lack thereof. Maybe Myrtle was right. Maybe she should give love a second chance. Her only date after the breakup had sucked but they can't all be as bad as that. And it would be nice to have someone to share things with. She hated to admit it, but she was lonely, not to mention bored. But was it worth the risk and possible heartbreak again?

She pulled open the heavy oversized mahogany door to the restaurant and the aroma of garlic and grilled meat wafted out to greet her. It was quiet inside, the murmur of conversations punctuated only by the occasional muted clink of silverware against china. She welcomed the sounds, they were comforting compared to the empty silence of the basement at work.

She walked past the hostess desk and nodded hello. Everyone here knew who she was because she frequently had lunch or dinner with her Uncle. She continued to walk to the back of the restaurant to their usual table, where Uncle Tanner already had her favorite lunch waiting for her. He was reading the daily newspaper and stood to hug her and pull her chair out when she approached.

"So, how's work?" he asked, fidgeting with the napkin on his lap and holding it up in the air to inspect the seams. He was always checking the quality of things, Harper had gotten used to it by now. He was a perfectionist.

Harper knew the question he really wanted to ask; how Gertie was doing. Uncle Tanner was infatuated with her. It didn't exactly surprise her, not only was Gertie a great person but she looked a lot like Uncle Tanner's late wife, Aunt Emily. And, she had the same spunky attitude as Aunt Emily too. Uncle Tanner had adored Aunt Em and missed her terribly. They both did.

"Work's okay. Busy this week because of the fashion show coming up on Friday night," Harper said as she poured more of the spicy garlic sauce onto her plate and dipped her steak into it. She closed her eyes and brought the fork to her mouth, savoring the deliciousness. She'd told Uncle Tanner more than once he should bottle the sauce and sell it, it was unique, and everyone always raved about it.

"Well that's good. I'm glad Gertie has gotten such high-profile events." Tanner's face lit up as he said

Gertie's name and he got a silly smile on his face. He grabbed a large breadstick from the basket and broke it in half, crunching down on it.

Harper knew he must be lonely, it had been five years since Aunt Emily died. Aunt Em and Uncle Tanner had taken Harper in when her parents had been killed in a car accident and had treated Harper as if she were their own child. Harper had loved them like parents and it had been horrible when Aunt Em died. She thought about her every day and knew Uncle Tanner must too. Until Gertie, he'd never shown any interest in another woman.

"So, I hooked up one of those GoPros in the storage area, you know, one of those video recording things? To see if anyone is messing around down there. I put it in the room that has all the lights. I remember you saying that would be one of the critical things someone might want to mess with," Harper said.

Tanner nodded his head in approval as he finished his mouthful of food.

"Great, that is exactly where I would have placed it. If I were going to sabotage the event, the lights are what I would mess with." He placed his cutlery down on his plate and paused for a minute. "I really wish I could do more for Gertie. I was horrible to her with those things I did. And I was horrible to you for asking you to do them for me, I will always regret it."

"No, Uncle Tanner, it's fine. Really, it is. I wish I had spoken up instead of letting you take the blame for me. That wasn't right, and I regret it."

"Harper, don't you dare speak up to Gertie about what happened! I don't want your reputation tarnished, and besides, you were only doing those things out of loyalty to me. None of that was your fault. I wish I could somehow make up for the wrong I did. I know Gertie has forgiven me, she's even working with me on making the restaurant more accessible to people in wheelchairs and with other constraints."

"She mentioned that."

"Did I tell you we are installing a separate salad bar and buffet lower than the standard height, so anyone in a wheelchair can easily access it? It's such a great concept, all thanks to Gertie. She's opened my eyes up to a whole new world. I just wish I could do more to show her how much I appreciate her."

Harper's heart warmed at the smile on his face when he spoke about Gertie. Even though he'd tried to ruin Gertie's last event, it did seem like Gertie had forgiven him. It wasn't uncommon for her to meet with him for lunch or dinner. Gertie always said it was business related, but Harper hoped that there was something more. She didn't know much about Gertie's love life, in fact she didn't know much about Gertie's past outside work at all, but she knew she didn't have any kids and Harper assumed she'd never been married. It seemed like work was her love and main priority.

Harper grabbed a piece of garlic bread. "Well, you're helping by giving me ideas on how to find the person who is trying to mess her business up. I think that's something Gertie would certainly appreciate."

Tanner nodded. "I want you to be careful, Harper. Whoever has been messing around will get more desperate to succeed as the event draws near, and I don't want you getting hurt. I couldn't bear to lose you."

Harper felt the same way as Uncle Tanner did, she couldn't bear to lose him either. He was all she had left. Her parents were gone. Aunt Em was gone. Even her fiancé had left her. Even then, Uncle Tanner had been there for her, lending his shoulder for her to cry on. It was no wonder she had abandonment issues and wanted nothing to do with a relationship, almost everyone she'd cared about in her life had left!

The restaurant manager came over to speak to Tanner about something, and Harper's mind wandered back to work. There were only four days left before the show, and she needed to figure out who was trying to screw things up before something bad happened. Hopefully that GoPro would give her a clue as to who it was.

LOGAN STOOD in the doorway of Gertie's office and smiled as he watched the antics going on inside of it.

The large glass conference table had been moved to the far end of her spacious office and she was wheeling around in circles, the long billowy sleeves of her blouse repeatedly getting caught in the wheels of her chair with every few spins she made.

"See? What the heck is this?! Does this look like it's easy to move around in? For crying out loud!" Gertie barked at Edward, who was standing off to the side looking like a scolded child.

"Well, those sleeves are extremely popular right now, Gertie. It's the hot trend."

"Well, me breaking my arm because all this fabric got hung up on a wheel isn't part of the trend, is it?! Look, tell your designers to have the bottom half of the arm taper in. From the elbow down. See? Look, here!" Gertie held her arm up and showed him exactly where she thought the material should taper in. "We want fashion AND function. Both! I know you're the expert, but I'm telling you right now, this blouse is a flop for anyone in a wheelchair!"

She spun around again and spotted Logan smirking in the doorway.

"Oh good, you're here. I need to talk to you." Gertie ushered him in and dismissed Edward, who now had a sour puss on his face. Logan couldn't get rid of his smirk, he loved Gertie's sass. She kept people on their toes. The fact that Edward was the CEO of Draconia Fashions, one of the most prestigious fashion houses in New York, didn't faze Gertie in the least. She had no problem telling him *exactly* what she thought of the design of the shirt she was wearing.

He shut the door behind him and walked over to her as she was still fumbling with the sleeves on her blouse. He leaned his hip up against the windowsill and watched as she spun herself around to loosen the fabric from one of the spokes on the wheels. Helping her business out made him happy, and he was surprised to find he liked being a Private Investigator better than he'd liked being a cop.

As a P.I. he got to choose the jobs he wanted instead of being told what jobs he would do. Plus, he didn't have to work with a partner. Which meant he didn't have anyone else to be responsible for. That was something he never wanted to do again. Not after what happened to his last partner. He thought about it every day. Nope, he didn't want that responsibility. From now on, he worked solo.

"So, how's the investigation going? Any news for me yet?" Gertie asked him as she fumbled with rolling up the sleeves.

"I've done some background checks on the people you were suspicious of and they all came back clean as a whistle."

Gertie frowned. "Is that all? You know I hated to have my employees' backgrounds checked in the first place. But I need this problem taken care of."

Gertie had argued with him about background checks when he'd suggested them. But he'd emphasized how important they were, along with the fact that she'd hired him to find the sabotage in the company and he couldn't do his job without running the employee's information through the system. She'd reluctantly agreed.

"No, that's not all. I have a few other things I am looking into, but I don't want to go over them with you until I have all the details." Logan thought it best that he avoided telling Gertie about seeing Harper in the storage area. Ordinarily he would mention something suspicious like that to her. But he didn't have any evidence she was up to no good and he didn't want her to get into trouble. Just because she'd gone down to the storage area it didn't make her guilty of anything. For all he knew she was only doing her job.

"Hmph," Gertie muttered, wheeling herself behind her desk.

Logan glanced out of Gertie's window to the area below it. It had to be the smoking area as it was the alleyway between O'Rourke's and the abandoned mill where he'd seen Ben emerge from. How stupid was that for them to smoke right under Gertie's office? She hated the employees smoking and they all knew it. Maybe they didn't realize her office was right above their spot.

Or maybe they knew it was futile to hide their activities from Gertie. She knew about them smoking anyway, no matter where they went. Nothing got past this lady. Heck, she'd probably start stocking the smokers' lockers with nicotine patches or set them up to go to smokers anonymous.

"I'll let you know as soon as I have more information for you, I'm on a tight timeline to figure out who it is so I should get back to it. Besides, I'm sure you have a ton of things to do as well," he said, walking towards the door.

"Okay, dear. Just be careful with all this detective stuff," she said. As she wheeled herself out from behind her desk, one of her sleeves catching yet again on a wheel spoke. "Dammit! Foolish sleeves! Now I know how a bug feels trapped inside a spider web!"

3

Harper fidgeted in her chair as Veronica went over the to-do list with her in her office. It was a long list, and a few times Veronica had already taken back a task she'd originally assigned to Harper, and it was making Harper very uneasy. She really liked Veronica and had been thrilled when Gertie had promoted her to Veronica's assistant. She'd been working hard, but no matter how well she did, she felt Veronica didn't fully trust her.

Befriending Veronica when they'd first met to get information out of her for Uncle Tanner had made Harper feel guilty. She hoped the more they worked together the closer they would get, and Veronica would fully trust her, otherwise this was really going to be a difficult working relationship.

"Let's see, what else is there …" Veronica's voice trailed off as she scanned down the checklist she had in front of her. "The desserts. Did you make sure there is a selection of bite-sized pastries? Mini cheesecake, éclair, carrot cake, and whatever else the chef comes up with?"

"Yes, I spoke to the chef and—"

"You know what? Never mind, I can check on this one instead. I have to speak to him anyway." Veronica cut Harper off, taking back another task to do on her own.

"I did speak to the chef about it and explained bite-sized desserts were what was needed versus the normal size pieces of cake or pies. He said it wasn't a problem and he would make them small to be passed around by the wait staff," Harper said eagerly, hoping Veronica would trust her with this minor detail.

"Mm … hmm, I'll just double check anyway. Thanks," Veronica replied dryly as she made a note on the paper.

Harper wondered if the note said, "Get rid of Harper, she's an idiot who can't even pick the right desserts out."

"Hello, ladies," a familiar voice said from behind, and Harper turned to see TJ Flannery entering the office.

She looked back over at Veronica. Her demeanor had totally transformed, and she had a lovey-dovey look on her face. It took all Harper's will not to roll her eyes. It was so obvious these two were in love. They made a cute couple and Harper was happy for them but the sappiness they exuded when they were together was a little annoying. Seeing them this way reminded her how alone she was, and she had the urge to leave the room. Especially if they were going to make goo-goo eyes at each other. Two's company, three's a crowd!

"Hi, TJ. Here, take my seat, I was just leaving. Veronica, I'll catch up with you later to update you on the list." She made a beeline for the door before anyone objected. Not that they would, they were too busy staring at each other.

"Whoa!" A hand shot out to keep Harper from running into its owner. She'd rushed out of Veronica's office so fast she hadn't bothered to look to see if anyone was in the hallway outside of the door.

"Sarah! Sorry. I was in a rush and wasn't paying attention." Harper apologized as she stepped to the side.

"No problem, I would be in a rush to get away from her too." Sarah tossed a narrow-eyed look at Veronica's closed office door as they walked past it.

Sarah's comment caught her off guard. Harper wasn't sure what to say. Sarah was TJ's sister, and while Harper had only dealt with her a few times, she seemed okay. They'd had a few run-ins at the last event, which had been a wedding reception for Edward Kenney's son and Sarah's best friend, Marly West, who also worked at Draconia. Sarah had been the bridesmaid in the wedding. There had been animosity between Sarah and Veronica then, but Harper thought it was all cleared up now. At least she hoped so for TJ's sake.

"Well, she and TJ sure seem to be in love, I think they are good together. You know, I mean good for each other," Harper said, stumbling a bit through her words.

Sarah remained silent and continued to walk down the hallway in the same direction as her.

"By the way, if you're looking for TJ he's with her in her office," Harper said.

"Thanks, but I'm not here to see TJ. I'm here to apply for a chef's job. It turns out working with your boyfriend isn't all it's cracked up to be."

Harper knew Sarah was referring to her boyfriend Raffe, who had a well-known restaurant in the city. The last she'd heard, Sarah and Raffe were doing well, and she had the impression they might end up getting married soon. At the wedding reception they'd seemed friendly. Then again, she knew from personal experience how fast that could change.

Something told her Sarah needed to talk. Even though they were only acquaintances Harper knew breakups sucked, she'd been there herself once upon a time and having a shoulder to lean on was always welcome. "Hey, do you feel like some coffee or something? I was going to make an iced coffee in the break room."

They both entered the break room, and Harper walked over to the fridge and pulled out a pitcher of iced coffee while Sarah took a seat at one of the café-style tables. The large break room was as immaculate as always, the stainless steel refrigerator gleaming, and the granite counter tops shining. Harper was grateful it was always stocked with coffee and treats, many times this was where she ate her main meals of the day.

She grabbed two tall glasses out of the cherry wood cabinet along with some sugar packets off the countertop and walked over to the table Sarah had sat at.

"So, how long have you worked with Raffe?" Harper asked her as she filled both of their glasses.

"Long enough to know it was a really stupid idea." Sarah took two of the sugar packets and poured them into her coffee. She grabbed a straw from the holder in the middle of the table and stirred her drink, then took a long sip.

"Raffe is a good guy. It's just … I guess … I don't know. It's hard taking orders from someone who is your boyfriend, you know? And it's impossible to leave work at work. Going out on date night, we talk about work. At work, we talk about work. Work, work, work. I feel like our relationship is just dying a slow death."

Harper nodded slowly as she listened to Sarah, her mind wandering back to her last relationship. It had blown up badly and so fast that, at the time, she remembered wishing she could fast forward her life to avoid going over all the drama in the weeks following a breakup. She couldn't imagine being in Sarah's position and having to work with the person you were having relationship issues with, that would be torture. No wonder she wanted to find a new job!

"I'm sure Gertie will hire you. I know we need another chef, and it probably doesn't hurt that TJ works here as well. Maybe working here will help your relationship, you know, because you won't be around each other so much?" Harper was trying to put a positive spin on the crappy situation.

"Yeah, maybe. I don't know. It's all confusing at the

moment. But I guess it will work itself out." Sarah stood and put her empty glass in the sink. "Thanks for the chat, I appreciate it. I should be getting down to the kitchen. Wish me luck!"

Harper wished her luck and watched her leave, stirring the rest of her iced coffee with the straw. She was confident Gertie would hire Sarah, not because she was related to TJ, but because Gertie had a huge heart and would basically hire anyone who seemed like they needed a job if they were capable and hard workers. It was a bonus if they were in an emotional turmoil Gertie could help soothe. Gertie was a people-fixer and Sarah fit that bill perfectly.

"Oops! Sorry!"

Big T turned and watched the blonde chef lady he'd bumped into hurry away down the hallway towards the elevator. He knew she was applying for the open chef position but hadn't known she knew Harper. How did she know her and what were the two of them yapping about together in the break room? Eh, it was probably just girl crap, talking about how stupid men are and purses.

He reminded himself not everyone was up to no

good, and besides, he had no issues with that lady. Harper was the problem one and the one who was up to no good. Big T had seen her snooping around in the basement and sneaking into the room with the lighting for the show. There was no reason for her to be in there, aside from being a snoop. He would have to be extra careful around her to make sure he didn't blow his cover.

He'd done well so far acting like a regular worker, not to mention making the occasional casual comment to place suspicion on someone else if anyone ever started to question certain things. No one would ever know he was the one causing the problems for Gertie, and it would stay that way.

He opened the door to the stairway and headed downstairs to the basement, his heavy work boots making a thud with each step he took on the cement stairs. He kept his head down as he passed a few employees in the hallway outside the stairwell. He wasn't in the mood to talk.

Opening the doorway that led to the loading dock he squinted, the afternoon sun beaming directly into his eyes. He reached into his pocket for the can of tuna he'd brought with him for the tabby cat that had been hanging around and peeled the metal lid off it slowly, as if the cat would hear the noise and come running.

Placing it on the ground he called out to the tabby, as he walked around the loading dock area. No one else was outside, which put him at ease. He didn't need anyone seeing him feed the cat.

Meow!

The cat ran out from the thick weeds, purring as it twined itself between his ankles briefly before running over to the can of tuna and eagerly chowing down. It devoured the food within a few minutes then sat, licking its paws.

Big T scooped up the empty tuna can and patted his feline friend goodbye, then walked back into the building. Tossing the empty can away in a nearby trash barrel he casually looked around to make sure no one was watching him, then he inconspicuously darted into one of the small cubicles that were located down there for the employees to share.

Each cubicle had a computer so that those who didn't have an office could use them to check email or do whatever they might need to online. He'd acted like he was computer illiterate around everyone at work but that was far from being true. He'd spent hours teaching himself about computers on all those nights his mom had had to work extra shifts and he'd been left home alone. He knew the knowledge would come in handy someday.

He clicked on a few buttons and the computer whirred to life. Instead of entering the ID he'd been given when he started working at O'Rourke's, he used an alternate one, changing the system user, then laughed softly as he messed around with the database.

Let's see how successful the fashion show is when all the bigwigs' invitations are sent to the wrong addresses!

4

Logan fidgeted with the empty coffee cup on the break room table as he peered through the blinds covering the glass window that looked out into the hallway. He debated filling it up again, but he'd already had three cups of coffee and that was more than enough to keep him on his toes. Camping out in here was boring, but he needed to keep an eye on Harper, and her office was a few feet down the hall. With the fashion show only a few days away he had the feeling the perpetrator might do something drastic, but he couldn't pin anything on Harper until he had proof it was her. He'd been shadowing her all morning and hadn't seen her do anything out of the ordinary. So far, anyway.

He heard a door shut and sprung up from the chair, knowing it had to be Harper's office door since she was the only other person on the floor at the time. He waited for her to walk past the window, then slowly crept out into the hallway, making sure to stay far enough behind so she wouldn't see him. He heard the familiar ding of the elevator and waited until he heard the doors open and close, then bolted towards it so he could see what floor she stopped at. The lobby.

He flung open the door that led to the stairway and ran down the concrete stairs to the lobby, skipping over two steps at a time and whipped open the door leading into the lobby as he entered, making a slight ruckus as he did so.

Harper was talking to Myrtle at the reception desk. The two of them looked over at him in surprise, Myrtle's glasses slid down her nose and her brows climbed her forehead.

"Logan! What's the rush? How are you? Say, have you met Harper yet?" Myrtle gestured towards Harper with a sly grin on her face.

Shoot! Now he couldn't follow Harper and see what she was up to. And he really didn't want to meet her. If she was the culprit, it would make it much harder to turn her in. It was too late now though, the two of them were staring at him, probably wondering why it was taking him so long to answer Myrtle's question.

"Hi, Myrtle, uhh, no. I haven't met Harper yet, but I've certainly heard some great things about her. Nice to meet you." He extended his hand out towards her as she juggled a large tote bag in her hands to shake his.

He eyed the bag suspiciously. It was too big to be a purse, where was she going in the middle of the work day with it, and what could be inside that would take up so much space? Whenever he'd seen her walking around she either had a clipboard in her hand or nothing at all, never this giant bag thing. Except for the time he'd seen her come out of the room with the lights.

She seemed way too composed for someone who was trying to ruin things for Gertie. She smiled at him and he tried to ignore the way her perfectly white teeth complemented her peaches and cream complexion. After a few beats, he realized he was still holding onto her hand and let go of it quickly, feeling unsure of himself. Awkward. He was usually smooth with the ladies, but this girl wasn't a lady. She was a suspect. He must be nervous about the fact she could be the saboteur.

He ripped his gaze away from Harper and focused on the receptionist. "Myrtle, your hair looks stunning as always. How's your day so far? Everything under control?" He swiftly turned his attention to Myrtle, who seemed to love it. He always made a point to be nice to Myrtle because he knew some people treated receptionists like crap, and the reality was, being a receptionist wasn't an easy job. Not to mention, receptionists knew almost everything going on with all the employees. He knew he needed to stay on Myrtle's good side.

"Oh, Logan, you are so fresh!" Myrtle chided him, pushing her lime-green glasses up on her nose, the black, white, and yellow beaded eyeglass chain dancing down from her ears.

"Help a girl out, would you? Gertie needs these papers right away. Can you take them up to her for me? I'm swamped!" Myrtle handed Logan a stack of papers from her desk as she gave him a quick wink.

"Of course I can, anything for you," Logan replied, winking back at her as he took the papers. As he turned to leave, he caught Harper's eye and was thrown off by the intense midnight-blue color of them. It reminded him of a moonlit ocean late at night. He hesitated for a minute before pulling himself away, muttering, "Nice to meet you, Harper."

As he headed quickly back upstairs, the unsettling feeling came over him that somehow this PI job had just gotten a lot more complicated.

Harper's heart skipped a beat as she watched Logan walk off. She'd caught a flicker of emotion in his eyes she couldn't place, but he'd turned away so fast she was thinking maybe she'd imagined it.

She always liked a tall guy and she guessed Logan was around six foot four. And his eyes! They'd been a dreamy caramel color, the kind that turned gold when the sun hit them just right.

Crap! What was she thinking? Nope. Don't go there, she scolded herself as she adjusted the thick straps on her tote bag. She had work to do, and besides so what if Logan was hot? After hearing Sarah's story about how much of a nightmare working with your boyfriend was she would never even consider getting involved with someone at work.

Her shoulder started to ache, the stupid giant tote bag was too heavy. Logan had looked at it a little suspiciously when they'd shaken hands. Did he think it was strange to have such a large bag or did he think she was hiding something inside of it?

Stop being paranoid.

She didn't even know him and why would he even care about her bag? She was being paranoid because *she* knew she intended to stick the GoPro in it.

"So, what do you think? He's hot, right?" Myrtle asked her in a singsong voice as she wagged her eyebrows, her multicolored eyeglass chain beads dancing in the sunlight.

Well, he certainly was attractive, that was for sure. And Harper did think it was nice how he'd flirted with Myrtle and made her feel special. It hadn't been cheesy and came across as genuine. Maybe he was a nice guy with a good heart. The kind that wouldn't dump his fiancé a week before the wedding. Then again, maybe not. It was hard to judge someone from a one-minute conversation.

"He was okay, I guess. I'm too busy to notice to be honest." Harper shrugged her shoulders to convince Myrtle she could care less about him. Trying to convince herself of it, too.

"Just okay? You're crazy. He's a sweetheart, and I saw that look between you two! Don't tell me there wasn't a little spark dancing around when you shook his hand!" Myrtle exclaimed as she side-eyed Harper.

Harper rolled her eyes sarcastically while simultaneously squelching the butterflies in her stomach. Was the chemistry between she and Logan really so strong Myrtle had noticed it? Wait. This didn't even matter right now. She needed to focus on getting the GoPro out of that room to see what it had recorded last night.

Just then, the glass lobby door swung open and Edward Kenney breezed in, dressed in his standard custom-tailored suit and looking as dapper as always. His immaculate dress shoes shined and click-clacked against the floor as he walked up to Myrtle's desk.

The door had barely closed behind him before he began barking out orders.

"Where are we with the fashion show? Is everything all set? Designs, what's going on with Gertie and the designs?" he demanded, looking from Myrtle to Harper then back to Myrtle again.

Harper stood in silence, unsure of whether to answer him. There were way too many things still left to do for the show, and she knew Edward didn't need to know everything. She also knew he should technically be dealing with Veronica, as she was the Events Manager and the person managing the show for him, but Edward didn't stand on formality, he basically demanded answers from anyone within earshot every time he showed up. Which, unfortunately, had been almost daily.

"Excuse me, but who do you think you are,

blowing in here and talking to us like that? You might be Mr. Big Boss over at Draconia, but here at O'Rourke's Signature Events you are no better than the rest of us, and I expect you to be polite and to treat us all with some respect!" Myrtle had stood and was chastising Edward, her hands on her hips and her spikey red hair moving back and forth like a bird's plume on top of her head.

"I beg your pardon? I am the founder of Draconia Fashions and I expect to be treated as such," Edward retorted.

"Well, that's your problem. You think you are entitled to special treatment here? Absolutely not! You come charging in here barking out orders and asking questions every day. That will stop, right now! We are all equals here, Gertie insists on it."

"Gertie insists on what, dear?" Gertie appeared in the lobby, wheeling herself up to Edward and Myrtle. Her thick, long grey hair had been pulled back off her face, a style few older women could pull off, but Gertie certainly did. Her olive skin glowed, and her green eyes sparkled as she looked at the three of them.

"I was just explaining to Edward you insist everyone here is treated the same and his daily temper tantrums won't be tolerated by me anymore." Myrtle looked at Edward over the top of her glasses, her hands still firmly planted on her hips.

"Well, duh. Of course, everyone here is equal, we are all on the same team. And yes, that includes you, Edward, so lay off the Mr. Important act and come with me so I can show you what's wrong with your designs. Chop, chop! I don't have all day for this baloney you know!" Gertie reached out and grabbed Edward's hand.

Harper took the opportunity while everyone was bantering to slip away down the back stairs to the basement. As she opened the door that led into the main storage area she clutched the tote bag close to her. She probably should have brought a clipboard or something to make it look more work related for her to be down here. Then again, her job required her to go all over the building. Besides, who the heck would be watching her so closely to even notice the stupid tote bag? She took a deep breath and told herself to stop worrying. She wasn't doing anything wrong, anyway, she was trying to help Gertie.

There were two large empty wooden dollies sitting in the main area. Harper knew they were used to move heavy items around, so she looked around to see who else was down there. As she walked farther into the area she realized they were doing some more staging to the runway. She hurried past to get to the room with the camera in it before whoever else was down there saw her.

She stopped when she was outside the room, looking around again to make sure no one saw her before she quietly slipped inside and grabbed the camera, quickly shoving it into the tote bag as she exited the room.

As she hurried back towards the stairs she saw two of the maintenance guys, Ben and Noah, pushing the dollies which were now loaded up with boxes of linens and plates.

"Hey, guys. I'm just checking up on how the staging for the runway is going for Veronica, she wants updates like every ten minutes." Harper rolled her eyes as she said the lie, knowing they would believe her. Veronica was a perfectionist, and everyone here knew it, so saying she was checking up because Veronica asked her to was totally believable.

Ben and Noah exchanged glances, making Harper feel a little uneasy. Maybe she was coming off as too weird or overly friendly? She hadn't really talked much to these two in the past.

"Ben, you were working on that weren't you?" Noah asked.

Ben frowned at Noah. "No. Well, yes. George is working on it now I think, isn't he?"

Ben leaned the dolly back upright on the floor and walked towards the staging area for the runway, calling out George's name. Harper followed a few steps behind him, smiling and acting like she was interested, but really wanting nothing more than to run away to her office and look at the images on the GoPro.

"What's up? I'm almost done here. Just tightening things up a bit." George was underneath the runway and had slid partially out, looking up at them. His tone sounded irritated at being interrupted.

"It looks amazing, George! I can't wait until the actual show. It's going to be such a huge success! Thanks for doing such a great job, guys, I'll let Veronica know everything's coming along fine!" Harper turned around, trying not to walk too fast away from them. She stuck her hand in the tote bag and fumbled around for the camera to reassure herself it was still in there and her hand felt a hard can. Tuna. Crap! She forgot she'd brought more tuna in for the stray cat.

She bypassed the stairs and kept walking towards the loading dock, stopping when she got outside. Opening the top of the tuna can she called out to the cat, placing the can on the ground as she looked around.

The cat didn't come. She called out a little louder and waved the can around, as if the cat would suddenly catch the smell of tuna in the air from wherever it was. But it still didn't come.

She hoped it was okay and nothing bad had happened to it. Maybe she should have taken it home with her when she'd last seen it. Even though she wasn't supposed to have pets in her apartment, she hated knowing the cat was most likely homeless and vulnerable to predators.

She placed the full can of tuna back on the ground and scanned the area one last time for the cat before leaving and going up to her office. If she could, she would have waited longer for the cat to appear, but she needed to look at that GoPro footage as soon as possible.

***

BIG T JIGGLED the vending machine, trying to shake the bag of pretzels stuck inside loose, so it would fall off the hook and drop down so he could grab it.

"Come on you stupid thing!" he yelled at it, tipping

it forward and watching the bag drop down from where it had been stuck.

He leaned over and stretched his arm up inside to grab the package, tearing it open before he stood again. As he shoveled a handful of pretzels into his mouth he thought about Harper. Why had she been downstairs again? Sure, he'd heard her say it was to check on some stuff for Veronica. But he wasn't buying that because Veronica had already been down there checking up on them earlier. Besides, she was carrying some big tote bag around with her and since when did anyone carry tote bags with them inside work?

His instincts told him she was hiding something in that bag, but it wasn't like he could look inside. He would have followed her when he saw her if there hadn't been people around, but there were, and he didn't want any witnesses.

He walked slowly over to one of the plastic chairs set in the open space near the vending machine and sat, the chair creaking under his weight. Reaching into the bag he popped another pretzel into his mouth, crunching on it as he thought about what he should do next. His patience was growing thin and Harper was getting on his nerves. His eye caught the security camera lodged up in the corner of the room, the red light flashing. Cameras.

Weeks ago, he'd hidden a few nanny cams around the entire building, including all the offices, so he could see what was going on. Maybe checking the one in Harpers office would be useful and would tell him exactly what she was up to.

Harper closed the door to her office quietly and rushed over to her desk, eager to see what the camera had recorded. She sat in the plush black leather chair, took the camera out of the bag, and placed it on her glass desk. Reaching into her drawer she pulled out a long HDMI cable and hooked the camera up to her monitor.

Hopefully this will work. Technology wasn't her strong suit, but she'd read through the directions a dozen times at home and was confident she could get this to work.

She turned on the camera and the video sprang to life on her monitor. Relief flooded over her as she watched it. The first few minutes were blank, then

Gertie entered the room, wheeling herself around, inspecting the lights then leaving.

Then there was nothing. A lot of nothing. After a while she started to fast forward the video. She pressed the button lightly, only speeding it up a little, so she wouldn't miss anything. Time dragged on, she'd bought a large capacity video card to fit the most hours of recording possible and was now realizing that meant having to painstakingly go through it.

Suddenly, Logan appeared in the frame. He stood for a while, looking around. Was he looking for something or casing it? He walked over towards the camera, and just as Harper thought he was going to grab it, he bent over and picked up some of the long wires from the lights.

Harper craned her neck, as if that would somehow let her see what he was doing. Is he tampering with the lights? His body was blocking her view! After a few minutes he left, seemingly empty-handed. It was hard to tell since his back was to the camera as he left the room.

What had he been doing in there? Had he done something to the wires? Her mind raced, thinking about her earlier interaction with him. It had been brief, but she'd kind of hoped he was a nice guy, someone she might want to get to know better. Now, she just wanted to know what he'd done in that room.

She removed the HDMI cable, grabbed the GoPro, and stood, eager to show Gertie the footage. She hesitated before opening the door. What exactly was she going to show Gertie? Logan walking into the room and standing there? Uncle Tanner's voice echoed in her head, telling her to make sure she had proof. What she had wasn't proof of anything, aside from Logan going into the room. For all she knew, Gertie had sent him in there. It would be really embarrassing if she burst into Gertie's office and accused him of something and was wrong. Maybe she should go check the wires first to see if anything was wrong with them. She already had proof he'd touched them, if something was wrong *then* she could approach Gertie.

Her thoughts were interrupted by a chirp signaling an incoming text. Glancing at the phone on top her desk she saw it was from Veronica.

My office, ASAP!

Harper cringed, and her stomach churned. Had someone seen her with the camera and told Veronica? How would she explain it to her if they had? Should she say Logan was acting suspicious or would that make her look like the suspicious one?

She knew Veronica didn't exactly trust her as it

was. If she'd been caught hiding the camera and she didn't have a solid answer as to why she was running around with a GoPro in her tote bag, instead of doing her actual job, then Veronica would not be happy at all.

LOGAN SCROLLED down the computer screen as he scanned Harper's background check. Nothing out of the ordinary there. In fact, she was as clean as a whistle. Never even had a parking ticket. His scrolling was interrupted by the ding of his phone. The screen showed a mysterious message from Gertie.

Sabotage trouble! Veronica's office ASAP!

He closed the screen, being careful to logout so no one could see what he'd been doing and hurried to Veronica's office. He knocked on the door and opened it immediately, not waiting for them to tell him to enter. Gertie and Veronica were seated at Veronica's desk with paperwork strewn all over it.

"Is everything okay?" he asked. Judging by the look of panic on Veronica's face and the scowl on Gertie's, everything was not okay.

"No, dear, it isn't. Someone has screwed with the attendee list for the show. The final invitations all have the wrong addresses somehow." Gertie's voice was laced with anger.

"I have absolutely no idea how this could happen," Veronica said. "I double-check everything, always! Lucky thing I triple-checked this time or the invitations would have been sent out to the wrong addresses, this is a disaster. They all had to be entered by hand in the first place and now the original file has the wrong addresses for all the attendees. We'll never get them out in time!" She looked at Logan in despair.

"Wait. The show is in a few days. Shouldn't you have mailed the invitations out already?" Logan asked. He didn't get invited to many parties these days, but when he did, there was usually plenty of notice. And since this was a very important show he assumed the invites would have gone out weeks ago, given the attendees were made up of important business people and minor local celebrities.

"We sent out save-the-date notices weeks ago. The actual invite is to be delivered two days before the show, we messenger them to everyone. The design for the invitation took weeks to finalize, it's practically a piece of art." Veronica explained, looking as though she was going to burst into tears.

"Can you trace who edited the file to see who made the changes?" Gertie asked Logan, giving him a look.

He knew the look meant to keep the fact he was undercover between the two of them, and not to let Veronica know. Since he'd been hired on as the IT guy, it made sense for Gertie to ask him about the file.

"Should we wait for Harper first? I already texted her and she should be here any minute. She's the only other person that would have accessed the file besides me. She's the one who entered everything into the database. Maybe she messed it up somehow," Veronica said.

Logan nodded his head yes, his suspicions about Harper being the perp growing. Never mind she was cute and had an innocent air about her and nothing in her background check. He'd gotten the distinct impression she was hiding something in the lobby earlier and he had seen her sneaking around near the light room.

Harper appeared in the doorway and looked away as soon as she met Logan's eyes. She shifted from foot to foot, looking from Gertie to Veronica.

"Is … is everything okay?" she stuttered. Fear? Guilt? She looked terrified, not at all the look of a criminal that goes around ruining fashion shows. He wanted to be wrong, he didn't want it to be her. But he had a job to do and that had priority.

"Harper, someone messed up the address list for

the attendees for the show. It's all wrong. They mixed up all the addresses. Did you check this stuff after you entered it?" Veronica's tone had an accusing note.

Harper's expression registered surprise. Her mouth opened and shut, but no words came.

Logan wondered if her reaction was an act or real. She was hard to read, and he was getting strange vibes from Veronica and Gertie. Veronica seemed to be directing anger at Harper, and Gertie seemed more like she was teaching her, or mothering her. Then again, Gertie did have a mothering spirit. Knowing her, she would take Harper under her wing and try to fix her, even if she was the one sabotaging the show.

Then again, maybe it wasn't Harper. Maybe Veronica was the perp. Her background check had included some things showing she wasn't as squeaky clean as she appeared to be. When he'd mentioned it to Gertie, the older woman had insisted Veronica had changed her ways, but he knew all too well; a leopard doesn't change its spots that easily.

"I didn't change anything on the list, and I double-checked it one last time earlier today, and it was perfect. But I will get it fixed. Don't worry, Veronica. I will make sure it's all done perfectly. I don't know how this could have happened." Harper gushed as she looked around the room, still avoiding Logan.

Logan watched her body language, looking for clues people generally give off when lying. He didn't see any, but he knew plenty of people were great liars. Maybe Harper was one of them.

HARPER'S CHEEKS FLAMED, and she cursed the trait that happened whenever she was upset or flustered. She hadn't screwed up the addresses on the attendee list. She'd double-checked them after each entry, it had taken hours. Someone else had messed that file up. But the way Veronica was shooting daggers at her, she didn't think her new boss believed her.

Veronica was about to explain again how meticulous she was about double-checking everything when Gertie spoke up.

"There must be a logical explanation for this. Veronica, is this list printed from the database?" Gertie held up a stack of papers.

"Yes, I had Harper enter the information from the list you gave me." Veronica stared at Harper as she answered Gertie.

"Well then, that means someone must have messed with the database after Harper entered them, right, Logan?"

"That would be the only way, yes," Logan replied, also looking at Harper.

Harper stood quietly, wishing she could run out of the room. The walls were closing in, and it was uncomfortable with everyone looking at her, especially Logan. She was sure her face was the same color as a cherry by now, thus making her look as guilty as they thought she was.

"Well then, maybe you can find out who changed everything. It's important to know if someone is messing around, but let's not get carried away with accusations. I think of everyone here as my family and I don't want any hard feelings. Maybe this was just a simple error that happened when the information was typed in. After all, there are over two hundred people on the list, and everyone makes mistakes," Gertie said.

"That's probably what happened, human error." Veronica's accusing eyes darted to Harper, then softened as they slid back to Gertie. "And, Gertie, it's so sweet of you to say we are all like family, that's why this has me so upset. I want everything to be perfect for you, we all do."

"It will be fine, I trust Logan to work it all out, dear. I don't want anyone prematurely blaming someone else. You guys are the only kids I have! I didn't raise any of my own, so this crew is what I've got, and I want to make sure we all work together. Now, let's move on. Logan will figure this out. It's good you caught it, no damage was done."

Harper stood in silence, irritated Logan hadn't taken his eyes off her since she arrived. Either he was intrigued with her candy-apple-colored face or he thought she was the one who sabotaged the list.

For a split second she thought about telling Gertie Logan had been in the basement room and had possibly messed with the lights. He was looking at her with his judgey eyes and he was the one who might be guilty!

But she knew Gertie trusted Logan, and given the speech Gertie just gave, it wouldn't be a good idea to accuse him without solid proof. It could backfire on her and make it look like she was trying to throw up a smokescreen to take the heat off her. She opted to keep her mouth shut about what she'd seen Logan do. For now.

Logan straightened out the picture on his office wall, stepping back to see if it was level. The sunlight shining in through the large windows glinted off the glass that held the picture in the black frame. He wasn't one for decorating, but this picture was one he'd always loved as a kid and his mother had given it to him many years after he'd moved out, right after he'd completed the police academy. It was a Norman Rockwell photo called "Runaway." Just a police officer sitting next to a kid at a soda shop from the 50's or so. It was generic enough not to blow his cover.

Satisfied it was straight enough, he looked around the small office for his coffee mug, he'd a bad habit of putting it down and forgetting where he left it. He spied it sitting on the top of his desk, a puff of steam still coming from the top, the strong aroma filling the air.

He sat in the plush leather chair and made a face as he tried to get comfortable in it. He'd originally grabbed one of the old metal and fabric chairs from the storage area for his office, but Gertie had insisted he use one of the new chairs she'd bought for all the offices.

They'd also argued over his desk. She had all these contemporary funky ones for the offices. Glass and metal, very sleek. But Logan had spent years with the standard police issued gun metal steel desks and there had been a few in storage, and Gertie had finally let him use one of them. The chair and desk didn't blend well together at all, but he didn't care. He was here to work, not to win a prize for office decorating.

He picked up his coffee mug and used his sleeve to wipe at the wet ring that had formed under it. He turned his computer on and took a big gulp of coffee while waiting for the PC to fire up. His mind drifted to Harper and how she'd seemed nervous when they'd met earlier. That was always a tell-tale sign of a guilty person when they were nervous. But his gut was telling him she wasn't guilty. He hoped he was right.

He entered his password then maneuvered onto the main server, so he could access all the files that every employee had uploaded. He clicked on the history for the file Harper had worked on and looked it over. She'd entered all the information as she'd said, and had gone back again the next day, but no changes had been made to the file. Must have been double-checking it maybe? Wait. What do we have here? Someone had accessed the file that same day. The login came from a computer located in the basement, where they keep the inventory. If Harper was the perp, why would she bother going down there to make the changes? Or was she smart enough to know it would throw up a red herring?

He leaned back in the chair and grabbed the warm coffee mug, pondering over Harper's innocence. He always trusted his instincts, and they were telling him she wasn't the one who had messed the addresses up.

He grabbed the manila file that held the details on the background check he'd run on her and looked it over. Hmmm. This is kind of an odd coincidence. Harper is related to that guy Tanner who seems sweet on Gertie. The same guy who had tried to pull some shenanigans on Gertie's wedding reception event last month. That was the reason Logan had been hired in the first place. Some strange things had been going on at O'Rourke's Signature Events, and according to Gertie it wasn't all by Tanner's hand. Tanner had confessed to a few things but there had been more that had gone unexplained.

He closed the folder and stared at the now empty mug then gazed over at the picture. Whatever was going on here was a bit more complex than he'd first assumed, that was for sure. It was time for him to do some more digging.

HARPER WAITED for the elevator impatiently, eager to leave for the day, even if it was only four o'clock. Hardly anyone in the building used the elevator aside from the employees with offices on the upper floors, so why was it always so damn slow? She tapped her foot as she pushed the button again and mulled the day over. She hadn't heard back about Logan finding out who changed the addresses. Then again, it was also possible he'd been the one who had changed it, and he was going to tell Gertie it was her. Then she would probably lose her job. Better to come up with evidence against him sooner rather than later so she could prove to Gertie what he was up to.

Turning around she headed back into her office, tossed her purse and coat onto her desk, then stormed off down the stairs to the basement area to see what exactly Logan had been doing with those lights.

She walked briskly through the storage area and into the room with the lights. She looked them over, paying close attention to the cords. Nope, everything seemed fine. Well, there might be a light missing. That would be odd though, and she wasn't sure since she hadn't counted them all when she'd been in here before. Besides, what would someone do with one light?

As she left the room quietly she caught Ben and George inside one of the small storage rooms out of the corner of her eye. They had a cart with a computer on it, piquing her interest. She approached them slowly, thinking what she should say. Maybe they knew who had access to the files on the server. Or, maybe one of them was trying to screw things up.

"Hey, guys. What's going on?" she asked them casually, nodding towards the computer.

"Nothing exciting here, just entering inventory," Ben replied in a bored tone. "It's never ending."

Harper took his lack of enthusiasm as a good way to pick their minds about the inventory system, which of course would lead to how they store the info on the server, who has access, and anything else that might help her figure out who had messed around with the file. She knew people loved to listen to themselves talk when they were asked for their opinion on something, no matter what it was.

"Really? That's pretty cool. Is it efficient? It seems like maybe just using paper and pen would be just as good, and you wouldn't have to worry about pushing that cart around and making sure there's power for the computer and all that kind of stuff," Harper said.

"Well, I guess it's efficient, it would take time to do the inventory for this place no matter what," Ben said.

Harper walked into the cube, making a show of looking at the computer setup. "My first job here was managing the inventory. But we didn't have this new system you guys have. Basically, I just had to keep track of everything manually, which was kind of a nightmare."

"Oh yeah, it's definitely better than doing it all manually, like with a paper and pen," George piped in. "We just enter it here, then once it's in the system, it's all set, and anyone can access it to make changes."

Harper watched as George showed her how he entered the quantity of each item into the database, quickly clicking through the screen.

"Have you guys ever used a scanner? You know, like bar codes?" she asked.

"No, but Gertie's mentioned it. The only issue with that is when we have temporary equipment, like this fashion show stuff, putting the bar codes on isn't really ideal."

Harper nodded her head in agreement.

"So, you guys can pretty much access all the files on the server, right?" Harper asked, using her most casual innocent tone.

George gave her a funny look. "Huh? Why would we even want to? We just go into the inventory program and update it. It's faster if one person does the count and reads it off and the other person enters the numbers."

"Yeah, I only know how to access the inventory program. The less I know how to do stuff in this system the better anyway, I don't do too much work in it. Leave that to the computer guy," Ben mumbled.

"Wouldn't it be easier if you had access to everything?" Harper asked, baiting them a bit. She knew it was a stupid question, but she was also playing the part of the dingbat office worker. Well, at least she was trying to.

George and Ben both looked at each other and shrugged.

"Not really," they replied in unison.

Noah appeared suddenly, handing a piece of paper to George.

"See, look here," George said, holding the paper out so Harper could see it. "This is how it all works. We input the inventory items into the system, then Noah makes a master list and turns it into a diagram. It's like a cool blueprint of where everything is physically located."

"Yeah, but I only know how to do that part, really," Noah said, looking at Ben. "Ben does most of the entering, like this morning you spent a lot of time on it didn't you?"

Ben looked at Noah weirdly. "Umm, well, yeah. The stuff has to be entered, like constantly. Usually, at least twice a day."

Harper nodded her head enthusiastically, said a quick thank you and headed back up on the elevator. It didn't sound like any of them had the know-how to change that file, was one of them putting on an act about not being very tech savvy? If so, which one?

As the elevator stopped and the doors whisked open she stepped out into the hallway and almost collided with Sarah.

"Ah! You scared me!" Sarah laughed, stepping to the side, and grabbing her chest.

"Sorry! We should really stop meeting like this." Harper laughed. "Feel like grabbing a quick iced coffee? We got some new flavors in that are pretty good."

Sarah nodded yes, and the two headed inside the spotless room.

"So, how are things going?" Harper asked, as she poured herself some vanilla mocha iced coffee from the container in the fridge. Since Sarah had confided about her problems with Raffe, Harper was feeling a bond with the girl. It wasn't that long ago she'd had major man problems too. Now she was past the hurtful stage, she found herself wanting to help Sarah through that too. Maybe Gertie's tendency to help those who were down-and-out was rubbing off on her.

"Okay, I guess. Gertie made me an offer to work here and I'm happy about that. I know she's super picky. And, based on the clientele, I will be able to make some great creative dishes and ones that are different for every event, instead of the same food off a menu, with an occasional special. But Raffe wasn't exactly thrilled when I broke the news to him I was leaving. I guess I assumed he knew this would be coming, but he seemed shocked. It threw me off guard and left me questioning my decision to be honest."

Harper nodded her head sympathetically, knowing all too well how it felt to question your decisions. "Follow your gut instinct. You've had the feeling for a while that working together wasn't good for your relationship."

They both sipped from their iced coffees in silence, the ice from the ice maker in the corner clinking loudly and breaking the silence.

"Overall, I think it's for the best. Change is good, plus I'll be able to see TJ more," Sarah finally said.

Harper could sense a "but" coming by the way Sarah was speaking.

"But, I'll be working with Veronica. And I don't really know if that's the best idea. We do have a bit of a history."

Harper was aware they'd had some problems in the past, but she hoped they could leave it there. Veronica could be a bit harsh, but deep down she wasn't that bad. Plus, Harper certainly didn't want any catty drama around here.

"Well, maybe getting to know her better will give you the opportunity to see she's good for your brother," Harper cheerily said, trying to be positive and upbeat.

"Working with her before wasn't exactly the best experience," Sarah said dryly.

"Well, maybe she's changed. I've only worked for her a short time but she's really not that bad." Harper was stretching the truth a bit, but that was okay. "The past is all over and done with. Don't dwell on it. Veronica's done some really good things since she's been here. She did go above and beyond to make sure Marly's wedding was perfect. And earlier this morning she circumvented another big problem for the fashion show. I don't think she would have done either of those if she was the same person who wanted to cause problems, right?"

"Yeah, you have some good points there," Sarah reluctantly said. "And Marly trusts her now, which is saying a lot. She says she has been really great with the fashion show planning. I guess I should just trust her too and not jump to conclusions about her intentions with TJ. It probably doesn't help I feel my relationship with Raffe is on its last leg. Maybe I am just taking out my negativity about relationships on Veronica. I don't even know what I want anymore, to be honest. Maybe I'm just not destined to find love."

Harper wondered the same thing about herself when it came to being negative about relationships. Truth be told, Logan was the only guy she'd felt even a small spark for since the big breakup, and she found herself hoping he wasn't doing something wrong in that room with the lights. But he was the IT guy, and as far as she could tell, there were no computers or servers in that room. So, what in the world had he been doing in there?

After her chat with Sarah, Harper grabbed her things and again made her way down to the lobby. Myrtle was seated at the receptionist desk, as usual. A sneaky smile crept across her face seeing Harper approach. Wait a minute, she knew that look ...

Myrtle's mischievous eyes drifted over Harper's shoulder and she whipped around to see Logan walking up behind her. Was he following her or something? Had he overheard her conversation with Ben and the others earlier, or possibly seen her in the storage room that had the lights in it? Why did he always seem to show up in the same place right after her? Shouldn't he be doing computer things? He was the IT guy, after all.

He continued to walk past them simply nodding his head instead of saying hello, then disappeared down the hallway.

"Well, it looks like you have a stalker!" Myrtle said in a singsong voice.

"Huh?" Harper asked, confused. Could Myrtle read her mind?

"Logan. Was he following you or something? First this morning and then now. And you did see how he looked at you, right?" Myrtle waggled her eyebrows up and down with a grin on her face.

"Yeah, right. Time to get your glasses checked." Harper shook her head. If anything, he was looking at her with suspicion.

"Well, I still think you two would make a cute couple." Myrtle tilted her head to the side, causing her spikey hair to sway to one side.

"I don't want to be a couple with anyone, Myrtle. Really. I am fine being alone, with no one to bug me." Or to lie to me and break my heart.

"Now, now dear, be careful what you wish for! I can sense you've been hurt, and I know how that feels, but you know the saying, when you fall off the horse you have to get back in the saddle! Besides, you're much too young to be so jaded about love. Save that for when you're ancient, like me."

"You should listen to her, honey, you deserve someone nice."

Harper spun around to see her Uncle Tanner walking towards her, holding a gigantic white and turquoise glass vase stuffed full of flowers. The arrangement was stunning, a mix of vibrant oranges, purples, and yellows, all nestled among greens and baby's breath. As Tanner came closer, Harper could smell the floral scent and see there were also lilac-colored roses scattered throughout the arrangement.

"Oh my, what beautiful flowers, Tanner!" Myrtle exclaimed. "You're here to see Gertie, I assume?"

"Yes, I am, and I hope she thinks these are just as beautiful as you do." Tanner winked at Myrtle as he held the giant vase up.

The front door opened again, and Edward came walking in, his smile quickly turning into a scowl when he saw Tanner holding the giant flower arrangement.

"You! What are you doing here?" he demanded of Tanner.

"I brought Gertie flowers to wish her good luck with the show on Friday, not that it's any of your business." Tanner held the vase higher for Edward to see, as if he couldn't already.

"Oh please. I am quite sure Gertie does not want your gaudy flowers." Edward rolled his eyes.

"Let's let Gertie decide that, not you," Tanner said.

"That monstrosity looks far too heavy for you to carry, I'll take it up to her." Edward reached for the vase and grabbed it towards the bottom, trying to yank it away from Tanner's grip.

"Hands off! I will take it to her!" Tanner yelled, his knuckles turning white as he tightened his grip and pulled the arrangement back towards him.

"Boys, boys! No fighting! Jeez! I will bring the flowers up to Gertie myself for crying out loud!" Myrtle had come out from behind her reception desk and grabbed the arrangement, setting the vase on her desk then turning around to face them both, giving them an over-the-glasses stare.

"Now, is there anything else, Eddie? Tanny?" she asked them, hands on her hips and eyebrows raised.

Harper knew that look meant both Edward and Tanner had better not say yes.

Edward's face was red with fury. He opened his mouth to say something then snapped it shut again.

"No, thank you very much, Myrtle. I'm sure Gertie is very busy," Tanner said, earning a pointed glare from Edward.

Edward immediately grabbed his phone, placed it

to his ear and rushed out of the lobby door like the building was on fire.

Harper and Myrtle exchanged a look Harper knew meant "men." Tanner turned and walked towards the door after Edward, saying goodbye to them over his shoulder.

Harper was smiling at their foolish shenanigans, but her smile quickly faded as she gazed over at the abundant arrangement. Flowers to wish Gertie good luck with the fashion show on Friday. It was now past five o'clock and she only had three days left to prove Logan was the culprit, or if he isn't, to figure out who is. She had a lot of thinking to do and it was best done at home in her lonely apartment where she wouldn't be interrupted.

"Hey, Uncle Tanner! Wait up, I'll walk out with you."

———

LOGAN WALKED BACK through the lobby, glancing outside to see Harper leaving with Tanner. Hmm, that was interesting.

That Tanner was her uncle, and he'd tried to ruin things for Gertie before, didn't sit well. Sure, Tanner made things right in the end, and, according to him, Harper had not been involved, but it gave one pause.

Could Harper and Tanner possibly be trying to work together to destroy the fashion show? Maybe, what happened at the reception had been practice runs, and a way for them both to feel things out here, before they did something big. He needed more details on exactly what happened at the last event, specifically, what Tanner had done to try to ruin the wedding reception.

While he was at it, he also needed to find out what Harper had been doing down in the basement earlier. She'd briefly gone into the room that held the lights for the show again, and he'd also seen her talking to Ben, Noah, and George.

The giant vase of flowers sitting on top of the reception desk broke his thoughts, and he stopped to look at them, rising on his tiptoes to peek over at Myrtle, who was sitting down behind them.

"This is quite the flower arrangement." He reached out and touched one of the vibrant orange lilies. "You must have an admirer."

Myrtle laughed. "Ha! It's not for me. You could help me out by delivering it to Gertie though, I'm pretty busy with these new invitations." Myrtle barely looked up, her polished nails clacking away on the keyboard.

"Of course I will." Logan reached out to grab the heavy vase.

The lobby door opened, and a delivery person walked in, holding another humungous vase filled with flowers, this one even bigger than the one Tanner had brought in.

"Gertie O'Rourke?" The delivery man raised a brow at them as he placed the flowers on Myrtle's desk, making a thud then wiping his brow.

"Yes, I'll take them. Thank you." Myrtle reached out for the card nestled inside the flowers and nodded her head grinning.

"Yup, just as I thought, from Edward. He called the florist when he was rushing out of here, to order flowers that would outdo Tanner's arrangement. There's no flies on him, that's for sure."

"Oh, so that arrangement is from Tanner?" Logan pointed to the other arrangement.

If Tanner had come here to drop off the flowers for Gertie then maybe he wasn't trying to plan something bad with Harper at all, Logan thought with relief. Then his cop instincts kicked in. Maybe the flowers were part of Tanner's plan.

"Yes. That one is from Tanner, now this one is from Edward, and the overwhelming floral scent is starting to make my head spin and my allergies flare up!" Myrtle stifled a sneeze, the motion causing her red, purple, and silver beaded eyeglass chain to clatter.

"I'll take them both upstairs to Gertie for you." Logan tried to maneuver the giant arrangements in both arms as he shuffled towards the elevator, tilting his head to the side so he could see the buttons for the elevator.

"Whoa, need some help there?" someone asked him from behind.

The flowers were so high Logan struggled to see around them, but he knew the voice was TJ, and he was more than happy when TJ grabbed the larger of the arrangements from him as they both stepped into the elevator.

"Thanks for the help." Logan pressed the button for Gertie's floor.

"No problem. These are probably the biggest flower arrangements I've ever seen," TJ said, laughing as he parted a few of the flowers with his hand so he could see Logan. "What's the special occasion?"

"Yeah, they are huge. One is from Edward and the other is from Tanner, wishing Gertie good luck for the show this week."

"Wow. Looks like Gertie has quite the fan club," TJ said.

"Those two definitely seem to like her, especially Tanner. Speaking of which, can I ask you something? About Tanner, I mean. I heard a rumor he tried to sabotage Gertie's last event, do you know anything about what happened?" Logan asked TJ casually, brushing some baby's breath out of his face.

The elevator came to a stop and the doors opened. TJ stepped out into the hallway, then used his shoulder to hold the elevator door from sliding shut so Logan could get out.

"Let's drop these monstrosities off at Gertie's then I can fill you in in my office," TJ said, the two of them walking down the hall.

Gertie's office door was open so they both walked in and looked around. She wasn't there.

"Should we just leave them on the conference table?" Logan asked, already setting his down on the large crystal clear glass table, the vase making a clinking sound as he did. TJ did the same.

They walked down to TJ's office, both taking a seat at the small round meeting table inside.

Just as Logan was about to speak TJ's office phone rang, and he excused himself to answer it.

Logan watched him briefly as he spoke and could

tell he must be speaking to Veronica, simply based on his sappy smile and the way he relaxed his shoulders as he spoke quietly into the phone. After a few minutes TJ came back to the table.

"Sorry, that was Veronica."

Logan nodded his head in acknowledgement and didn't say anything. His last girlfriend hadn't worked out well for him. They'd also worked together like TJ and Veronica. They'd been partners. She'd been a risk taker and had always kept him on his toes at work. Then one day things had gone bad, real bad. She'd been shot during a robbery and that had changed everything for him. He hadn't been able to protect her, and the guilt had ended up killing their relationship. Heck, it had killed his career, too. He ended up quitting the force over it eventually.

"So, you wanted to know something about Tanner?" TJ's voice pulled him out of his thoughts.

"Yeah, if you don't mind. I heard some rumors about him messing around with the wedding reception and I wanted to hear the story from someone who might really know what went on. You were working here when it happened, right?" Logan asked, hoping TJ would spill the beans.

"Yes, I was working here. There were a few things Tanner messed around with that I heard about. First, he had the wedding gown made way too small, then he had the cake topper which was custom-made ruined, and then he tried screwing around with the tent poles."

"Tent poles?" Logan asked, not sure what TJ was talking about.

"Yeah. We used one of those huge tents set up outside, you know one of those big white ones. And Tanner tried to swap out the good poles for bad ones, which would have caused the tent to collapse. You know Gertie, she's kept everything that came with this place as well as any inventory lots she bought. So, there's some junk included, and she never wants to throw anything away, it's always donate, donate, donate. So, the old poles were supposed to be donated or something eventually."

Logan laughed. Gertie was known for making sure every little thing was used and never wasted.

"But, how did he get away with these things if he wasn't working here, then?" Logan asked, trying to put the pieces of this sabotage puzzle together.

"I'm not sure about that. He wasn't working here, you're right, but I guess he could have snuck in or something?"

"Was Harper working here then? Do you think she was maybe doing it for Tanner?"

"Yeah, she was working here, and there actually was a rumor she was involved, but at the end of it all Tanner confessed, and he said Harper didn't know anything about any of it. He actually made things good, he fixed the tent poles, and the reception was a huge success. Everyone was happy."

Logan mulled over what TJ was telling him.

"Harper doesn't exactly fit the bill when it comes to someone who would sabotage things, does she? She's always pretty helpful as well as being kind of on the quiet side," TJ said.

Logan thought the same about Harper but knew better than to eliminate someone as a suspect just because they seemed nice. Or looked good, like she did. He still couldn't cross Harper off his list, even though he basically felt the same way TJ did.

"No, I was just curious. I don't even know what someone could do to try to ruin a fashion show anyway," Logan replied, shrugging.

"I guess the worst thing someone could do would be during the actual show so that the press and everyone would see and ruin Gertie's reputation. Now that I think about it, whoever tried to ruin the wedding could still be here. They could have been doing things all along, exclusive of what Tanner was trying to do. Someone moved luminaries around at the wedding reception, and they could have set the tent on fire. But I know that wasn't Tanner."

"Hmm." Logan pieced some of the puzzle together as he spoke. "So, basically Tanner caused some issues, but none of them were anything that could have hurt or killed anyone. Well, the tent pole thing, yes, but that's when he stopped and 'fessed up and fixed it from what you've said. So, in theory this person has been working here since Gertie opened the place."

"When you put it like that, yeah, I guess so," TJ replied.

"And you're positive Tanner didn't move those luminaries at the reception?" Logan asked.

"If Tanner moved the luminaries, then he would have wanted to die in the fire they would have caused. So, yes, I'm pretty sure it wasn't Tanner. Unless he wanted to die in the fire himself."

Harper walked slowly along the busy sidewalk, stifling a yawn as she haphazardly dodged the rush of oncoming hurried workers. She'd tossed and turned all night long, trying to figure out who could possibly be trying to ruin things for the fashion show. It was already Wednesday; the show was in two days and she was desperate to figure out who the culprit was before they sabotaged anything else.

She'd spent her night trying to think like a detective and had narrowed down her list of suspects through a process of elimination. When she was done, Ben and Logan had ended up at the top of her list. Logan was there because she'd seen him acting suspicious on the GoPro. Ben was there because he always seemed overly uninterested in whatever job he was doing, and it made him stick out to Harper. Plus, there had been that incident with the butterflies at the wedding reception. She bet he assumed she'd forgotten about that.

As she came to the front of the office she walked around towards the back of the building down by the loading dock, reaching into her bag for the small carton of cream and Tupperware bowl she'd brought with her for the stray cat. She leaned over and set the bowl down on the concrete ramp of the loading dock and started to pour it out when the door suddenly swung open. She jumped up and hid the carton. She didn't want anyone seeing her feeding the cat for fear of them possibly causing an issue, like scaring the cat away or calling the animal control officer. She scrambled to try to stand in front of the bowl as someone stepped out the door. Logan. Of all people.

She stiffened up a bit as she forced herself to smile at one of her suspects. Was he following her again? Maybe she should move him to number one.

"Oh … er … hi," Logan said, stumbling through his words as he juggled something in his hands which he was clearly trying to hide from her.

"Hi." She glanced nervously at the fence hoping the little cat wouldn't choose this moment to appear.

Logan's brows furrowed as he followed her glance.

"What are you doing here?"

What did he think she was doing? Sabotage? Veronica had certainly implied she messed around with the invitations and Gertie had sent Logan off to investigate who had altered the file. What if whoever had done it had somehow rigged the file to make it look like she was the one who made the changes and Logan was here to confront her ... but if so, what the heck did he have behind his back? A pink slip?

She shifted on her feet. "Getting some fresh air. What are you doing?"

"Same."

She craned her neck to try to see what he had behind his back and he jerked his arm away from her view. His grip must have loosed though because he fumbled, and something clattered to the ground. A can of cat food.

"Wait a minute. Are you feeding the cat too?" Harper stepped aside so he could see the bowl of cream she'd set out.

His worried look turned to a sheepish smile when he saw the bowl she'd been hiding.

"Yeah, I've been doing it for a while now. No wonder he's getting a big belly. I didn't realize two of us were feeding him." Logan picked up the can and opened it, then placed it next to the bowl of cream.

Mew!

The cat ran over to him, purring as it rubbed itself on his leg before turning its attention to the food.

"And to think, I was worried this cat might starve to death." Harper crouched to pet it behind the ears. "Instead it's becoming the best fed cat around."

"Yeah, go figure."

She glanced up and their eyes met. His eyes softened, and she saw a flicker of interest before he looked away.

"So, did you get everything all straightened out?" Logan asked her as they both watched the cat eat.

What did he mean, get everything straightened out? "Did you ever figure out who changed the file for the invitations?" Harper ignored his question and continued to pet the cat who was now indulging in the bowl of cream.

"No. It could have been anyone, really."

"What do you mean it could have been anyone? Can't you tell who logged in? You can tell exactly which computer and login was used, right?" Harper's suspicion grew. He was the IT guy; shouldn't he know how to do that? Why did each employee have a different login if they couldn't be tracked?

"Well, yeah. Whoever did it used a system admin to log in. The file showed after you entered all the information the first time, you went back and opened it, then it was accessed once more after your session."

"So, that proves I didn't do it." Harper couldn't keep the relieved tone out of her voice.

"How so?" Logan asked.

"Because, obviously, someone accessed the file after me. Why would I go into it twice? If I wanted to screw it up, I would have done it the first time."

Logan nodded his head slowly in agreement.

Meow.

The cat glanced pointedly from them to the empty dishes, the gold flecks in its eyes sparkling in the sunlight.

"Nice try," Logan said. "I think you had enough for breakfast."

Meow. Judging by the cat's tone, he did not agree.

"Sorry," Harper said to the cat.

The cat glanced from Harper, to Logan, to the building. Then, apparently realizing no more food was coming from either of them, he darted towards the door.

"Oh no!" Harper noticed the door had been left ajar.

Logan made a comical grab for the cat, but it was too quick. In a flash, it had slipped through and disappeared into the building.

LOGAN RUSHED inside the building right behind Harper. The basement was a maze of rooms and passages. The cat could easily get lost in there. Or hurt. He'd gotten rather attached to the little animal and didn't want something bad to happen to it.

"Over there!" Harper pointed towards the room where they were staging the catwalk and he saw the tabby jump onto the runway, pausing before it ran down one of the long ramps.

Harper ran after it, jumping up on one of the long wooden ramps on the runway. The cat sprung off the side of the ramp and Harper stopped abruptly, turning towards Logan.

Logan watched as her body started to sway, then noticed in horror the ramp was starting to buckle underneath her. Without hesitation, he rushed over, holding his arms out and catching her before she fell off the shoulder-high structure onto the floor.

She landed in his outstretched arms, as if it were a scene from some cheesy movie. Everything around them stilled as he stood there holding her, her perfume wafting up to him, and her long red hair tickling his arms. He looked into her eyes and noticed, up close, they were an even deeper blue than before.

MEOOOW!

The loud meow from the cat interrupted his thoughts, reminding him they were at work and he had a job to do, which was to find whoever had obviously now tried to sabotage the runway. But first, they needed to wrangle the tabby.

"We better get that cat before someone else sees it." He gently placed Harper down as the cat weaved its way around the metal staging underneath the wooden planks.

"Err, thanks for catching me. I guess the runway wasn't checked yet for sturdiness, huh?" Harper straightened her ivory silk blouse and brushed at her tan skirt.

"I guess so, even though it looks like it's all set up to me. Is this it or is there more that needs to be done to it, you know, like added to it?" Logan asked, grabbing one of the metal pieces on the bottom and shaking it. It wasn't sturdy at all, and it seemed to be missing most of the screws to hold the underlying metal supports in place.

"I don't think so. The plan is to pre-stage it here, then move it outside the day of the show. It looks like it's all set in terms of layout," Harper said as she twirled one of her red curls between her thumb and forefinger.

"What's wrong?" Logan asked her, able to tell by the way she was playing with her hair she was thinking about something. His ex had done the same thing whenever she was deep in thought.

"Oh, nothing. I just feel like something is, I dunno, off, I guess. I'm not sure that was an accident. The ramp on the runway buckling, I mean. But again, maybe they aren't through with the setup yet."

He watched her as she continued to look around the room. Her level of concern was very telling. And it was telling him she wasn't the one messing with things. Her concern was too genuine.

"Oh, there it is! Under there!" She pointed under the runway and ran over to where the cat had just scampered, crouching down to look for it underneath the structure.

"Lose something?" Veronica's voice startled Logan and he spun around to see her standing in the doorway, arms crossed, and brows mashed together as she bent to look under the runway at Harper.

HARPER GLANCED NERVOUSLY BEHIND HER, looking at where the cat had disappeared to. She didn't know if Veronica would take kindly to a homeless cat running around the building and wasn't sure what would become of the cat if Veronica wanted it gone. Plus, chasing a cat around wasn't exactly on the to-do list Veronica had given her.

"We were just checking on the staging," she replied, glancing quickly over at Logan. Her heart warmed when she noticed he was maneuvering himself in front of where the cat had run, trying to hide it.

"I don't remember telling you to check the staging," Veronica said stalely.

"Oh, I know you didn't, I was just trying to be proactive." Hopefully, Veronica would believe that.

"Oh, good. Anyway, are you sure you entered the right addresses for those invites? I still don't understand how they got messed up."

The question didn't exactly surprise Harper, given all the shenanigans that had gone on before with the wedding reception. She knew Veronica assumed Harper had messed the invites up on purpose, and no matter how many times Harper explained to her she didn't, it was going to take a lot for Veronica to believe her.

"Veronica, I checked all the logs and Harper wasn't the last person to access the file. So, she wasn't the one who messed them up," Logan piped up. "She could have used another login to throw people off track. But, whoever accessed the file, did it two minutes after she accessed it for her final check, and they did it from one of the shared computers located downstairs in the cube area. It would be impossible for her to make it from her office upstairs down to that area and log on within two minutes. I timed it."

Harper jerked her head towards Logan. He'd timed it? Is that when she thought he was following her? She was surprised by what Logan had said regarding the timeline for the files being changed, he hadn't mentioned that part to her earlier. But the fact Logan was sticking up for her felt nice, it was good knowing he had her back. And it also meant maybe she was wrong thinking he might be a suspect.

Veronica pursed her lips and look puzzled, as if unsure whether she should believe him, but her attention was distracted by the runway. She was frowning now, and her head was moving back and forth from side to side, as if she was confused.

"I don't think this is set up the way it should be. On the plan I have, the long side is way over there, so they come in from behind reception area then around and back. The way its set up now, they end up on the river side. Who changed this?" Veronica asked.

Harper and Logan exchanged a quick glance.

"I have no idea. I know I have the original plans in

my office, I can check," Harper replied slowly, as she was thinking how the runway had seemed off to her when she'd first seen it.

"Let me know what you find out. This has to be set up exactly as the plans say."

Meow!

Harper's chest constricted as the cat loudly meowed from behind Logan.

"What was that?" Veronica asked, looking towards where the sound had come from.

"Oh, that was just me. Sorry," Logan said, coughing. "I've had a weird sounding cough the last few days."

Veronica gave him a strange look and left, turning, and looking back at them once more before disappearing through the doorway.

As soon as she was gone, Harper and Logan scrambled over to the area where the cat was. Logan picked it up, the cat purring as he held it in his arms.

"I'm going to take this escape artist back outside before he gets in trouble here," Logan said, as he rubbed the cat's head.

"Okay, I'm going to check out those plans." Harper gave the cat a pat on its head and headed towards the elevator, wondering if the runway had been built the wrong way by mistake … or if someone had done it on purpose. She had a feeling she knew which one it was.

Big T stooped to pet the cat, rubbing it behind its left ear as it purred loudly and leaned against his leg.

"Well, this is it, buddy. What's on this piece of paper is the most important thing I'll ever read. This could turn everything around for me."

The cat let out a loud meow and stared at him for a minute, as if to agree with him then it sat back on its haunches and started to clean its paws, pausing briefly to look at some long blades of grass swaying in the light breeze.

Big T slid his finger under the flap on the envelope slowly, careful not to rip anything. He gently pulled out the piece of paper inside, unfolded it, and started to read the results he'd waited a lifetime for.

He stared numbly at the piece of paper for a few minutes, his face getting redder with every passing second, then he crumpled the paper into his fist, making a ball, turned, and threw it at the brick wall next to him, startling the cat. The cat let out a loud meow and ran away through the fence and into the overgrown weeds, leaving Big T alone staring at the crumbled wad of paper. The red DNA lab logo was still visible, glaring at him, taunting him.

Not a match, it had said. How could that be? How was this possible? He couldn't even question the results, it said it was 99.9999 percent accurate.

He stamped his foot on the ground with a loud thud as his boot hit the cement. Nothing ever went right for him. Nothing! Since birth! Even before he was born, for that matter! Well, that's okay. He'd make it right. At least now, he knew for sure. He had nothing to lose. This wasn't about him anyway; this revenge was for someone else.

He walked over to the ball of paper and snatched it up, stuffing it angrily into his pocket. It wouldn't be good if someone stumbled on this, read it, and guessed the truth.

Well, that was it then. He knew there was only one thing left to do. He needed to step up his game. It was time to do something now he knew the answer for sure. None of this would be happening if it weren't for that old bag Gertie. Miss Popularity, the one with the growing collection of flowers in her office. Every time he'd snuck by her office the number of flowers she had lying around seemed to double. She sure had quite the list of admirers. Bet if they knew how evil she was and what she'd done, they wouldn't be sending her anything at all.

A chill went down his spine when he thought of the flowers, they reminded him of the hospital. The thought of someone in the hospital made him even more angry. And more determined than ever.

HARPER LET OUT A LONG SIGH, rolled out the giant blueprint for the runway onto her desk, and sat, eager to figure out what was going on with the design issue. After she'd left Logan downstairs, she'd been busy with one thing after another all day, including bringing yet another giant vase of flowers up to Gertie's office. It had been so big she could barely carry it, and Gertie's office was filling so fast it was starting to look like a dang flower shop. She hoped the interruptions would stop soon so she could finally focus on the runway setup.

As she examined the prints it became obvious the runway, set up downstairs, was *definitely* different from the blueprints. She doubted it was a mistake. Her mind started to race, worrying Veronica might think she was involved in messing it up, since she'd just found her in there and questioned Harper about what she was doing. She forced herself to stop thinking negative thoughts, replacing them with encouragement, reminding herself Logan had stuck up for her. By now, he knew she wasn't the one sabotaging things, and she knew she could find out who it was if she focused carefully on what her next steps would be.

So, how could she use this runway situation to capture the culprit? She stood and paced around her office, her heels clicking as she patrolled the wooden floor.

The show was in two days, and she needed to stop this person before they did something major, ruining everything for Gertie and everyone else who worked there. She stood next to the window, basking in the late rays of the sun which was slowly creeping down behind the buildings and closed her eyes to concentrate.

Wait a minute! She ran to the drawing, spinning it around so it was facing her and looked at it again. Why change the setup? What was this person trying to achieve by doing it? The models could still go along the runway, so why did it matter where the weak spot was? She squinted as she looked at the drawing, trying to envision the runway downstairs versus what it was supposed to look like according to the drawings.

Her heart froze when she realized what was going on. The way the runway had been set up, the part of the catwalk that would be next to the river, was where it had buckled when she'd stood on it. If it happened with a wheelchair model on it, the platform would pitch forward at a steep angle, and the model would plunge into the river in her wheelchair! Given many of the models couldn't use their legs, this would certainly kill someone. What kind of sicko would want to do that, and why?

She already knew it *could* be Ben, but she'd also seen George downstairs near the runway. Really, there were a lot of people involved in the construction of it. So, how could someone make changes, and have it built the wrong way without anyone realizing? Or did this person sneak in after hours and change it on their own? Whoever it was must have a serious axe to grind with Gertie to risk potentially killing someone.

Harper knew Veronica had already instructed the maintenance guys to repair the weak spot in the runway before they dismantled it, so they could rebuild it outside in readiness for the show on Friday. If someone wanted to make sure the runway was sabotaged, odds were they knew the damage was now being fixed. They would also know they only had tonight to mess it up again. Meaning they would have to go in after-hours when no one was around and mess with the supports again, or whatever it was they planned on doing to sabotage it.

She glanced at her watch, it was approaching five o clock. Snatching up her cell phone, she headed downstairs bracing herself for a long night. If someone was going to tamper with things she would be there, phone in hand, ready to capture it all.

Logan crammed himself into the small closet across from the runway, the cold brick wall making him wish he'd worn his jacket. He left the door slightly ajar, so he could see out, hopeful whoever was causing the problems would show up.

He'd looked at his copy of the blueprints, and Veronica had been right; the runway configuration had been set up differently than it should have been. Sure, there was the slim possibility it had been set up wrong by mistake, but after he'd taken the cat outside, he'd gone back and inspected the runway where the supports had started to buckle. They'd been tampered with, so it wasn't obvious from the outside, but they would buckle when pressure was applied. If the runway was set up outside in this configuration, the pressure would cause it to tilt down, forcing whoever was on it to go right into the river. That meant, whoever was walking first had to be the target. Everyone knew the first person along the runway was supposed to be Gertie.

He shifted uncomfortably inside the dark closet and rubbed his hands together. The last person to access the invite file had done so under the admin login. What didn't make sense was how the perp had gotten everyone to build the runway the wrong way? It took several employees to build, and they all knew how to read a blueprint. The only thing that made sense was if the person had given them a new blueprint, but Logan had scoured through the files and hadn't found one.

Since he'd made sure everyone on staff knew the faulty supports were going to be fixed, and it was also well-known the entire runway would be rebuilt outside tomorrow, he was hoping the perp would come back tonight to try to mess with the supports, or something else, to damage the runway again. When he, or she, showed up, Logan would be ready.

Suddenly, he heard a faint noise; someone was approaching. He held his breath and peeked out through the crack in the doorway. He could see a shadowy object in the darkened room. It was moving slowly, and while he couldn't make out who it was, he knew by their size it was a person.

"Stop right there!" he yelled, bursting out of the closet, turning on the flashlight he'd brought with him, pointing the bright light at the figure. For a minute he reached instinctively for his gun, an old habit from his policeman days.

"What? You stop!" Harper shouted, taking several steps back and holding her hand up to shield her eyes.

"Harper? What the heck are you doing down here sneaking around in the dark?" Logan moved the beam of the flashlight away from her face, so she could see.

"Me? What the heck were you doing hiding in the closet? You nearly gave me a heart attack! I came down—"

"Shush. Someone's coming." Logan reached out and grabbed her by the sleeve. He pulled her, before she could protest, towards the closet and pushed her in before him, pulling the door behind him but leaving it open a crack so they could still see out.

He shut his flashlight off and neither of them said a word. They were facing each other, crammed into the tiny area together. Her hands were pressed against his chest, making him lose focus on why they were there. She turned her head to peek out the doorway, and he caught the faint scent of her perfume, a beachy smell that reminded him of the ocean.

"I know him!"

Harper's whisper jolted Logan back to reality, and he peeked out to see who she was talking about. He watched in silence as Ben came into the room, grabbed a screw gun, and left.

They stood, frozen, for what seemed like hours but was only a few minutes. Then Logan opened the closet door and stepped into the room.

"Do you think Ben's the one who has been messing with everything?" He turned the flashlight on and shone it around the room.

"I'm pretty sure it's him. I've suspected him from the start."

"Well, there's one problem. He didn't do anything, aside from take the screw gun. If he was going to sabotage the runway, he would be doing it right now, wouldn't he?" Logan walked over to the light switch and flicked it on.

"Maybe he heard us? I don't know. I guess you have a point. But he could also walk in again."

They both looked at the door as if Ben would burst through it any minute and announce himself as the troublemaker.

"What made you think of him as a suspect, anyway? What did he do?" Logan leaned against the wall. He kept the flashlight at hand, ready to use it as a weapon just in case someone did come bursting through the door and tried to start some trouble.

"Well, the last event we had was a wedding reception. It was important because it was Gertie's first event and was also two well-known people. The bride wanted butterflies to be released during the reception. Butterflies are a major nightmare, they have to be kept at a certain temperature or else they will die."

"Butterflies?" Logan laughed, shaking his head.

"Yes, butterflies! Anyway, they were in this special temperature-controlled box, and Ben opened it up and looked in it. When questioned, he said Gertie had told him to make sure the box remained at a certain temperature."

"So, he did what Gertie told him to. I'm confused."

Logan was unsure why that would have made Ben a suspect to Harper.

"Well, yes, but I'm not convinced Gertie told him to do that. You know she has a habit of covering up for people when she feels it's just a minor detail. Plus, even if she did ask him to do it, he didn't need to open the box up. The thermometer was external and could be seen from the outside."

"Hmmm. Yeah, I guess that could make him a suspect." Logan was uncertain there was enough evidence to make Ben the perp. Whoever had changed the runway configuration and messed around with the support beams knew what they were doing, and he was unsure Ben had that knowledge.

"Well, what's our next step? Do we sit in here all night?" Harper spoke as she looked around.

"Well, the night's still early and I feel whoever is messing things up will want to screw with the runway again, and they might come back tonight. Everyone knows first thing tomorrow morning it will be moved outside. If they weaken the supports like it appears they've done here it's likely that no one will notice when they put it back together. You can't tell unless you inspect it and since it's supposedly already been inspected in here, they won't be looking too closely when they move it outside."

"Yeah, I had the same thought."

"You go ahead and go home. I'll hang out here for a while, to see if anything happens. I would be mad if I wasn't around tonight and the guy—or girl—screwed with the stuff again." Logan looked around the room.

"Uh, no way. I want to be here if something happens too." Harper pulled an old metal chair out from the corner and sat on it, her stomach growling.

"Tell you what. I'll order some takeout for us, you go grab it upstairs when it arrives, and I'll stay here. We can eat it here, if you're okay with that. I mean, it's not the nicest spot for a picnic."

"Deal. I'm starving!"

"Good. Maybe we can put our heads together and figure this thing out while we're at it."

Harper hurried down the dimly lit hallway with the giant bag of takeout food. She'd tried to be as quiet as possible when she'd run up to the reception area to open the door for the delivery guy, and she hadn't seen anyone else in the building. Maybe, whoever it was had decided they wouldn't try to mess with the setup again, but it was better she and Logan stay, just to be sure.

"That smells awesome," Logan said as soon as Harper approached him with the food. He'd ordered so much of it she was sure the entire building smelled like it now. If the perp was here and hungry then they would definitely make an appearance after smelling this!

She shut the door behind her and walked over to

where Logan had set up two chairs with a cart in between to use as a makeshift table. For a minute, she thought about asking if they should maybe shut the lights off and use a candle instead, but that seemed overly dramatic and possibly suggested something romantic, and she didn't want to make a fool out of herself. Besides, the main door was shut and there were no windows. If someone was going to come in here, they probably wouldn't see the lights on from outside the room anyway.

She sat and helped him pull the various boxes of Chinese food out of the bag, grateful they'd thrown in some paper plates and plastic utensils as well. She handed him one of the bottles of water then arranged all the boxes in the middle of the cart, so they could each grab food from them easily.

"Well, I think you ordered enough food for about ten people. I guess you were as hungry as I am, or you just really like Chinese food," she joked, as they both eagerly dug into the food.

"So, I have a confession to make," Logan said, in between bites of pork fried rice. "Gertie hired me to find out whoever is messing things up. I'm not really an IT person by trade, I'm a Private Investigator."

Harper dabbed at her mouth with a napkin and nodded her head. It made total sense to her, and it also explained why he didn't seem to be a whiz with computers.

"Well, that doesn't exactly surprise me. Things came down to the wire at the last event, and if it hadn't been for Tanner having a change of heart, Gertie's first event could have been her last. Hiring someone to get to the bottom of things was a smart thing for her to do."

Logan stopped chewing, looking questioningly at Harper.

Harper finished chewing her food, knowing she needed to explain her last statement.

"Well, you probably know Tanner is my Uncle, if you've investigated me, which I'm sure you have." Harper said this hoping to get a reaction from Logan, she was sure he already knew everything there was to know about her, but his reaction didn't give him away if he did. "So, there is a bit of history with him and Marly, the girl who had her wedding here. He thinks she ruined his fashion business, and he wanted to try to screw her wedding up."

Harper sighed heavily, unsure how Logan would react to what she was about to say next.

"So, I got the job here basically to help my Uncle mess up Gertie's first event. Not to get back at her for anything, she was just collateral damage. He had an issue with the bride, Marly. Anyway, as time went on we both agreed what we were doing wasn't right and Uncle Tanner fixed it all. The wedding reception went off without a hitch and was a huge hit. I still feel guilty for what I did, Gertie has been nothing but great to me. So, that's why I want to catch whoever it is that's screwing with things. I want to make sure no one messes things up for Gertie. She's a good person and doesn't deserve to have her business ruined. Plus, my Uncle adores her, and he would be heartbroken if she was hurt in any way, and I can't even think about seeing him like that again."

Harper waited for Logan to say something, but he didn't. Was he shocked? He reached for a sparerib, maybe he was just hungry and hadn't even heard what she'd said.

"Oh, and I also put a GoPro in the room with the runway lighting. I saw you on it. You messed around with the wires."

Logan looked up from his plate and wiped his mouth with a napkin.

"Guilty. You got me. But, I wasn't messing around with the wires. I was checking them, and they'd been screwed around with. As in cut."

"What? Someone cut all the wires for the lights for the show? Why are you only telling me this now?"

Harper was irritated Logan hadn't mentioned this before, and now knew she would have to scramble to replace all the lights.

"I didn't say anything because I didn't want everyone to panic. I didn't know who did it and didn't want everyone here slowing down on getting ready for the show. It's too important. So, I had a buddy of mine replace the lights, and I still don't know who did it."

Harper couldn't really argue with him over that. He was right, if everyone knew about the lights being sabotaged they would focus more on trying to figure out who had cut them versus get ready for the show. Plus, he'd already taken care of getting them fixed.

"I guess that all makes sense. It seems to me maybe one of the maintenance guys could be the suspect. They are down here all the time and putting this stuff together."

"Funny you say that. I did see Ben skulking around outside. He didn't really belong there," Logan said.

"I saw Ben, Noah, and George with a computer. You know, the ones on the carts they use for inventory. Can't they access the files from there, the ones on the main server? If so, then in theory it would be easy to change things without arousing suspicion."

"That computer has the same access as the others,

if the person has the right login and password, and if they know some system commands, they could change the rights, and access the files from the command line," Logan explained.

"In English please," Harper said.

"They could access the blueprint and invitation files from there." Logan laughed.

"Well, it looks like we're in for a long night then. Considering the suspects, I think we need to make a list of things we need to triple-check for the event and cross them off, one by one, tonight."

BIG T WALKED into the room where the runway was being assembled and saw George and one of the other maintenance guys, Hank, working on it, tearing it down. He wanted to scream but kept his composure, he'd worked hard to make sure the runway had been perfect, and it had been when he'd left the night before. Now they were screwing around with it and he didn't like how it looked.

"Hey, can you help us out T? We need to move this around. It was set up wrong and everyone is flipping out about it," George asked him as he struggled with one of the giant pieces of wood.

Big T nodded his head yes and started to help them, his face turning bright red from anger. First, he'd gotten the test results that were not what he'd expected, and now this. His plan had been ruined! He knew exactly who had done it, too. Harper. She'd been snooping around down here way too much lately.

He'd caught her on more than one of the nanny cams he'd set up around the mill, including in her office. He'd watched as she hid a GoPro in the room where all the lights were. The same room he'd already hacked apart wires in the day before. Ha! Too late!

But then she'd hooked up that GoPro and watched a bunch of footage from it in her office. He couldn't see her monitor, but he could see her face and tell she'd seen something that might be incriminating. Maybe she'd seen him doing something else. He didn't know if she had any other GoPros around, he couldn't hide his nanny cams everywhere without them being seen. She'd also been asking all those dumb questions about the computers the other day. Why did she even care?

He knew she was trying to trap him, but the joke would be on her. He was way too smart for her. He would take care of her, and Gertie, in one fell swoop. It would happen so fast, neither one of them would know what happened.

Harper entered the lobby humming, a noticeable spring in her step as she walked across the floor.

"Well, someone certainly seems to be in a great mood this morning. And look at that updo, if I didn't know better I would ask if a certain young man has anything to do with this great mood," Myrtle said to Harper, causing Harper to blush as she smiled. She started to reply but was interrupted by Edward, who came bursting through the doors with his usual dramatic flair.

"Did Marly bring the clothes for the models? Where are they?" he demanded as he marched up to her desk and looked around, as if Myrtle was trying to hide them.

"Oh, hello, Edward. Perhaps if you asked me a bit nicer I would be more inclined to give you the answer to your question," Myrtle said, sounding like she was scolding a child.

Harper stifled a giggle.

"Oh fine," Edward replied in a huff, sighing loudly. "Good morning, Myrtle. You look stunning today. By any chance, would you happen to know if Marly is here with the clothes for the models for tomorrow's fashion show?"

Myrtle smiled approvingly and nodded her head.

"Well, yes, Edward, as a matter-of-fact she is with Veronica in her office right now. However, Gertie requested you leave them be so they can work everything out and have it all set up before you get involved."

Harper watched as Edward's face turned into a scowl.

"But, well I ..." he stammered.

"Eddie, I know you like to control things but ..."

Harper scurried out of the lobby, almost positive there was some bizarre flirty spark between the two of them. She was torn between wanting to watch the show, but also knowing she needed to get things underway to find out who the perp was.

She and Logan had gone around the building late

last night and ensured things were as they should be for the show, that nothing else had been altered. After that, they'd kept an eye on the runway in case the person tried to mess with it again. Whoever it was hadn't come back, and she and Logan had spent hours just talking. He'd lived an exciting life as a cop, he had so many stories. Harper loved listening to them all and had joked to him he should think about writing a book.

She headed towards Veronica's office, eager to see the outfits. When she'd first heard Gertie was working with Marly and Edward on a fashion line for wheel-chair-bound people she'd thought it was strange, but after Gertie explained things to her she'd felt a bit stupid for assuming all clothing was the same, aside from sizes.

She knocked on Veronica's door and entered her office, her eyes widening as she saw how the room had been transformed into a massive dressing room.

There were racks and racks of clothes, each rack had a name assigned to it, which Harper assumed was for the model who would wear the clothes on it. The clothing seemed to cover all styles: sporty, casual, elegant. From gowns to jeans and yoga pants, Harper could see them all neatly lined up.

Gertie was in the middle of the room, wearing a

gorgeous lavender top. The sleeves flowed loosely at the very top then tapered down towards the bottom. As she walked closer to her she could see the top had thin strips of silver woven into the material. It was stunning.

"What do you think, dear?" Gertie asked Harper, as she zipped around the room in her wheelchair, pulling out different styles and checking the material and sizing.

Harper wasn't sure how to answer her, was she asking about the clothes or her speed in the wheel-chair? Both were impressive as far as Harper was concerned! She opted to answer about the clothing.

"The blouse is gorgeous. I assume it's the sleeves that are tailored to be for wheelchair-bound people?" Harper asked.

"Yes! And the pants. See? They look like normal pants, but they have a special waistband and are cut a tad longer at the bottom, so they don't ride up. Only took about ten tries before these people got it right!" Gertie winked at Marly as she said it.

"Yes, it's been a challenge, but I think we finally nailed it, Gertie. Thanks to you." Marly looked exhausted. Harper knew it couldn't be easy to have been right in the middle of Gertie and Edward's design sessions as Marly had been.

Harper smiled, at the same time still worried someone might still be plotting to screw things up. She wasn't sure if she should say anything about what she and Logan had talked about the night before.

As if reading her mind, Veronica caught Harper's eye and shook her head subtly, as if to say to keep quiet. Harper wasn't sure that's what it meant at all but opted not to say anything, and, instead, thumbed through some of the designs on the racks.

"Okay, so, Harper, if you can take these down to the dressing area that would be great." Veronica motioned to a rack of clothes that was set aside. "Some of the models will be coming in and trying the clothes on today, so I'm trying to get as many outfits down there as I can."

Harper took the rack, wheeling it out of the office and taking the long way to the elevator, past Logan's office. As soon as she walked by and saw he wasn't inside she felt stupid. What was she doing? Acting like a high-school girl, that's what. She hurried down the hallway and got on the elevator, pressing the button inside for the lobby as she squeezed herself close to the door to avoid brushing up against the clothes.

The elevator dinged, and the doors whooshed open, and as she pushed the rack through the lobby she heard a familiar voice talking and she peeked over them, seeing her Uncle Tanner in the lobby.

"What are you doing here?" she asked him as she moved some of the clothes around on the rack to space them out more.

"I'm taking Gertie to a private breakfast to show her the new buffet setup at one of the restaurants, it's a new layout that's specific for wheelchair height. I'm trying to make things up to her ... you know. She's been asking about this for a while, no other restaurants have it! So, this is a great start, at least, I think it is."

Harper did know what he meant about making things up to Gertie.

"Yes, I think that is a great start," she said as she smiled at him, happy he seemed happy.

"Yes, well it's just minor really. I caused so much pain I need something really, really big to redeem myself."

Gertie wheeled into the lobby and Tanner's smile widened.

"You just missed Mr. Big Pants, he's in the men's room," Myrtle said to Gertie, referring to Edward.

Harper watched as Tanner's smile turned into a frown as soon as he figured out to whom Myrtle was referring. Both he and Edward were obviously smitten with Gertie, she thought it was kind of cute how they both fussed over her. At the same time, she thought Myrtle and Edward might have a little flirty thing going on, they were always bantering whenever she saw them together. Then again, that was Myrtle's style, she liked to be the boss up front and anyone who tried to mess with her, or Gertie, got an ear full.

"Oh, for crying out loud, why do you insist on hanging out around here?" Edward's voice boomed through the lobby, his question directed towards Tanner.

"I'm not hanging out. I'm consulting with Gertie on the changes I am making in my restaurants for handicap accessibility that goes above and beyond what everyone else does. It's a first in the restaurant world. What are you doing? Checking out the bathroom design?" Tanner asked, a smirk on his face.

"Ha! I'm creating an entire line of clothing with Gertie for people with disabilities! And it will be shipped worldwide!" Edward shot back, a triumphant look on his face.

Harper watched as Myrtle swiveled her head back and forth between the two men, as if she were watching a tennis match while they tried to best each other with who was doing more for Gertie.

"Boys, *Boys*!" Gertie clapped her hands loudly, like a

teacher would to a kindergarten class to grab their attention.

Harper took the opportunity to scoot off to the dressing rooms with the rack of clothes. She couldn't help giggling as she heard Gertie's words as she left the lobby. "There's enough of me to go around."

LOGAN WALKED DOWN THE HALLWAY, pausing in front of Harper's office. What was he doing? Embarrassed, he quickly walked away, shaking his head at himself. He needed to focus. He was trying to figure out who was sabotaging things and hanging outside Harper's office like a lovesick puppy wasn't going to help him.

He walked to Gertie's office and stepped inside. She wasn't in, or at least if she was, he couldn't see her amidst all the flowers. It was like a funeral home there were so many giant arrangements all over the place. The air was heavy with their perfumed scent, there were so many arrangements that some were on the floor as there was no more room on her desk or conference table.

He walked towards the window and moved one of the large flower sprays with his hand, so he could see out of it, his eyes catching the card in the flower. It was from Tanner. Out of curiosity he grabbed the arrangement to his left and looked at that card. It was from Edward. The one behind it was from Tanner. The one on the right from Edward. He laughed out loud, he could cross those two off his list of suspects. They would never hurt Gertie unless they were trying to kill her with flowers.

Looking down at the smoking area below he didn't see anyone out there smoking, and there didn't seem to be any cigarette butts laying around on the ground either. Gertie was so strict, maybe the smokers picked them up and threw them away every time they smoked? Then another thought struck him. Had Ben lied about that being the smoking area? Why would he do that?

He left Gertie's office and went farther down to one of the conference rooms, which was almost directly above the smoking area. There was a dumpster and an area a few feet away from it was littered with cigarette butts. Noah was there. As he watched, Noah bent over and stubbed his cigarette out on the ground. He must have just gone down for a quick smoke since he hadn't been there a minute ago when Logan was watching from Gertie's office.

Something moving behind the chain-link fence caught his attention and the tabby cat emerged from between the overrun weeds. He'd thought more than once about bringing the cat home with him, but he knew his landlord probably wouldn't like it. The old abandoned mill building loomed behind the fence. That was most likely where the cat lived. He knew the building had that rickety old water wheel inside it and didn't want the cat to get hurt. He watched as the cat scurried away. When he looked back towards the dumpster, Noah was gone.

He decided to check on the catwalk and see how they were progressing with setting it up outside. In theory, everyone had the right set of plans, but he wanted to ensure it was built the right way and wasn't at risk of collapsing again.

"Hey, guys, how's it going?" he asked as he approached the crew. Ben, Noah, and George all grumbled hello to him, none of them looking too thrilled to be there.

"It will be better once this thing is all set up. I'm sick of building it, taking it apart, building it again!" Noah whined as he grabbed a heavy piece of the metal support.

"Relax, we are almost done," George said, rolling his eyes at Logan.

"So, has it just been you guys that built it? I've only seen you three working on it any time I've been down in the basement and now out here. No wonder you're sick of it."

"Yep, just us lucky ducks," George said, pausing for a minute. "Well, Harper was around, too. Actually, she just brought a rack of clothes into one of the rooms set up as a dressing room."

Logan nodded his head as if he already knew Harper had been around them before, but inside, all he could ask himself was why.

12

Hurrying off the elevator Harper went straight to the break room, opening the fridge and grabbing some iced coffee. She poured some of it into a giant mug, thankful there was always a large carafe of it waiting for her in the fridge. She grabbed a straw from the gleaming stainless steel dispenser and headed to her office, sipping on the cool drink. After she'd dropped off the clothes downstairs she'd checked on a few other things and had found herself thinking again about the conversation she and Logan had the night before over their makeshift dinner, trying to figure out who was sabotaging things.

As she walked into her office she stopped for a minute and looked back at her door. Weird. She almost always left it closed when she wasn't inside. It was just a habit, but she was sure she'd shut it earlier. Then again, she had a lot on her mind so maybe she'd left it open. It didn't matter anyway, it wasn't like she was trying to hide anything.

She took another sip of her coffee and placed the mug on her desk, making a clinking sound against the glass. As she was leaning over to her side drawer she noticed something in her in-tray. Odd, because she could have sworn the tray was empty. She picked it up, squinting to see it.

Her heart froze.

The picture was black and white, and the quality was that of a very grainy printout. But she could see it well enough to know it was a picture of her, walking into the room where the lights had been stored. It must have been taken when she'd put the GoPro inside.

Someone had been watching her. And, whoever it was, wanted her to know it.

LOGAN LEFT the guys outside to finish setting up the runway. He wanted to investigate Ben further, but since he was busy he couldn't really hang around for too long without it being blatantly obvious he was checking up on someone. There was no way the runway could be altered now anyway, there were too many witnesses. So, if it was Ben who had messed around with it, it was at least safe, for now anyway.

He pulled open the heavy wooden door and walked towards the dressing room, wanting to see if Harper had discovered anything new since they'd spoken last night. He slowed his pace a bit after he entered the building and second-guessed his eagerness to keep Harper involved in the investigation.

Someone he'd cared about a lot had already gotten shot while working on an investigation with him, and he didn't want that to happen again. That person had been his partner and girlfriend. He hadn't been able to protect her, and it was something that would haunt him the rest of his life. He didn't want Harper getting hurt because of him.

At the same time, he knew Harper wouldn't stay away from the investigation until the person was caught. She wanted to redeem herself, and he sympathized with that. She'd clearly put herself out of her comfort zone to help capture the person, and he couldn't really say the same about himself. If anything, he'd stayed in his comfort zone, minimizing risks. He shook his head at himself, feeling like a coward. If Harper hadn't given him a little push he probably wouldn't be as far as he was now in the investigation. He picked up his pace. He'd do whatever he could to help Harper figure out who the culprit was, then he'd let her be the one who brought him—or her—down.

He caught a whiff of a familiar smell in the air and stopped walking and looked around. With all the construction going on the smell reminded him of a power tool that had been used too much, as if it were overheating. Except no one was working inside here, they were all outside. And it couldn't be coming from the kitchen, that's all the way at the end of the building. Strange.

As he walked closer to one of the dressing rooms, he sensed something was wrong. Turning the corner, he immediately smelled smoke. The dressing room door was closed, but he could see bright orange and red flames flicker from the gap at the bottom and a cloud of smoke pouring out.

His adrenalin kicked into high gear and he yelled, *"Fire!"*

13

Harper wrung her hands nervously as she stared at the grainy black-and-white picture of herself lying on her desk.

Whoop! Whoop! Whoop!

She jumped out of her chair, startled by the screeching of the fire alarm. Bolting out the door she instinctively ran down the hallway towards Gertie's office, yelling Gertie's name out as soon as she burst through her door. She had to push some of the vases of flowers out of the way to see if Gertie was behind her desk and craned her neck to look in the corners of the office. She didn't want Gertie trapped if there was a fire, but she didn't seem to be in there.

"Gertie!" she yelled again as she stood in the middle of her office, looking around.

"Harper! There you are! Let's go!" Veronica's voice echoed in the office, and Harper turned to see Veronica standing in the doorway, motioning with her hand to hurry up. "Gertie isn't back yet, let's go! I don't know what's going on, but I know this wasn't a planned test on the alarms!"

Harper ran quickly out of the room and down the stairs, right on the heels of Veronica. Had Veronica specifically come looking for her to make sure she got out? Maybe she'd won a few points with her by looking for Gertie as soon as the fire alarm had sounded. It was a small victory, but she would take it, it felt good to know that maybe things had turned a corner with Veronica.

She stopped suddenly as they rounded the last set of stairs, her heart lurching. What about Logan? She should go check his office!

"Come on!" Veronica yelled, grabbing her arm, and pulled her down the rest of the steps and out the side door as the fire alarm continued to wail inside. They hurriedly walked away from the building and towards the parking lot where the other employees were standing. In the distance she could hear the fire engines approaching, their sirens getting closer by the second.

"Veronica!"

Harper turned to see TJ rushing towards Veronica, the two of them hugged. She looked away, feeling lonely suddenly. She felt a bit jealous of TJ's obvious concern for Veronica, no one was worried about Harper making it out safely that was for sure. Well, Veronica had been, but she meant someone who would have the same lovey-dovey look in their eyes as TJ had right now.

"Are you okay? What's going on?" TJ asked, looking at the two of them as the fire engines roared into the parking lot and screeched to a halt near the building.

The firemen jumped out of the bright-red fire engines, and Harper watched as Logan ran up to them, seconds later they all raced into the building.

Everyone stood in silence for what seemed like hours, Harper finally breaking the silence.

"What the hell happened?" she asked out loud to no one in particular as they all stared at the building.

"There was a fire in a dressing room downstairs." They all turned to see Logan walking up to them from the side of the building, his clothes and face covered in soot. "Are you okay?" he asked Harper, reaching out and touching her arm. Harper nodded, taken aback by his genuine concern for her.

"Were you in the fire? Are you okay?" Harper asked him, brushing some of the black off his forehead.

"Yeah, I'm okay. I grabbed one of the fire extinguishers and was able to put the fire out, but not before it pretty much ruined everything in the room."

"This is horrible!" Marly cried, running around the parking lot like a mad woman, her hands in the air. "The clothes were all hand-sewn. We're going to have to work nonstop to get them made again for tomorrow! What a bad time for an accident!"

Harper, Logan, and Veronica all exchanged looks. Marly was right, it *was* bad timing, but it was also not an accident.

BIG T CROUCHED down in the overgrown grass across from the loading dock and patted the cat. After he'd helped that dimwit Logan put out the fire in the dressing room he'd come out of the building through the loading dock door and looked around for the cat. There was so much commotion going on he'd just wanted to make sure it was still okay and hadn't gotten hurt in all the hoopla.

The cat meowed as it rubbed up against his leg and lightly batted at Big T's arm which had a streak of soot. He rubbed it off and stood, watching as the cat ran through one of the holes in the chain-link fence, turning and looking at him before it scurried off, disappearing through the thick weeds. For a minute Big T felt as though the cat might be judging him, almost like it knew he'd been the one who set the fire. But that would be impossible, it was just a damn stray cat.

He walked to the parking lot and headed towards the huddle of employees. Marly was talking about how all the clothing was ruined by the fire and she didn't know how they would ever get them all made again by tomorrow's show. He struggled to force himself not to smile when he heard that. Mission accomplished, clothing ruined.

"What the heck is going on? Is everyone okay?" Gertie emerged, her face showing panic. Big T watched as she wheeled herself over to every employee, asking them if they were okay, grabbing their hands and patting them. When someone mentioned the clothing was ruined, she barked out she wasn't worried about the clothes, only about her family, the employees.

For a split second Big T felt a stab of remorse over what he was doing. No. Don't start getting soft and ruin what you've started, he told himself. Gertie was a wolf in sheep's clothing. Always making people think she was so kind. Well, he knew better. He knew something none of these people did. Gertie had done something bad in her past, and now she would pay for it.

Karma was a bitch.

14

The firemen started to trickle out the building, giving everyone the okay to go back inside. Apparently, there had been no structural damage as the room was mostly brick. It was pretty much only the clothing damaged from what Harper heard as she walked past the firemen who were talking to Gertie. She was insisting they stay for some food, telling them she would have the chef make something nice for them.

Logan had insisted on walking her back up to her office and Harper didn't mind. His protectiveness over her felt nice, it was comforting. Even though she knew the fire was over, she was still a little jittery, especially when she thought about the picture. Was there any relation between the person who left the picture on her desk and the fire? She assumed there was, and it scared her.

They entered her office and she walked over to her desk and reached for the picture, looking at it again to make sure she was right, and it was indeed her in the picture. Positive it was, she handed it to him without saying a word and sat in her chair.

"What's this?" he asked, squinting his eyes while holding the picture close to his face. "Wait a minute, is that you? Who took this?"

Harper could tell he was upset by his tone, it was more of a demand than a question.

"I have no idea. Whoever it was, left it on my desk earlier. Shortly before the fire."

"What? That's creepy." Logan looked disturbed. "This isn't good."

"Tell me about it."

"I think you should leave the snooping around and investigating to me from now on. Obviously, this person is on to you, and they are dangerous, they just tried to burn the place down, for crying out loud."

"What?" Harper asked, surprised at his reaction. "Of course I'm still going to investigate, don't be ridiculous."

"I'm serious, Harper. Leave it to the expert—me— to get this guy, okay?"

Harper couldn't believe what she was hearing. Only yesterday he was all about them being a "team" and working together to find the person. Now he wanted to just drop her and find the person himself. It reminded her of her ex-boyfriends: especially her ex-fiancé, always so eager in the beginning to work together then, *boom*! They want to do it on their own and she was left out, alone. Well, not this time. Logan wasn't her boss, even if he was "the expert."

"*The expert*, really? Well you might want to think again since this has gone on for a while, and your list of suspects is the same as mine. You've gotten no further in your "investigation" than I have! So, excuse me while I go do some work. I have an actual job to do here besides just "snooping around!"

With that, she stormed out of her office, leaving Logan staring at her open-mouthed.

She marched into the break room and grabbed a can of tuna from one of the cabinets, then took the back stairs to the loading dock. She'd started keeping a stash of tuna for that stray cat. Feeding it always gave her some comfort. Plus, she wanted to make sure it was okay after the fire.

She walked out of the stairwell into the basement and could see the area around where the fire had occurred was all taped off with bright-yellow caution tape. There were some policemen and another person standing there talking. She walked towards the loading dock area slowly, still looking back at where the fire had happened.

"Coming through!"

Harper turned to see Sarah, who was rushing towards her with a cart full of food in plastic containers. The food must have all been ruined in the fire! Wait. That wouldn't make sense. The fire had only happened in one of the dressing rooms, and the kitchen is located way down the mill at the opposite end of the building.

"What's that for?" she asked her, leaning over, and peering into one of the large containers.

"The giant walk-in fridge broke, and everything inside it spoiled. We've had to replace it all! That fridge was brand new, too!"

"Wait a minute, you started here already?" Harper asked, suddenly realizing Sarah wouldn't be doing this unless she'd gotten the job.

"Yes! Today, actually. Take it from me, don't ever get a job working with your boyfriend. Boy, was that a nightmare. I've only been here a few hours and I already know I made the right decision."

Harper nodded her head, recalling the previous conversation in the break room she'd had with Sarah about Raffe. It only made her feel stronger about keeping Logan at arm's length now, strictly on a professional level. Which kind of stunk, because there was no way the fridge breaking was a coincidence. Gertie bought brand-new equipment for the kitchen and made sure it was always maintained. Someone had messed with that fridge on purpose, and she would like to tell Logan about it. But, since he was the expert as he'd pointed out to her, he would just have to find that out on his own.

"Well, I'm glad you're here. I think you'll like it. I know you're in a hurry, so I'll let you go, but if you need anything just give me a yell."

"Thanks, Harper, I appreciate it." Sarah took off down the hallway towards the kitchen.

Harper continued down the hall and out the loading dock door, pulling the tuna can from her pocket. She peeled the top off and placed it on the ground, calling out to the cat as she looked around for it.

Behind her she heard the door open. *Crap!* She stepped in front of the can as she whirled around to see …

Veronica was standing in the doorway, her face registering surprise at seeing Harper as she quickly tried to hide something behind her back.

"What are you …" Veronica's voiced trailed off as she craned her neck to see what Harper was hiding.

"Are you …" Harper craned to see what Veronica was hiding.

Meow!

The cat jumped up onto the loading dock and greeted the two of them, rubbing up against both of their legs as if to say hello, then turning its attention to the open can of tuna behind Harper.

"Are you feeding the cat, too?" Harper figured with the way Veronica's face had lit up when she saw the cat, it was a sure bet that's why she was out here.

Veronica laughed and pulled a tuna can out from behind her back. "Guilty. I saw him my first day here and I've been feeding him ever since."

"I was worried something might have happened to him, you know, with the commotion from the fire and everything," Harper said as she watched Veronica lay down the second can of tuna.

"Me too. I'm even more worried about what's going to happen next. I think we can all say the fire was no accident."

"Yes, I agree that was no accident. But who could want to do all this? Whoever it is started it at Marly's reception. They obviously want to put Gertie out of business. What I can't figure out, is why?" Harper said, bending over to pick up the empty tuna can as the cat moved on to the next one.

"What do you mean, whoever it is started it at Marly's reception?" Veronica asked.

Harper hesitated for a minute, then explained about the lanterns at Marly's wedding. She knew by saying this she was opening herself up to more judgement by Veronica, since some of the things that had happened at Marly's reception were done by her and Tanner.

"Wow, and to think I assumed it had been your Uncle that pulled that stunt," Veronica said in an icy tone as she stared at Harper.

Harper's eyes dropped. She could feel her cheeks start to burn from embarrassment.

"Veronica, I'm sorry. I did do some of those things, too. My Uncle had totally convinced me to do them, and while it's no excuse, he's all I have for family. I felt like I should do whatever he said to help him. But I didn't do everything that happened. I absolutely did not move those luminaries! And, that's why I've been trying to figure out who is doing this. I want to right the wrong I did and catch this person." Harper couldn't resist the tears welling up as she spoke, she felt horrible and knew she'd probably just sealed her fate. Veronica would fire her for sure.

"It's okay. I get it, actually. I don't really have any family either." Veronica put her arm around Harper. Harper was shocked. "And I know about wanting to right wrongs, turning over a new leaf. Trust me. I've done some pretty crappy things in the past and I know people can change. I'm living proof!"

HARPER LOOKED at Veronica with new eyes. No longer did she see that hard-as-nails boss. She saw the vulnerability in her and felt a small bond forming.

"Thanks." She wanted to say so much more but didn't know how to form the words. Instead she tried to do one good deed. "There's something else."

"Oh?"

"Yeah, I just saw Sarah, TJ's sister, running around trying to make sure the food doesn't spoil. Apparently, there was some fridge incident."

"You think it was this person? The same one that messed around with the invitations?"

"Maybe."

Veronica sighed. "Okay, I'll go find Sarah."

Harper smiled as she watched her boss walk away. Since Veronica was in a consoling mood, she hoped that would spill over to Sarah. And if she could help bring Veronica and Sarah together, then at least something good would come of this whole mess.

She hurried back into the building. She wanted to do more than just bring people together, though. She wanted to stop the one person who was determined to ruin it all, never mind what the "big expert," Logan Carter, wanted. She could do this. And she didn't have much time.

15

Logan crouched down to pet the cat, who was licking his paws. There was a can of tuna on the ground, most likely left by Harper he assumed. He knew she was mad at him for telling her to stop playing Nancy Drew and trying to find whoever was sabotaging things, but he also didn't want her in any danger. The fact the person had left that picture on her desk was really telling. He'd seen a lot of sickos when he was a cop, and the ones who taunted people were the worst. There was no way he would let Harper get near this guy. Maybe he was being a little overprotective, but too bad, Harper was starting to become important to him and he wasn't about to let her get in harm's way.

He stood and looked around, thinking about how he was going to catch the person. He'd scanned the crowd in the parking lot when the fire happened, and George had been missing. It didn't necessarily mean he'd set the fire, Logan knew a few people had exited towards the back of the building during the alarm, and it was totally possible George was one of them. Harper had also mentioned Ben, he'd been in the parking lot. Then there was Noah, he'd been in the smoking area and seemed kind of sketchy.

George and Ben both had access to the room where the lights were, as well as the rooms where the runway had been staged, and the makeshift dressing rooms. But he'd done extensive background checks on them both, and for the most part, they were clean. Minor problems in their past, and they'd worked together before, but that wasn't unusual. Coworkers often recommend friends or people they worked with in the past to be hired. He'd noted each of them must have had hard times financially based on their addresses and poor credit scores. It even looked like each had been homeless for a while. But did that have anything to do with this case? Logan couldn't figure out how it could.

Maybe the dressing room was the best place to start. Maybe, whoever it was that had set the fire, had left a clue behind.

He made his way to the dressing room, lifting the yellow caution tape up so he could walk under it.

"Sorry, only authorized ... hey, Logan! Long time no see!"

Logan shook hands with the burly cop, someone he'd known for years back on the force. After some small talk he looked inside the room.

The brick walls were smattered with black soot. The ceiling was the original high exposed one with no ceiling tiles and just the metal ductwork. That had been good, because if everything had been wood or Sheetrock the place would have completely lit up and spread outside the room. Instead, it was just the clothes that had burned, their charred remains scattered all over the floor.

Gertie was already inside, barking orders at everyone. Logan chuckled because even the cops and the arson investigator were deferring to her.

He approached the arson investigator, someone else he knew from his past.

"Any idea how this started?" he asked, looking around at all the burned clothing and trying to make some sense of it.

"The only thing we found out of place was the remnant of a cigarette butt. Camel, non-filter. We think that's how the fire started, someone used it to light some cloth then tossed it aside."

Logan nodded his head slowly. He knew Ben and Noah smoked. Who else did? And what brand did they smoke? He needed to find that out, *now*.

***

BIG T WALKED SLOWLY DOWN the hospital corridor, the overhead fluorescent lights humming softly. The grey and white industrial tile floor pattern seemed to go on forever, the colors blending into the drab off-white walls. He hesitated before he opened the door to his mother's room, dreading what he was about to tell her.

The machines inside her hospital room whirred and beeped as usual, the constant noise having no effect on Big T's mother's sleep as she lay quietly in the bed. Her eyes opened as Big T sat in the chair next to her bed.

"Bad news, Mom. The DNA wasn't a match." He struggled to get the words out, knowing he'd failed her. He'd been positive they would have been a match. That this would have fixed everything and given his mom the kidney donor she needed.

His mother nodded her head a little, the tubes that carried oxygen into her nose moving slightly. "It's okay," she said softly.

"No! It's not okay, Mom. Our lives would be so much different if this hadn't happened to begin with."

"Don't think that way. She did what she had to, I don't hold any grudge against her. You should know that, I raised you better than to blame others for things going wrong in your life. It is what it is, dear, everything will be fine."

She closed her eyes after talking, as if it had taken so much energy to say the words that she needed to rest. It killed Big T to see her like this.

"I'm going to make things right, to make her pay for what she did. If it's the last thing I do, I will make things right!" he said, his face getting red from anger and his hand tightening into fists.

His mother opened her eyes and sat up a little, pointing her frail finger at him.

"I don't like the way you are talking! I know you have a lot of anger, but you need to let it go. Forgive. It is not good for you to carry around all this anger."

Big T knew he was upsetting her and settled back into his chair, reaching out for her hand.

"Sorry, Mom. I just wish things could be even."

"Be careful what you wish for." She squeezed his

hand lightly then closed her eyes, drifting off to sleep again. Big T stood slowly and left the room as quietly as he could, wondering if, maybe, he should follow her advice and let things be. Nah. Maybe his mom could forgive and forget, but he couldn't. He needed revenge, and he would get it. Besides, he was too smart for those dimwits at O'Rourke's. He knew Logan was a PI and he'd been putting cameras all over to monitor what's going on, but the joke was on him, everything was arranged to throw him way off track.

And tomorrow night, well, tomorrow night would be the perfect opportunity for him to finally get his revenge.

16

The next morning Logan's stomach was in knots. He hadn't been able to eat breakfast; his mind was too preoccupied, and he'd just wanted to get to the office, so he could nail the perp once and for all.

He knew whoever it was would likely choose to strike again tonight. They'd caused some damage with the fire, ruined some food with the fridge sabotage, tried to get the invitations sent to the wrong places, and sabotaged the runway. Yet, with all that, they still hadn't been successful in stopping the event. Whoever, was most likely pissed off at that fact and would be looking to cause some major problem to stop the show, they would be almost desperate at this point, and Logan needed to ensure that didn't happen.

He entered the bustling lobby and was greeted by

people rushing around, getting ready for the show that was to be held later that night. Myrtle was standing in the middle of it all, directing the various employees around as well as telling the delivery people where to go. She was dressed to the nines, wearing a cobalt-blue dress that made her cranberry-colored hair pop. Her familiar quirky glasses were perched on the end of her nose, this time the frames were turquoise and black, and the eyeglass chain consisted of matching colored beads on them. She caught Logan's eye and winked at him as he rushed past her.

"Looking more gorgeous than ever!" he threw out at her as he whisked by, catching the smile on her face as she heard him say it, then chastised a delivery boy who had flowers in his arms, reminding him not to crush the arrangement by holding it so close to his chest.

He rushed up the stairs, catching a glimpse of Harper and Veronica as they hurried past him with some clothing, neither one of them looking like they'd slept much. He knew Marly must have had her employees stay up all night to make new sets of clothing to replace what had been lost in the fire. As far as he knew it had been a total loss with the clothing, nothing could be saved.

He tried to catch Harper's eye as she quickly passed

by him, but he may as well have been invisible to her. She was mad at him and it sucked. He wished she realized he was just trying to keep her safe. Once this was all over maybe she would be more forgiving. He would make it up to her then, if she let him.

Walking by Gertie's office he overheard her bickering with Edward, who was trying to change some of the show even though it was starting in just a few hours. She was suggesting to him that maybe he go jump in the river to cool his jets, and that she had everything under control and needed to leave for some interview. Logan chuckled at her sense of humor and sassiness.

He went to his office and sat at the desk, eager to review the footage from the various cams he'd placed throughout the mill. He impatiently tapped his pen on his desk as he watched the footage then stopped, leaning forward to be closer to the monitor. Was that George? He was walking around the runway slowly, he seemed to be looking at it for some specific reason. But George didn't smoke, and Logan was pretty sure whoever was doing all this smoked. Then again, George had been the only one suspiciously missing when the building had been evacuated for the fire. Maybe George was trying to make it look like Ben was the perp when it had really been him all along.

Logan stood and headed downstairs. He needed to have a talk with them and check the final build of the runway to make sure it was safe and in no danger of collapsing tonight.

HARPER RAN around the building like she was on fire, checking all the various last-minute things before the show that evening. After taking the rest of the clothing downstairs with Veronica, she had double-checked every dressing room was set up correctly, then had gone back to her office to make some calls. She hung up the phone, happy she'd finished her calls to all the PR people. That was one more thing she could cross off her to-do list.

She hurried down to the kitchen to check on the food. She knew Sarah was an amazing chef, she'd heard nothing but positive reviews about her when she'd worked for Raffe at the restaurant. All the local food critics had given the restaurant the thumbs-up, and all had pointed out the unique menu items Sarah had created. It was just a formality for her to check the food, she had no doubt Sarah had it all handled.

Entering the kitchen through the heavy swinging doors she followed the sound of laughter to see

Veronica and Sarah standing by a tray of desserts. TJ was on the opposite side of the stainless steel table talking to them while moving his arms wildly in mid-story.

"Wow, those desserts look amazing!" She glanced down at the pastries. Miniature éclairs, brownie bites, and teeny cupcakes. "I just came down to make sure everything is all set for tonight. Can I do anything, do you need any help?"

TJ stepped in between Veronica and Sarah and put his arms around them, squeezing them both close towards him.

"I think my two girls have it all covered, Harper," he joked.

Harper noticed Veronica seemed thrilled with him calling them his two girls, but Sarah looked a bit annoyed. Veronica was giggling, and Sarah was just standing there, her smile looking forced.

"Actually, there is something you can do for me. Can you hunt Gertie down?" Veronica looked down at her watch. "She left almost three hours ago to do some interviews and I haven't seen her since. She should have come back by now."

"She's probably in her office, lost amongst all those flowers," Sarah chimed in, making everyone laugh.

"Sure, no problem, I'll go find her and I'll call you

when I hunt her down," Harper said, and left the trio in the kitchen to go back upstairs.

Her smile faded as soon as she was in the hallway. It wasn't like Gertie to run late, and especially not before an event. She remembered Gertie had not been too thrilled about this interview being on the same day as the show to begin with.

She pulled out her phone and called Gertie, hoping there was some reasonable answer why Veronica hadn't been able to get hold of her. Maybe Gertie had been too busy and found the phone calls annoying and shut her phone off. Harper knew she was grasping at straws, Gertie would never shut her phone off. The line rang several times and voicemail picked up. She called two more times. Still no answer. She had a strange feeling about this, and it wasn't a good one.

Harper knew whoever the saboteur was would definitely try to mess things up today, and that picture they'd left in her office proved they were creepy and wanted to scare people. She still had a strong suspicion it was Ben.

She turned towards the other end of the mill where the setup crew was. If Ben was there, which he should be, she wanted to see how he was acting. And if he wasn't there, well she would go tell Logan her suspicions and they would need to find Ben. She didn't really want to talk to Logan, but this was too important, she would swallow her pride if she had to.

She could see Noah as she approached the area, stacking chairs to be brought outside for the guests.

"Hi, Noah. Have you seen Ben around?" she asked him nonchalantly, not wanting him to sense any urgency.

"Yeah, he left a while ago." Noah eyed her up and down. "He's probably outside somewhere, I've been down here doing something for Gertie so don't really know what he's up to right now."

"Gertie? You know where she is?" Harper felt some relief Gertie was back and had been down here ordering people around. She remembered in certain areas of the basement cell phone reception was spotty so that would explain why she and Veronica hadn't been able to reach her when they'd tried. Now it all made sense!

"Sure, she's right over there."

Noah pointed towards one of the storage rooms that had been turned into a dressing room, and Harper hurried over to it.

"Gertie?" she called out as she knocked on the door, unsure why Gertie would be in the room with the door shut. She didn't need to be dressed for the show for a few hours still.

She knocked again, trying the door handle as she did and opening the door slowly. She stepped inside the dark room and yelled out Gertie's name again as she took a few steps inside, asking herself what the heck Gertie would be doing in a dark dressing room. The ceiling fan whirred high above her, making a whooshing sound in the otherwise quiet room. Gertie wasn't in here. Noah must have been wrong about which room she'd gone into. Harper turned around to leave the room.

"Hey, Noah, she's not—" Before she could finish her sentence, her head exploded in pain and everything faded to black.

17

Logan crawled out from underneath the runway and stood, brushing off his pants. He'd spent almost three hours checking to ensure it was safe and was now sure it was. He hadn't planned on it taking that long to check, but it was so big and had so many areas that could be messed with he'd had no choice but to go over every inch of it.

The place was abuzz around him with everyone getting the area ready for the show. The wait staff were placing the crisp linens over the various tables scattered around to hold the food and swag bags. There were some people placing flowers all over the place, and another person was carving an ice sculpture for the middle of where the buffet was to be set up.

The maintenance crew was hard at work setting up and wiping down all the chairs as well as setting up the outdoor bars for the after-party. Logan scanned the whole area intently, looking for any signs of something, or someone, that looked out of sorts. He didn't see anything unusual, which made him even more suspicious and on high alert.

He decided to go find Ben, to see if he could figure out what kind of cigarettes he smoked. He also wanted to speak to George and find out where he'd been when the fire started. He figured the two of them would be working together today. Hmm, could they both be in on this together? He hadn't thought about the possibility of two people working together to do these things, but anything was possible.

Veronica interrupted his train of thought as she yelled his name from down the hallway and hurried over to him, a worried look on her face.

"Have you figured out who it is yet? Have you seen anything?" she asked him in a low tone, looking around as she did so.

"Nothing yet. I did check out the runway, and it's safe. So, no worries there at least."

"That's good." Veronica didn't sound as happy as Logan assumed she would be.

"It took almost three hours to do it."

"I'm sorry, I mean that is great. Really. I'm nervous about this person doing something really crazy today, and to make things even worse, I can't find Gertie. She left for an interview hours ago and I haven't been able to get hold of her since. It's totally not like her to just disappear on me."

Logan ran his hands through his thick dark hair. Veronica was right, Gertie going MIA was completely out of character. He knew Gertie liked to be on top of things here, and that usually meant she was always hovering around.

"Where have you checked for her?" He took his phone out and called Gertie.

"Well, I called and texted her a bunch of times, looked in her office, asked Myrtle if she'd seen her and told her to keep an eye out for her. Oh, and I asked Harper to go look for her. Wait. That was over an hour ago and I haven't heard back from her, either."

Logan put his phone back in his pocket, his call to Gertie going to her voicemail. Learning both women were missing told him something was really wrong. He didn't want Veronica to know he now considered both Gertie and Harper might be in danger, that would only cause her to panic.

"I'm sure they are both fine, maybe Harper found Gertie and they are just in the middle of something for the show. You know how Gertie gets when she is busy, so focused she doesn't want to be disturbed."

"Yeah, I guess. But—"

"I know you have a ton to do right now. I will take care of finding them, okay? I'll check back with you as soon as I do," Logan said to Veronica reassuringly, relieved when she agreed with him and went on her way.

He immediately rushed to the back of the building where the runway was, hoping to catch the setup crew. He knew Noah, Ben, and George were all involved with setting things up, and he also knew one of them had to be in on whatever was going down. This guessing game would end right now, he was determined to find out who was causing all the problems. And Ben was first on his list.

"You okay? Looks like something's wrong, with the way you just rushed in here. There's not another fire is there?"

Logan turned to see Noah looking at him, holding one of the dozens of chairs he was setting out for the guests. He didn't want to blow his cover, so he took a deep breath and tried to think fast.

"Nah, nothing's wrong. I'm just trying to get

through checking all the computers, to make sure they are all set for the show."

"Yeah, sorry, I can't help you with that. I don't know jack about computers."

"It's good, I'm almost done anyway. I was craving a cigarette and came out here because I thought Ben might be here. He smokes Camels, right? Non-filters? I left mine in my car I guess."

Noah looked at him, his eyes narrowing as if he were trying to remember.

"Yeah, I think he does smoke those. Actually, he's over there smoking right now I think." He jerked his head towards the smoking area.

Logan thanked him and left, picking his pace up to get to the smoking area. He could see Ben and George standing and talking, each of them smoking. He paused for a moment just to watch them, neither one seemed to be in a rush or in fear of being watched. They weren't standing close to each other and whispering or looking around cautiously. They looked like two employees taking a smoke break.

As he approached the two of them they turned quickly towards him, both with guilty looks on their faces and exchanging glances quickly. Logan could tell they'd been talking about something they didn't want him to overhear.

"How's everything going?" he asked them.

"Good. We're just taking a quick break and will be back to setting up again in five minutes," George replied quickly, taking a long drag on his cigarette afterwards.

"Don't worry, I'm not here to babysit you two. But I do have a question I need answered." Logan looked directly at Ben as he spoke, his eyes staring intently and not blinking once. He'd learned to do this when he was a cop, it always seemed to help get the importance of what he was about to say across.

Ben shifted uncomfortably, and Logan leaned in closer towards him, still not breaking eye contact.

"Why did you lie?"

"Huh? What are you talking about, what did I lie about?" Ben looked at George and shrugged his shoulders.

"The other day, when I saw you walking away from the alley you told me you had been smoking over there, but that's on the other side of the building. The smoking area is here, obviously." Logan took in the body language of Ben and George as he said this, noting they both exchanged nervous glances and shifted on their feet.

"Is that a Camel non-filter?" Logan asked, pointing to the cigarette in Ben's hand.

"Yeah, so?" Ben replied as he held the cigarette up and looked at it.

"So? So where were you when the fire started?" Logan asked him.

"What? Why would you ask me that? Who do you think you are, a cop?" Ben asked in an annoyed tone, standing up a little straighter than he'd been.

"Why were you in the staging room the other night? And where were you coming from the day I saw you out on the loading dock?"

"What are you trying to get at?" George asked gruffly.

"What I'm getting at is your buddy Ben here has been screwing around with things, causing issues for Gertie. And, you might be doing it too. In fact, you were the only one not accounted for during the fire."

Logan nodded his head as he saw them both move nervously after he made his statement, the two of them looking at each other.

"That's right, I'd be nervous too if I were you. And, if you know what's good for you, you'll spill the beans right now and tell me what's going on. If you speak up now I can help you both, otherwise, all bets are off and you're on your own." Logan stepped closer to them as he said this, and he could sense their panic. Their facial expressions gave them away.

"Okay! Alright already! I lied about smoking that day. Yes, I smoke. But that's not where I had been coming from when I saw you. I was feeding the homeless. I sneak food to them," Ben said.

"What?" Logan asked incredulously, not prepared for the explanation Ben had just given him.

"Uh yeah, that's also why I wasn't around when the fire alarms went off that day. I was taking food to them. The homeless people, I mean," George chimed in.

Logan stared at the two of them, at a loss for words.

"We sneak the food out of the kitchen. That's where I was when the fire started, the kitchen. I was getting it together to give to George. We only use the food that's going to be thrown away, though. We didn't think anyone would mind, but if it's that big of a deal then—"

"You were in the kitchen when the fire started?" Logan asked as he cut Ben off.

"Yes. You can ask that new chef lady, Sarah, if you don't believe me. She was helping me out because her brother was homeless before and she knows how hard they have it."

"Does anyone else here smoke Camel non-filters?" Logan asked. He'd already determined after years of questioning suspects these two weren't guilty of anything aside from feeding the homeless.

"Um, what? I'm not sure. Not too many people that work here smoke besides us two. One of the servers, Christina, does, but she smokes those long brown cigarette things," Ben said, making a face.

"What about Noah?" Logan asked.

"No, Noah doesn't smoke," they both said in unison.

"I'm pretty sure I saw him out here before, though." Logan looked back and forth between Ben and George.

They both shrugged, and Ben tossed his cigarette down, grinding it out with his heel.

"Well he's never joined us to smoke. As far as I know, he doesn't smoke at all. And we see him a lot during the day. So, are we in trouble for the food, we will cover the cost."

Logan wasn't hearing a word Ben was saying, he was too busy putting new clues together. Ben had just stubbed out his cigarette with his foot. Like everyone else who smoked did. Yet, when he'd seen Noah the other day, he'd been leaning over to put his cigarette out with his hands. Except that wasn't what he'd been doing, that's what Logan had *assumed* he'd been doing.

What he'd really been doing was picking one up.

He'd picked up one of Ben's cigarette butts and there could only be one reason for him to do that. He wanted to frame Ben for the fire. And there's only one reason he would want to do *that*. Noah had been the culprit all along.

18

Harper opened her eyes slowly, the back of her head throbbing. She felt groggy, and when she went to rub her head she found she couldn't move her arms. As she became more alert she soon realized she was taped to an old wooden dolly, unable to move her arms or legs.

Looking around she could tell she was in an old mill. Where the mill was, she wasn't sure. It wasn't O'Rourke's. The inside was a large wide-open space and had deteriorated badly. There were windows that had broken through the years, allowing the outside elements access to the inside. Some of the wood had rotted because of this, and there were weeds growing in random cracks in the floor. The large windows were fogged with dirt built up over the years, a few of them cracked and others had holes in them.

She told herself not to panic and tried to remember what had happened before she'd passed out. Work. She'd been at work, downstairs in the basement. Looking for Gertie.

She suddenly heard some movement towards her side and jerked her head as far as she could to try to see what it was, barely making out a dark shadow walking towards her. She could tell it was a person.

"Why are you doing this, Ben?" she asked loudly, refusing to let her fear come through in her voice, even though she was scared.

A male's laughter echoed throughout the large open space, making her head pound even more.

"Ben? Is that who you think is behind all this? That's the best news I've heard all day! That means my plan worked. Let's just hope that nosy IT moron thinks it's Ben, too."

Harper was too shocked to say anything, immediately recognizing the voice.

It wasn't Ben, it was Noah.

She slowly started to piece together the clues from the past few days. Looking back, she realized she should have known it was him all along. Noah had been the one with the blueprints the day she'd seen he and the others downstairs. And he also had access to the computers and could have generated new plans for the runway to be reconfigured. He'd done plans for the inventory and if he knew how to do that, then he could have accessed all the files. He'd played dumb when she asked, but of course he would if he were the culprit.

"Why are you trying to ruin Gertie's business? What did she ever do to you? And what do I have to do with any of this?" She watched as he paced around aimlessly.

"I did it because that old bat deserves to be ruined. She's a horrible person and now there's no hope for my mom. Gertie's gonna pay for it. And you? You snooped around too much. With your stupid GoPro and your stupid questions. And trying to find her, why do you care so much about her anyway? If you had just minded your own business, you wouldn't be here. But instead you got in my way."

Harper had no idea what he was talking about. He sounded unhinged, and judging by his frantic pacing, he was at his wit's end. Maybe he was delusional. What did his mother even have to do with anything? She immediately thought the worst for Gertie and knew she needed to get herself free, so she could find her. Hopefully, Logan was looking for her, maybe he'd already figured out it was Noah that had been doing the sabotage all along. She looked around again, realizing wherever she was it wasn't at work. How would Logan even know where to find her?

"What do you mean, there's no hope for your mom?" she asked him, wriggling her wrists behind her, and trying to get them out of the duct tape while keeping him busy talking about his mom.

"My mom is sick. Real sick. She's been in the hospital for months. She needs a transplant."

Harper feigned sadness, trying to sympathize with him.

"Oh no! That's horrible. But, what does that have to do with Gertie? Does your mom know her?" Harper was still clueless where this was heading. She knew Gertie didn't have any kids, and she'd never really talked about any family either. She'd always referred to the employees as her family. Clearly, Noah was nuts. He'd always seemed normal to her when she'd dealt with him at work, but it hadn't been very often.

"Ha! She never told you, huh? Wow, what a shocker. Yeah, she was always ashamed of us. But that's gonna change. I'm gonna show her. She's about to see what it feels like to wish you were dead. It's been a long time coming! You wanna watch?"

Harper tried not to look horrified as she looked at

him, sweat dripping from his hairline onto his forehead. Was he really talking about killing Gertie?

"Err, no I don't want to watch. Are you saying Gertie is your—"

"Grandmother. Yep, she's my grandmother who abandoned us, and now my mom is gonna die. And none of this would be happening if Gertie had stepped up. You guys all act like she's this nice old lady, and she isn't. She's a bad person who threw my mom away when she was a baby like she was a piece of trash."

"I'm still a bit confused, Noah, but I know if my mom was still alive I would be at the hospital with her, not kidnapping people! She needs you, doesn't she? What if something happens to her and you aren't there?"

"You don't know what you're talking about, Red! I can't help her! Don't you get it?!" Noah yelled, obviously irritated as he kicked at a piece of wood on the floor, sending it skittering across the room, the noise echoing eerily throughout the mill.

Harper didn't get it, but she wasn't about to tell him that. At least not how she wanted to, which was by whacking him like he'd done to her. Noah was a big guy and she knew she couldn't take him.

"Why can't you help her?"

"My mom needs a kidney, and I'm not a match."

Harper still couldn't piece together what this had to do with Gertie. Was Gertie really Noah's grandmother? How was that even possible? He must be delusional, and this was some story he'd made up in his mind. Despite how crazy it all was, Harper realized this could be her ticket to freedom if she played her cards right.

"Hey, wait a minute. If Gertie is your grandmother then she could donate a kidney, couldn't she? She would be a match, right? I'm sure she would do it! She likes me, and I can talk her into it if she isn't sure. But we need to hurry, I'm sure time is really critical for your mom."

Noah stared at her, his big arms crossed at his chest. He was such a big guy, and Harper had no idea how she could get away from someone who probably weighed twice as much as she did. She might be able to outrun him, but she also knew Gertie was in this mill somewhere and she couldn't leave her here with this nutjob.

"You think she would listen to you, huh?" he asked her, staring at her intently.

"Yes! She would listen to me! But, she would be mad if she saw me like this. She isn't going to focus on what I'm saying if I am tied up. So, let me go, and let's take care of this."

19

Logan stormed into Gertie's office calling out her name. He weaved through the array of flowers and plants that had been sent to her and made his way to the window, looking below to see if she or Harper were outside. His instincts told him Noah had them both. He still didn't know the reason why, but he was positive it was Noah who had been causing all the problems.

As he rushed out of the office he ran into Tanner.

"Is she here? I have been calling her for hours!" Tanner brushed by Logan and stepped into Gertie's office, making a face at all the flowers inside.

"No. Have you talked to her at all since she left this morning, did she call you after she left?" Logan watched Tanner's facial expression when he realized

Gertie wasn't there. He knew something was wrong, Logan could see it on his face.

"What is going on? Harper has been telling me someone was sabotaging things, are she and Gertie okay? Where are they?"

Logan hesitated to tell Tanner the truth. He didn't want to assume Tanner could help him out with this. He knew he'd caused problems before for Gertie, but he also knew he'd tried to fix what he'd done. And, he knew he loved his niece, Harper. He was also pretty sure he had a thing for Gertie too.

"Logan, I know every trick in the book when it comes to trying to ruin a business. If something's going on, I might be able to help you," Tanner said.

Logan explained to Tanner everything he knew as they walked downstairs to the basement area. They weaved their way around the storage rooms and hallways and ended up on the loading dock, with no sign of Noah or the two women.

"So, right now we need to figure out where Noah could be, and hopefully that will lead us to Gertie and Harper," Logan said, looking around the empty loading dock.

Meow!

The cat jumped up onto the loading dock and

trotted over to him, winding itself between his legs as it purred.

"Sorry, buddy, I don't have time to feed you now," Logan said absently. The cat jumped back down and scurried through the hole under the fence, trotting towards the decrepit old mill that loomed in the background.

Logan watched it weave through the grass towards the abandoned mill. He started to feel uneasy, his instincts kicking in.

"Is that mill abandoned?" Tanner asked Logan.

"Yep."

"Oh no." They broke into a jog after the cat.

Logan shivered as he remembered the last time he'd been inside that building, back when he was on the force. It was isolated, and no one could hear what was going on inside. He recalled the creepy water wheel, the water still inside the building. That building was dangerous in more ways than one.

20

Big T paced around the old abandoned mill, second-guessing his decision. He'd been so focused on himself being the only person who could donate a kidney to his mom, he hadn't even thought about Gertie being able to do it. Of course, Gertie could donate her kidney, it was her own daughter that needed the kidney, they had to be a match!

But what if Gertie refused to donate? She wouldn't refuse. Now that Harper knew about it, of course Gertie would donate, she wouldn't want anyone thinking she was a horrible person! Besides, what Harper had said was true, Gertie liked her. She could probably talk the old woman into donating her kidney. Things had finally fallen into place for him! He would make sure his mom got the kidney now, no matter what. Things were looking up!

He ran over to Harper and moved swiftly behind her, grabbing at the duct tape on her wrists and tearing it off, then did the same with the tape around her legs and upper body.

"Follow me!" he yelled at her as he ran across the large room then went to the right, heading off through a wide opening.

The room had a giant water wheel inside, which had seen better years. It was made of wood and run by huge mechanical metal gears that were now rusty and looked as though they would break in half at any moment.

Big T's heart lurched as he looked at the giant wheel. He'd balanced Gertie's wheelchair on one of the huge paddles. His intent had been to make the old bat suffer, to sit and look helplessly at the dark water below her, and not be able to get away. But the wheel-chair now sat empty. They were too late; either she'd jumped or fallen into the water below.

"What have you done?" Harper screeched.

"Hey! Is someone up there? Get me out of here! Noah Timmons!"

Harper and Big T looked at each other with their mouths wide open then ran to the edge of the water wheel where the water was. About ten feet down in the black water was Gertie, floating around and looking up at them.

"What the hell is wrong with you people? I have a show to run! Get me out of here, now!"

"Gertie, you're alive!" Harper yelled excitedly.

Big T, or Noah Timmons, as Gertie called him watched as Gertie bobbed around in the murky water below them, amazed at the woman's feistiness. He'd just wanted to make her pay for all the years of misery he and his mom had endured. Hopefully, she wouldn't hold that against his mom now.

He could see Harper walking closer to him from the corner of his eye, shouldn't she be trying to help with getting Gertie out? This wasn't a time to mess around, he'd let her go so she could help. He turned towards her to remind her what they should be doing.

Thwack!

Sparks flew inside his head and the cold wooden floor rushed up to greet him as everything faded to black.

HARPER DROPPED the giant piece of old rusty metal she'd just hit Noah over the head with and rushed over to the hole to save Gertie. She glanced back over at Noah, unsure if she'd hit him too hard and possibly killed him. She couldn't see his chest moving. Was he dead? She didn't want to kill him, she just needed to disable him, so she could help Gertie. Whether Gertie was his grandmother or not, the guy needed some serious therapy!

"*Hello!* Is someone going to help me out of here or not!" Gertie yelled out in an agitated tone.

"I'm coming, Gertie!"

"Get my chair first! Don't let it fall into the water for crying out loud! That chair was custom-made just for me!"

Harper struggled with the wheelchair that was teetering on one of the massive paddles, being careful not to have it, or herself, go tumbling into the water below. Gertie continued yelling instructions at her, her arms flailing around. The old woman really was a piece of work!

She moved to the back of the wheel and slowly turned it by leaning on each paddle until the wheelchair reached her and she could safely remove it. She pulled it towards her and pushed it off to the side then ran over to the hole where Gertie was. She laid down on her stomach and stuck her hand down for Gertie to grab.

"Here, try to grab my arm!" she yelled down, realizing that getting Gertie out of the hole was going to be much more difficult then she'd thought. Her arm wasn't long enough to reach Gertie.

"Hold it right there!"

Harper shrieked and jumped up on her feet, holding her hands up in the air as she turned around. It was Logan and Tanner, both of whom immediately ran over to her.

"Oh, for crying out loud!" Gertie's voice drifted up from the hole.

"Are you okay?" Logan asked Harper as he looked around. "Where is Gertie? I hear her but don't see her anywhere?"

"Gertie!" Tanner yelled, looking around the room with a panic-stricken expression on his face.

"I'm down here, are you all deaf? Get me out!"

Logan and Tanner peered over the edge of the hole, Tanner started rolling up his sleeves. They worked together to maneuver Gertie up and out of the hole, Tanner taking the lead and holding her in his arms as she dripped water all over him and the floor.

"Put me down!" Gertie scolded Tanner, beating at him lightly with her fists. "Put me in my chair, I don't need to be carried like a child!"

Tanner carefully placed Gertie in her wheelchair

and she looked over at Noah, who was still lying on the ground motionless.

"What's with him?" she asked.

"Well, that's kind of a long story, Gertie," Harper said, hesitant and unsure of what to say to her.

"Well, can you give me the short version? I have a show I need to run," Gertie snapped back impatiently as she wrung the water out of her long silver hair.

"Short version. Right. Well, the short version is the guy lying on the floor, Noah, says you are his grandmother. His mother needs a kidney and for some reason he is blaming you."

Harper explained to everyone what had happened while Logan walked over and felt Noah's wrist for a pulse.

"He's still alive," he said, looking at Gertie along with everyone else.

"What? Why are you all gawking at me? Okay, okay, for crying out loud. I had a child when I was younger. Too young, to be honest. My parents said I couldn't take care of a kid and they took her away from me, and that was that," Gertie said matter-of-factly, as everyone's jaw dropped, and they continued to stare at her.

"But I thought you said you didn't have any kids?" Harper asked her.

"No, dear, I said I never *raised* any kids. There's a difference." Gertie looked over at Noah and continued, her tone softening. "You see, I tried to find my daughter, but my parents had set up the adoption as a closed one. No one would give me any information on my own daughter! I even hired detectives to find her, but they always came up empty-handed. I'm sure she felt abandoned her whole life. And now you say this is her son, my grandson? He was a sweet kid when I interviewed him, seemed quiet to me. He was talking about karma when he did this to me and I couldn't figure it out. Now I guess it makes sense."

Harper watched Gertie look at Noah lovingly. Most people would be mad after what he'd just done, but not Gertie.

"Poor kid. He did all this baloney for his mother. She's raised a good kid, I mean underneath all that anger and bitterness, but can you blame him for being like that? When he interviewed here with me he told me he'd had a tough life. Big kid too, huh? He said they called him Big T because of his size and last name. Well, I better get a move on. If what you've said is true, Harper, then I have a kidney to donate and a daughter to reconnect with!"

The group looked at each other, confused.

"What about the show?" Harper asked.

"What?! *No!* Gertie you can't donate your kidney! You need to rest immediately after this ordeal. You're fragile and—" Tanner snapped his mouth shut when Gertie cut him off.

"Fragile?! I'm no more fragile than any of you! And this is my daughter! I can't change what happened all those years ago, but I can try to make up for it!"

"You're right, Gertie, you aren't fragile. That's why I would like to see if I'm a match to donate my kidney instead. I have some making up to do too, you know," Tanner said.

"Okay, everyone, slow down for a minute," Harper said. "First, I think we need to call the cops." She looked at Gertie as she said this, unsure Gertie would approve. Despite trying to burn her business down and kidnap people, Noah was Gertie's grandson, and she wasn't positive Gertie would press charges against him.

"Why are you looking at me? He's going to have to answer to the police about what he did, to take responsibility. Just because he's my grandson it doesn't mean it's okay he hurt other people!" She wheeled herself over to where Noah was still lying unconsciously and watched him for a minute. "Go ahead, dear, call the police. And everyone else, move it! We have a show to put on!"

"Can I go now?" Harper asked the policeman as she looked around at all the activity in the abandoned mill. He'd been taking her statement for what seemed like hours. She was grateful Logan had stayed by her side, he knew the cop, and that had made things go much smoother, especially as they'd wanted everyone to go down to the station to be questioned. Harper didn't have time for that!

The cop nodded his head as he continued to make notes in his pad, and Harper looked over at Gertie who was talking quietly with Noah. He'd come to, and immediately been placed under arrest, but Gertie had insisted she be able to speak with him before they hauled him away.

Uncle Tanner was on the phone with the hospital,

trying to see how quickly he could get tested to see if he was a match to donate a kidney, even though Gertie was still insisting she be the one to donate. Harper didn't have the energy to grab the phone away from him and stop him, besides, she had a fashion show that still had to happen tonight. What were the odds he'd be a match, anyway?

"Ready?" Logan reached his arm out to her, grabbing her hand. Harper felt butterflies in her stomach and decided to let them be, instead of chasing them away. Who knew what would have happened if Logan hadn't come looking for her and Gertie? Maybe it was time for her to take down the wall she'd built up.

"Yes, let's just wait for Gertie," she said to him, squeezing his hand. "By the way, thanks for saving us."

"Well, if you two can break this lovefest up I'd like to get the heck out of here. Harper, we need to clean up and get this fashion show underway!" Gertie said, grabbing Harper's other hand, and squeezing it as she gave both Logan and her a wink.

They all went next door, Logan maneuvering Gertie's wheelchair through the overgrown brush and into the parking lot of O'Rourke's. It was late afternoon, and guests were already starting to arrive.

"Take me in through the rear doors, dear," she said,

pointing towards the back of the building as Logan rushed along pushing her.

They entered through the rear door, which brought them to the basement area abuzz with activity. The models were rushing around, their clothing looking stunning in different styles and colors.

"GERTIE!" Veronica screamed, running towards the trio. "I've been worried sick about you! All of you!" she exclaimed. "Where the hell have you all been?"

"It's a long story, dear, I can explain later," Gertie said, looking around.

"Wait, are you wet?" TJ asked as he approached them all, a confused look on his face.

"Guys, we can explain later what happened. Right now, we need to get Gertie changed for the show!" Harper said.

"Bring her in there," Veronica said, pointing to one of the dressing rooms. "I'll go get her clothes upstairs."

Harper wheeled Gertie into one of the dressing rooms, where some makeup artists were waiting and rushed over to her. Veronica backed away as Gertie started to swat at the makeup people trying to dote on her.

"Watch it! Just a dab of some lipstick and powder

my face, that's all I need! I don't want to look like a clown for crying out loud!"

Harper stepped back and turned to leave, wanting to give Gertie some privacy to change, as well as needing to go get herself cleaned up and help run the show.

"Harper!"

Harper froze, Gertie's voice making her flinch. She turned around slowly to look at her.

"You did good, dearie." Gertie winked at her and gave her a grin.

Harper left the room almost floating on air, Logan waiting outside for her. She'd helped Gertie and there would be no more sabotage at O'Rourke's. As Logan grabbed her hand she welcomed the butterflies in her stomach again.

EPILOGUE

Two weeks later …

Harper watched the various blips on the hospital monitors nervously, the noises they made echoing throughout the room. Logan squeezed her hand, making her relax a bit. She was happy he was there with her, although she was still a little miffed about him wanting to kick her off the investigation. But she knew he'd done that to protect her, and after what had happened, he'd made a good point about not wanting her to get hurt.

"Stop worrying about me," Tanner said to her. "I feel great!"

Harper smiled as Uncle Tanner held his arms up as if in victory, the IV hooked into the back of his right hand swaying as he did so.

"There's my hero!" Gertie's voice sang as she wheeled herself into the hospital room grinning from ear to ear. It had turned out that due to some health issues she couldn't donate her kidney, but Tanner was indeed a match. Despite everyone telling him he didn't need to do it, Tanner had insisted Gertie's daughter, Lily, be given his kidney. The operation had gone smoothly, and so far, everyone was doing great.

"How's Noah?" Logan asked Gertie, who had now wheeled herself over to Tanner's bedside and was patting his hand. Harper noticed Tanner had the same lovestruck look in his eyes as Veronica and TJ usually did.

"He's good, dear. I'm getting him some help, you know, he needs some therapy, mentally. The poor kid just made assumptions his whole life about me. Same with his mom. All he ever wanted was for me to acknowledge I had a grandson, and hell, I didn't even know I had one! He never knew I had tried to find them. It's all good now though, thanks to Tanner, my beautiful daughter, Lily, has a new lease on life and Noah will get some help!"

Harper's heart swelled to see Gertie so happy, and Uncle Tanner, too. In fact, she hadn't seen him so happy since before Aunt Emily had died.

"I've seen enough flower arrangements to last me a

lifetime!" a voice said from the doorway, their face hidden by a huge arrangement.

It was TJ, flanked by Sarah and Veronica. Everyone laughed, knowing he was referring to Gertie's office that had been filled with so many arrangements. Harper was surprised to see them but assumed with the end result of things they must have forgiven Tanner. His grand gesture to give up a kidney for someone he didn't even know had redeemed him for sure.

Harper watched as everyone chatted, TJ and Veronica holding hands, and Veronica practically gushing when she looked at him. Sarah, on the other hand, didn't seem very happy. Not that she seemed upset to be there, there was just a general sadness about her, as if her mind was preoccupied.

"Gertie, we received a big delivery today of cat food. Do you know anything about that?" Veronica asked Gertie.

"Oh yes, dear. That stray cat that's been hanging out by the loading dock, have any of you seen it?"

Harper exchanged looks with Logan and Veronica.

"Right, that's what I thought. Anyway, I'm officially adopting the cat as O'Rourke Signature Events mascot. I'm naming him Kidney."

Everyone burst into laughter as Gertie said the cat's name.

"Well, I wanted to come give you the good news in person but it sounds like you're already in a great mood!" Marly said as she walked into the room.

"What good news?" Gertie and Harper asked in unison.

"The fashion show was a huge success. The buyers at the show have all placed orders. Big ones! The disabled clothing line is going to make Draconia even more profitable thanks to you, Gertie. Now, I just hope this news lifts Edwards spirits, he's been a bit grumpy since Tanner's been getting so much attention from you!"

"Pfft. Edward needs someone to take him down a peg. He fought me every day about the damn designs for these clothes, if I had just let him go with his ideas it would have been a huge flop," Gertie said.

"Oh, Eddie will be fine. Besides, it isn't like he can one-up Tanner with what he did, giving his kidney and all," Myrtle said as she stood in the doorway. "Besides, I plan on keeping him plenty busy, now I've been promoted to Gertie's right-hand assistant."

Wearing a canary-yellow blouse and matching colored beads for her glasses, Myrtle certainly stood out against the drab off-white-colored walls in the hospital room. While her choice in clothing, and beads, were always rather eccentric, Myrtle always pulled it off, looking fashionable and never gaudy. Harper loved her sense of style and plucky attitude, as did everyone else.

TJ and Veronica excused themselves, needing to get back to the office. Harper knew she should get back, too, but she didn't want to leave Tanner. That, and she really didn't want to let go of Logan's hand.

She caught Sarah looking down at the two of them holding hands and felt a pang of guilt. She knew Sarah and Raffe hadn't spoken in a while, even though Sarah's food at the fashion show had been written up in several papers as a standout. Harper wasn't sure if Raffe was mad that Sarah had left working for him, or mad she was doing so well, or maybe he was mad at both.

"Ah, well, I see I was right," Myrtle said to Harper.

"Huh? Right about what?" Harper asked her, oblivious to what she was talking about.

Myrtle looked down at Logan and Harper's hands clasped together, then back at Harper.

She winked at her, a broad smile on her face.

"Like I said to you before, be careful what you wish for."

****

Join my email list and receive emails about my latest book releases - don't miss out on early release discount on the next book in this series: http://www.leighanndobbs.com/leighann-dobbs-romantic-comedy/

If you want to receive a text message on your cell phone for new releases, text ROMANCE to 88202 (sorry, this only works for US cell phones!)

Join my Facebook Readers group and get special content and the inside scoop on my books: https://www.facebook.com/groups/ldobbsreaders

OTHER BOOKS IN THIS SERIES:

In Over Her Head (book 1)
Can't Stand the Heat (book 2)
What Goes Around Comes Around (book 3)
Careful What You Wish For (4)

ALSO BY LEIGHANN DOBBS

Contemporary Romance

***

Reluctant Romance

Sweet Romance (Written As Annie Dobbs)

Firefly Inn Series

***

Another Chance (Book 1)

Another Wish (Book 2)

Hometown Hearts Series

***

No Getting Over You (Book 1)

A Change of Heart (Book 2)

Cozy Mysteries

Lexy Baker Cozy Mystery Series

* * *

Lexy Baker Cozy Mystery Series Boxed Set Vol 1 (Books 1-4)

Or buy the books separately:

Killer Cupcakes

Dying For Danish

Murder, Money and Marzipan

3 Bodies and a Biscotti

Brownies, Bodies & Bad Guys

Bake, Battle & Roll

Wedded Blintz

Scones, Skulls & Scams

Ice Cream Murder

Mummified Meringues

Brutal Brulee (Novella)

No Scone Unturned

Cream Puff Killer

Kate Diamond Mystery Adventures

***

Hidden Agemda (Book 1)

Ancient Hiss Story (Book 2)

Heist Society (Book 3)

Silver Hollow

Paranormal Cozy Mystery Series

***

A Spell of Trouble (Book 1)

Spell Disaster (Book 2)

Nothing to Croak About (Book 3)

Cry Wolf (Book 4)

Mooseamuck Island Cozy Mystery Series

* * *

A Zen For Murder

A Crabby Killer

A Treacherous Treasure

Mystic Notch

Cat Cozy Mystery Series

* * *

Ghostly Paws

A Spirited Tail

A Mew To A Kill

Paws and Effect

Probable Paws

Blackmoore Sisters

Cozy Mystery Series

* * *

Dead Wrong

Dead & Buried

Dead Tide

Buried Secrets

Deadly Intentions

A Grave Mistake

Spell Found

Fatal Fortune

Hazel Martin Historical Mystery Series

***

Murder at Lowry House (book 1)

Murder by Misunderstanding (book 2)

Lady Katherine Regency Mysteries

***

An Invitation to Murder (Book 1)

The Baffling Burglaries of Bath (Book 2)

Sam Mason Mysteries

(As L. A. Dobbs)

***

Telling Lies (Book 1)

Keeping Secrets (Book 2)

Exposing Truths (Book 3)

Betraying Trust (Book 4)

Romantic Comedy

***

Corporate Chaos Series

In Over Her Head (book 1)

Can't Stand the Heat (book 2)

What Goes Around Comes Around (book 3)

Careful What You Wish For (4)

***

Sweetrock Sweet and Spicy Cowboy Romance

Some Like It Hot

Too Close For Comfort

————

Regency Romance

* * *

Scandals and Spies Series:

Kissing The Enemy

Deceiving the Duke

Tempting the Rival

Charming the Spy

Pursuing the Traitor

Captivating the Captain

The Unexpected Series:

An Unexpected Proposal

An Unexpected Passion

Dobbs Fancytales:

Dobbs Fancytales Boxed Set Collection

————

Western Historical Romance

***

Goldwater Creek Mail Order Brides:

Faith

American Mail Order Brides Series:

Chevonne: Bride of Oklahoma

————————————————————

Magical Romance with a Touch of Mystery

***

Something Magical

Curiously Enchanted

ROMANTIC SUSPENSE

WRITING AS LEE ANNE JONES:

***

The Rockford Security Series:

Deadly Betrayal (Book 1)

Fatal Games (Book 2)

Treacherous Seduction (Book 3)

Calculating Desires (Book 4)

Wicked Deception (Book 5)

ABOUT LEIGHANN DOBBS

USA Today bestselling author, Leighann Dobbs, discovered her passion for writing after a twenty year career as a software engineer. She lives in New Hampshire with her husband Bruce, their trusty Chihuahua mix Mojo and beautiful rescue cat, Kitty. When she's not reading, gardening, making jewelry or selling antiques, she likes to write cozy mystery and historical romance books.

Her book "Dead Wrong" won the "Best Mystery Romance" award at the 2014 Indie Romance Convention.

Her book "Ghostly Paws" was the 2015 Chanticleer Mystery & Mayhem First Place category winner in the Animal Mystery category.

Find out about her latest books by signing up at:

http://www.leighanndobbs.com/newsletter

Connect with Leighann on Facebook
http://facebook.com/leighanndobbsbooks

Join her VIP readers group on Facebook:
https://www.facebook.com/groups/ldobbsreaders
/

This is a work of fiction.

None of it is real. All names, places, and events are products of the author's imagination. Any resemblance to real names, places, or events are purely coincidental, and should not be construed as being real.

80258948R00124

Made in the USA
San Bernardino, CA
25 June 2018